THE GOD
OF OUR FATHERS

Belting the globe with the Gospel

Marcus Thomas

AMBASSADOR INTERNATIONAL
GREENVILLE, SOUTH CAROLINA & BELFAST, NORTHERN IRELAND

www.ambassador-international.com

The God of our Fathers
Belting the globe with the Gospel

Copyright © 2016 - Marcus Thomas
All rights reserved

Paperback: ISBN: 978-1-62020-196-1

Printed by Bethel Solutions

"Scripture quotations taken from the New American Standard Bible® (NASB),
Copyright © 1960, 1962, 1963, 1968, 1971, 1972, 1973,
1975, 1977, 1995 by The Lockman Foundation
Used by permission. www.Lockman.org"

Ambassador International
Emerald House
427 Wade Hampton Blvd
Greenville, SC 29609, USA
www.ambassador-international.com

Ambassador Books and Media
The Mount
2 Woodstock Link
Belfast, BT6 8DD, Northern Ireland, UK
www.ambassadormedia.co.uk

our first century
APOSTOLIC CHURCH UK 1916-2016

To Pat, a precious gift from God

THE LOTUS SCHOOL, PAKISTAN

All proceeds from this book will go towards the Lotus School in Pakistan. This is a project of ActionOverseas, which is the mission department of the UK Apostolic Church.

The Lotus School in Pakistan is located in Charsadda, a pro-Taliban area in Peshawar in the North of Pakistan. In 2010, Pastor Andrew Jenkins visited the area on behalf of ActionOverseas to see the damage caused by flooding and an earthquake, and from here the school found its beginnings.

The school was established to help and teach children from the very poorest families in the area and to date, June 2016, a total of 287 children have been able to receive basic education through this project. It also provides employment for nine people, including teaching and ancillary staff.

Pastor Tariq Masih, who is responsible for the support and running of the project, says, "Through your constant prayers and financial support, we are able to give education in a less privileged and neglected area of Pakistan. We are also able to reach the unreached people in this area and tell them about Jesus Christ."

Pastor N. Bainbridge,
ActionOverseas Administrator,
The Ark, Noah's Ark Road, Dover, Kent, CT17 0DD

CONTENTS

	Acknowledgements	9
	Foreword	13
	Preface - A Story to Challenge	15
Chapter 1	Wales in 1916 – The Context	19
Chapter 2.	The Big Picture – Restoration	37
Chapter 3.	Daniel Williams – World-wide Mission	55
Chapter 4.	Andrew Turnbull - Scotland	85
Chapter 5	Cecil C.Ireson - China	105
Chapter 6.	James McKeown - Ghana	127
Chapter 7.	William Cathcart - Australia and New Zealand	149
Chapter 8.	Jacob Purnell – Monmouthshire	183
Chapter 9.	Omri Jones - Wales	205
Chapter 10.	William Thomas - Italy	227
Chapter 11.	Cyril Rosser – Nigeria and Ghana	255
Chapter 12.	Our Response	285
Appendix 1	A Cloud of Witnesses	289
Appendix 2	Memories	331
Appendix 3	The Ultimate Cost	355
	Bibliography	365

The Apostolic Church has its origins in the first independent Pentecostal denomination in Britain, the Apostolic Faith Church, founded in 1912. Because of its teachings about the present day ministry of apostles and prophets it developed separately from other Pentecostal denominations in the UK. Through its mission work, especially in West Africa, this relatively small denomination became international, and some of the largest Pentecostal churches in West Africa trace their existence to the Apostolic Church. Many of the contemporary forms of Pentecostalism have been influenced by the ecclesiology of this denomination. It has therefore made an impact far beyond its size. I am pleased to congratulate the Apostolic Church on the occasion of its centenary.

Prof. Dr. Allan H. Anderson
Professor of Mission and Pentecostal Studies,
Department of Theology and Religion,
University of Birmingham.

At the mid-point of the Great War, 1916, the Lord unleashed one of his choice battalions for the Greatest War, the battle for the hearts and souls of people for Christ. Thank God, I say, for the Apostolic Church, deeply committed to the Lord Jesus, his Word and his gospel. May your tribe increase until the King, victorious, returns!
(Message sent to the Centenary Celebration, January 2016)

Dr. Rev. Steve Brady
Principal
Moorlands College

The temptation for Pentecostals has always been to tone things down. A previous generation were in danger of priding themselves on having an experience of 'Pentecost with dignity'. The history of the Apostolic Church is a reminder that we were not birthed into that way of thinking. Our mothers and fathers in the faith believed that God was disruptive of our committee meetings, directive in our decisions, involved in our ongoing journey. Perhaps we need to hear their voices now more than ever. We are in danger of believing that we have all we need to make a difference. We can believe that we have the resources we need for the task ahead of us: finance, people, buildings, education. And these gifts are not to be despised; but our history reminds us that we need more. At a time when early Pentecostals were trying to work out what it meant to have received the Spirit, the Apostolic Church was a provocation. At times, the other Pentecostal denominations played it safe, marginalising prophecy, afraid to use the Pauline terms for ministry. But the Spirit that soared over the deep at the beginning of time, and will cry 'Come' at the end of time, is never about safety. As we reflect on the gift that the Apostolics have been to the wider church, may we hear the call to launch out into the unknown, drawn by the power of the Spirit.

Dr. Neil Hudson
Pastor Salford Elim Church
Director, Imagine Project, The London Institute for Contemporary Christianity.

"We don't honour our fathers by following their ways but we honour our fathers by knowing their God."
(Unknown)

ACKNOWLEDGEMENTS

Many people have helped with the preparation of this book and I am grateful to them all.

It was Pastor Andrew Saunders who, after consulting with the leadership of the Apostolic Church, gave me the go ahead for this project to start. That was some three years ago. At that time it was just an idea, so thank you for saying "yes". Andrew also provided me with some invaluable material from the Apostolic Church Archive Library.

Peter and Val Williams did some research for me and lent me a fine collection of old Apostolic magazines, which provided a rich source of information and Peter Bridgens shared his collection of past Apostolic publications with me. Thank you. I want to thank my father who, I discovered, also had a treasure trove of magazines and books which I could use.

Others who have kindly loaned or given books and old publications include, Pastor Abraham Sackey, Pastor Emmanuel Mbakwe, Pastor Jonathan Black, Maurice and Ruth Marshall, Pauline Lewis, Brian Robinson and Bryn and Marion Morgan.

I am further indebted to many individuals around the world

who have helped confirm and detail some of the history of the Apostolic Church. These people include, Barry Chant, Pastor John Hewitt, Pastor Omri Davies and Colin Bevan.

I must mention my gratitude to Dr. Pastor Neil Hudson, Professor Dr. Alan H. Anderson and Rev. Dr. Steve Brady for their contributions, and to Dwaine Hanna at New Creations for his globe and belt design.

There are a number of retired Pastors in the U.K. who have been kind enough to listen, to help and to provide answers to the various questions I have asked and confirmations I have sought in preparing this book. These include Pastors Warren Jones, Danny Thomas, Ernest Williams, Brian Powell, Bryn Thomas, Maeldwyn Howells, Frank Parker, Ian Ross and Jackie Harris. They have been very patient and I would like express my thanks to them.

In the course of research, I have been in contact with some families and friends of those who feature in the book. Thank you to the Ames, Cathcart, Parks, Powell, Robling, Fuller, Thomas and Jones families for the material which you kindly provided. I would also like to thank those who have contributed to the Memories Appendix.

I want to specifically thank two retired pastors: Pastor Samuel McKibben who wrote the foreword, which really sets the scene for the chapters that follow, and Pastor Philip Powell who prepared the article, Ultimate Cost, which is included in the appendices.

I must also thank my wife, Pat. My skill as a wordsmith is limited. Pat has spent many hours editing the book and preparing the material so it is readable and well ordered. Thank you. My three daughters, Elspeth, Joanna and Angharad have been a constant encouragement to their mother and have helped in the editing process.

Thank you to the leaders and members of the Bridge

Community Church, Lurgan, who have followed the progress of the book with patience and great support.

Thank you also to Mark Linton from Ambassador for his help in bringing this project to completion. I am so grateful for the "God moment" in March 2016 when I was led to speak to Ambassador. Since then the journey has been brilliant.

Finally, I want to give thanks to the Lord for the privilege of putting down on paper the story that He has written through the lives of many of the leaders with whom He has blessed the Apostolic Church over the first hundred years. I have tried to capture as many of these individuals as possible. If God had not called them and revealed Himself to them, if God had not saved them by His grace and filled them with the Holy Spirit, then they would have passed into eternity unknown. However, because of the Lord, a story of faith, sacrifice, obedience and service has been written to challenge us for the next one hundred years.

Marcus Thomas
July 2016

FOREWORD

Every building needs a good foundation and Marcus Thomas has made it very clear that the early Apostolic Church, in accordance with God's Word in Ephesians 2:20, was built on the foundation of apostles and prophets, producing millions of believers throughout the world. Such truth is dear to the heart of the writer and clearly was his inspiration to produce this book.

The accounts you will read are as accurate as is humanly possible. They are the result of tireless hours of investigation, reading, international phone calls, emails etc, etc. Many of the happenings described remained fresh in the minds of those who related them, often years later. I am convinced that this is the result of the permanent effect of "God happenings" in the lives of people.

It is with regret that it has not been possible for Marcus to include every apostle and prophet who played a part in the making of Apostolic Church history. It would take more than one book to do that, but, without a doubt, most of the major contributors are included. It is noticeable that some of these great men of God came from difficult and often broken backgrounds. Most of them did not have the opportunity for any form of higher education. How inspiring this becomes for anyone reading this book to know that it is possible for all of us to step into the life of divine anointing beyond our greatest dreams.

If as a reader you do not happen to have some knowledge of the beginnings of the Apostolic Church, may I say, you are in for a treat. The restoration of the ministry of apostles and prophets, laying the foundations of new churches and building up established churches, brought Christian experience back to the days of the New Testament. The sick were being healed, demons were being cast out and people were not only hearing but seeing the power of the Gospel of Christ. If you have had any doubts about the continued recognition of apostles and prophets, this book will dispel them.

I think you would want to thank Marcus for committing himself to this large task which, without doubt, will bless the Body of Christ. I am also sure it will be an inspiration to all its readers and birth a desire for God to work in similar ways through our lives.

Pastor Samuel McKibben,

Inverness, Scotland,
July 2016

PREFACE

A STORY TO CHALLENGE

The following story is told of Duncan Campbell, the famous revivalist of the twentieth century, when he was in his mid- forties. He was in his study, preparing sermons for a preaching engagement at the well-known Keswick Convention, when his fifteen year old daughter came in to see him. As they talked, she asked this question: "Dad, why doesn't God use you like He used to?" "My dear, what is it that you mean?" he replied. "Dad, you've told me stories of what used to happen when you worked in the Faith Mission Movement. Why doesn't God do that with you anymore?"

Campbell said, "I made some lame brain excuses and tried to theologically talk through it so I wouldn't lose face in front of my daughter. I held my composure... until she left the room. When she did, I fell on my face and said, 'God, she is right!' With my face in the carpet, I wept hot tears and said, 'God, if You will give me back what I had, I will do whatever You tell me to do.'" (Tenney, 1999)

As you read about the lives and ministries of the people in this book, I trust you will have the grace and courage to ask a similar question to that which Duncan Campbell was asked by his daughter: "Why doesn't God use The Apostolic Church like He used to?"

In seeking to answer that question, various ideas have been suggested - for example the centralised administrative structure of the Apostolic Church; a failure to release apostolic and prophetic ministries or a loss of the vision of being a movement, rather than a denomination, to mention just a few.

Many of our recent leaders have tried to confront these issues and changes have been made, but we must still ask the question, "Why doesn't God use The Apostolic Church like He used to?" or "Where is the God of our fathers?"

Thank God for every evidence we see of His power in our lives. Of course, we have to be careful not to look back at the past with rose-tinted spectacles, but we can and must learn from the past.

One of the men highlighted in this book is Andrew Turnbull. Andrew and his family lived in Portobello, just outside Edinburgh. His son Tom was saved, filled with the Holy Spirit and had received the gift of prophecy. It was 1915 when Tom, at the age of twelve, prophesied to his own father: "I would have My servant go to a large city in the west of Scotland. He is to rent a large house, conducting services in one of the rooms. A large spiritual fire will be lit in the west of Scotland, and the sparks will fly out and ignite and commence many assemblies in Scotland."

This was a huge challenge to Andrew, but move he did. He began a meeting in his home, in Alexandra Park, Glasgow, in July 1915, and within weeks over thirty people were attending. Numbers continued to grow, a hall was rented and through prophetic guidance the church was named "The Burning Bush". From this church, not only were other churches planted in Scotland, but men were also launched out to other nations to touch the world with the Pentecostal experience.

Some of these men will be mentioned in later chapters. Their stories will challenge us in regard to sacrifice. Their attitude is best illustrated by a conversation I had with Maisie Rankin, widow of Pastor Jack Rankin. Talking to her about the sacrifices that they had made over their many years of ministry and missionary service, and the very hard family and personal experiences they had gone through together, she said, "Jack and I didn't call them sacrifices. There is only One who gave a sacrifice. That was Jesus."

The first Apostolic Church pastor to die on the mission field was Pastor William Taylor, on 1st July 1938 at Kaduna, Nigeria. There is a memorial stone to him in the Old Temple, Penygroes, South Wales. He went to Nigeria knowing that he might die there. On his death bed, dying of dysentery, he said "If the Lord wants me to be the first, I am quite willing!" What a response! But the story doesn't end there.

In August 1938, a month after William Taylor's death, his family were attending the Apostolic Church International Convention in Penygroes, South Wales. During an appeal for missionaries to go to Kaduna, in Nigeria, his son volunteered to take his father's place.

The attitudes and desires that gripped our past fathers and their wives and families can be summed up by the following poem by A.L. Greenaway, later to become an Apostolic missionary himself. There was no other way for them than living for God and knowing His perfect will.

In writing this book I have not set out to give a step by step history of the Apostolic Church. Instead its pages tell the stories of some early Apostolic pioneers and much of that history will unfold as you read the amazing things which God accomplished through their lives.

Lost in Thee

Oh! that my longing soul might be
Utterly lost, my God, in Thee!
Silent and yielded, lying still,
Glad to embrace Thy perfect Will!

> Lost in Thee! Lost in Thee!
> Hidden from all and lost in Thee!

Oh! Grant that I in Thee may hide,
Safe from the guilt of sinful pride;
Myself I can no longer see
When I am lost, my God, in Thee!

> Lost in Thee! Lost in Thee!
> Hidden from all and lost in Thee!

Oh! That in Thee I might abide,
Content to trust, whate'er betide;
Dwelling in Thee by day and night –
My blest abode the Infinite.

> Lost in Thee! Lost in Thee!
> Hidden from all and lost in Thee!

Oh! God Eternal, Thou canst hold;
Within Thyself Thou canst enfold
All that I am or yearn to be;
Then let me now be lost in Thee!

> Lost in Thee! Lost in Thee!
> Hidden from all and lost in Thee!

A.L. Greenaway (Greenaway, 1926)

I read of a well-known minister to whom God said, "I've seen your ministry, now do you want to see Mine?" The stories in this book demonstrate how God does church. I hope they will inspire you. I want them to challenge you to declare over your own life and the life of your church – GOD HAS NOT CHANGED. HE IS STILL IN THE BUSINESS OF BUILDING GREAT PEOPLE FOR HIS GREAT CHURCH.

Marcus Thomas
Lurgan, Northern Ireland, July 2016

CHAPTER ONE
WALES IN 1916

"Bend us, Lord, bend us; Oh, bend us for Thy Son's sake."
Evan Roberts, Blaencwm, December 1904

The Apostolic Church in Wales came into being on 8th January 1916. In this first chapter I want to consider briefly the social, economic, political and spiritual context into which it was born. Despite many adverse conditions these early Apostolic pioneers boldly preached the Gospel and moved forward undaunted in the purpose of God. Understanding this will, I hope, increase our confidence in the power of the same Gospel which we also declare and in the continuing purpose of God which we desire to be fulfilled in our own lives and in the life of the Church in this generation.

Our early fathers did not find themselves in an easy situation. The First World War brought significant changes to Wales, and to

Great Britain as a whole. Our forefathers were products of their time, but let us not forget, they were also "new creatures in Christ Jesus". They were able to overcome the challenges that they faced post January 1916. They saw the Gospel flourish initially in their Jerusalem - the villages and towns of South Wales. Then, as they linked with others, they saw a vibrant church spread throughout Great Britain and beyond into other parts of the world.

In Romans 8:31 (AV) the Apostle Paul wrote: "If God be for us, who can be against us?" The lives and achievements of these men give testimony to the truth of this scripture and it stands true for us as we look ahead to the next one hundred years.

THE FORMATION OF THE APOSTOLIC CHURCH IN WALES

Pastor Jonathan Black, in his blog, *Happy 100th Birthday to the Apostolic Church*, gives us a snapshot of how things developed from that initial day in January 1916: "What started with a small number of Welsh churches a century ago has spread far beyond Wales and that handful of assemblies, through the preaching of the Gospel. Today, the Apostolic Church has over 15 million members around the world in 100 countries. (Someone has worked out that that means that, on average, one person has become an Apostolic every 10 minutes for the last hundred years.) 100 years ago, the Apostolic Church consisted mostly of poor miners and farmers in rural villages in Welsh-speaking West Wales. Some of our earliest leaders struggled to learn English. There were no great financial resources, no hugely influential people in society, and they were far, far away from London and the great communication centres of the Empire. Yet they had Christ and His Word. And Christ, the Head of the Church, built His Church among them, and from those humble beginnings, He used them to 'belt the globe' with the Gospel." (Black, 2016)

How the Apostolic Church in Wales came into existence in January 1916 will be dealt with in more detail in the following chapter. Suffice to say here that it resulted from a split in a Pentecostal denomination called The Apostolic Faith Church, which was led by William Hutchinson and had its headquarters in Bournemouth.

Jonathan Black explains: "On 8th January 1916, a meeting took place in Ammanford Apostolic Church which saw the breaking of ties between nineteen Welsh Apostolic assemblies and William Oliver Hutchinson and the Apostolic Faith Church movement which he led. Hutchinson was beginning to significantly depart from evangelical Christianity, and so all British Pentecostals, not only the Welsh Apostolics, cut all ties with him and his movement." (Black, 2016) The Welsh churches, nineteen in total, under the leadership of Pastor Daniel Powell Williams, formed the Apostolic Church in Wales.

POST-REVIVAL WALES

Revival came to Wales in 1904 and lasted until 1905. It was a true visitation of God to the "Land of Song". However, the issue with revivals is that they are difficult to sustain. What, therefore, was the spiritual condition of Wales in January 1916?

The Daily Mail published an article in August 2014 with this headline: Sex, cocaine and epic binge drinking. What history books DON'T tell you about life in Britain during the Great War. Included in the article was an incident from Wales, which caught my attention: "In 1917, Mr. Justice Lawrence who, in sentencing a young collier to three months' imprisonment at Glamorgan Assizes for bigamy, told the court: 'This crime is rampant. Respect for the marriage ceremony seemed to be dying altogether.'" (Charman, 2014)

Many of us have heard how the Revival impacted the social and community life of Wales. Rick Joyner, in his book on the Welsh Revival, *The World Aflame*, writes: "Before the Revival there had been almost a plague of drunkenness and gambling. During the Revival taverns were either closed or turned into meeting halls. Instead of wasting their earnings on drinking and gambling, workers started taking their wages home to their families." (Joyner, 1993)

Eifion Evans, in his book, *The Welsh Revival of 1904*, describes how "the pit ponies could no longer understand the miners' instructions because of the absence of oaths and curses. The most notable effect of the Revival was the precipitous decline in drunkenness... Convictions for drunkenness in Glamorgan fell from 10,528 in 1903 to 5,490 in 1906." (Evans, 2000)

The Revival impacted Welsh society as a whole, but it also impacted the existing churches. Historic prejudices and quarrels were healed and church barriers were broken down. One outstanding feature of the Revival was the deep sense of conviction of sin which many experienced. This had an effect not only on the unsaved but also on the churches. The sins of bitterness and resentment were confessed and, as a result, churches were transformed by a renewed vision of the cross of Jesus Christ.

It was a Wales-wide revival with approximately 100,000 being brought into the Kingdom of God, although some estimates are higher. As the population of Wales in 1901 was just over two million, this means that between 5 and 7.5 percent of the population were converted. Churches which had been struggling to remain open prior to the Revival had an influx of new converts, especially young people. But it did not last.

Rick Joyner suggests one reason for this: "...multitudes, who were touched by the Revival and had a genuine encounter with the Lord, were also lost again to the world because there were not enough workers to care for them." (Joyner, 1993) Noel Gibbard, in his book, *Fire on the Altar,* writing about the increased numbers that some churches received, commented, "Such increases posed problems. Chapel buildings did not afford the most suitable accommodation for dealing with such a volume of converts... In many churches, arrangements for meeting the needs of new converts were not satisfactory. In other cases worthy attempts were made, some of them successful, but others lasting for only a brief period." (Gibbard, 2005)

Many of the converts did turn back to the world in the years following the Revival. There is a view that the Revival did nothing to effect real changes in Welsh society. One historian says that as many as seventy-five percent turned away. The truth is that we cannot be certain of numbers, because some of the converts did not join the nonconformist churches. They began to attend the many mission halls that sprang up around Wales as a consequence of the Revival.

James Worsfold, former apostle and church historian, points out a paradox: "The Welsh Revival was on the wane and by 1906 there were complaints that, for instance in the Rhondda Valley, the old sinful ways were returning and drunkenness and evil behaviour were breaking out. Yet at the same time many revival converts began to experience the Pentecostal baptism of the Spirit with the accompanying sign of speaking with tongues." (Worsfold J. E., 1991)

Pastor D.P. Williams, the founding father of the Apostolic Church, explained the paradox this way, "A large number of the converts, not taught to wield the weapon of the Spirit against their human and spiritual assailants, grew discouraged in their efforts to hold forth the standard of life and truth obtained. The sand of the wilderness had blinded others from seeing what God really aimed at. The conflicts and combats became increasingly more terrific. Some hearts became chilly, whilst others became fiery. A great upheaval such as the Welsh Revival brings certain reactions." (Williams, D.,1933)

THE FIRST WORLD WAR 1914-1918

The website Cymru'n Folio – Wales Remembers paints this picture of the situation on the home front during the First World War: "To wage war on an industrial scale the state mobilised all its resources, including its civilians.

From 1914 onwards, the Defence of the Realm Act (DORA) gave the government increasing powers over matters it had never controlled before. It could be a crime to fly a kite or buy binoculars. Alcohol could be sold legally only for six hours between noon and 9.30pm, with a gap in the afternoon. For the first time the government took control of essential industries such as coal mining, railways and shipping.

The control of public opinion was important to the war effort and a new Ministry of Information took responsibility for propaganda. The Ministry could choose which newspapers it gave information to and it could even close down a newspaper altogether.

The high casualties continued and in 1916 the government introduced conscription, which forced men to join the services or do work for the war effort. Over 80,000 women served in the forces as non-combatants and others took on jobs left temporarily vacant by the men. Food was rationed and even time was controlled – British Summer Time gave more hours for war production. Later, people said that the war produced nothing but 'widows, wooden legs and taxes'.

To win the war the state took control of its citizens. It needed millions of civilians to produce weapons, support the soldiers and look after casualties." (Home Front, 2014)

Worsfold sums up the main preoccupation of the day: "The overriding interest in Wales at that time (January 1916) was the course of the war." Wales, being part of Great Britain, was in the middle of "the war to end all wars." (Worsfold J. E., 1991)

There was a huge poster recruitment campaign to encourage men to join the armed forces. The iconic poster of Lord Kitchener with the slogan "YOUR COUNTRY NEEDS YOU!" was the most successful. However, propaganda was not just about recruitment. It infiltrated other areas of life and included misinformation about German atrocities in order to stoke up anti-German feeling. Newspapers and letters sent home from the troops were censored.

Support for the war in Wales was initially high. Many Welshmen felt that in some way this was "their" war and so large numbers enlisted. The headline in magazines and papers was, "What Wales has done in the war." The war was seen in apocalyptic terms of good against evil and God versus the Devil. Few saw the war as a clash between the interests of two nations. Denzil Morgan, theologian, explains, "It was when people realised that the war would not be 'over by Christmas', when battle scarred men returned for leave with horrendous stories of life in the trenches and when the body count reached thousands... that popular idealism cooled and doubts as to the wisdom, if not the justice, of the war cooled." (Morgan D. D., 2011)

Another mood changer was the introduction of military conscription. By 1916 the British Army needed more soldiers. In the February many miners declared their opposition to the threat of military conscription and nearly went on strike over it. Nonetheless, in March 1916 the Military Service Act was passed by Parliament. This specified that all single men between the ages of 18 and 41 were liable to be called-up for military service unless they were teachers, clergymen and workers in key industries. On 25th May 1916, the requirements were changed to include all married men. Conscription started on 2nd March 1916.

As a consequence of forced conscription, some men declared themselves pacifists. There were approximately one thousand conscientious objectors in Wales. The Apostolic Church in Wales, newly birthed in January 1916, decided to support those members who became conscientious objectors. Pastor Omri Jones, from Llwynhendy, whose story is told in chapter 9, was one such person.

Conscientious objection was anything but an easy option for the young men involved, or for their families. The men were imprisoned, some being sentenced to hard labour or even death, although the death sentence was invariably commuted. The families experienced public mockery and many were sent a white feather as a symbol of cowardice.

By the end of the First World War, it is estimated that some 280,000 Welshmen had served in the army, navy, and air force. Kenneth O. Morgan in his book, *Rebirth of a Nation* writes: "Welshmen... enlisted in such vast numbers that the proportion of the male population engaged in the armed forces... eventually outstripped that for either England or Scotland." (Morgan K. O., 1981) This was a shocking and a dreadful war.

It is difficult to underestimate how far-reaching, and in many cases how devastating, were the consequences of this war upon the mental, spiritual and emotional well-being of the men who survived the trenches and returned home. One serving soldier explained, "It was utterly impossible to preserve a clear conscience. Assuming we survived, the question of whether our conscience survived too depended on whether we believed in the forgiveness of sins." (BBC History Website)

The BBC History website records that some 40,000 Welshmen died during the war. However, there is no record of how many came back injured either physically or mentally or both. Chris Wrigley, in his book *The Impact of the First World War*, writes, "The post-war world had many veterans who were maimed or damaged by shell shock. In 1921, 1,187,450 men were in receipt of pensions for war disabilities, with a fifth of these having suffered serious loss of limbs or eyesight, paralysis or lunacy". (BBC History Website)

Although the war was fought in Europe and beyond, those at home were also deeply affected by it. On the outbreak of war in 1914 the Government passed a law, the Defence of the Realm Act (DORA), which gave them power over all aspects of British life. This legislation was wide-ranging, covering issues such as the brightness of lights on a car or in a house; the striking of a match at night on a street; spreading false reports; suspicious conduct; giving of information; sedition; careless words. Any infringement resulted in a court appearance and a fine. In addition, the threat of a German invasion was ever present and for the first time British cities experienced the terror of aerial bombardments.

On the economic front, inflation more than doubled between 1914 and its peak in 1920. The Welsh miners went on strike in July 1915 because a new wage structure was required, in the face of rising prices and the profits that the mine owners were receiving. There were over two hundred thousand miners in Wales. The war cost Britain four million pounds every day and Britain went from being the world's largest overseas investor to being its biggest debtor, with interest payments consuming around forty percent of the national budget. (History of the United Kingdom During World War I)

Jessica Flynn in an article, *World War One Centenary*: How Wales reported the start of the Great War, gives us this overall picture of the effect of the war on these islands: "But this war affected everyone whether they were the men on the front line or the women and children left at home. Nobody was exempt from the poverty and hardship that it caused." (Flynn, 2014)

While the men were fighting for our country, women played their part in the war, looking after their homes and children and filling the jobs the men had to leave behind. Around 1,600,000 women joined the UK workforce between 1914 and 1918 in Government departments, public transport and the post office. Some became business clerks, land workers or factory workers, and many worked in the dangerous munitions factories, which were employing 950,000 women by Armistice Day.

One of the largest munitions factories and weapon stores in Wales was at Pembrey, near Llanelli, where dynamite and TNT were produced: from 1916 women were employed on the shop floor, alongside the men. In July 1917 an enormous explosion left four men and two women dead. But it was the funeral of the two female victims, Mildred Owen, aged 18, and Mary Watson aged 19, that drew the most mourners, including from among their fellow workers, some of whom wore their overalls to the service. (Shinn, Pulpits, mutinies and 'khaki fever': World War One in Wales)

The Declaration of War on 4th August 1914 was made under a Liberal Prime Minister, but the Liberal government fell in May 1915 due to inadequate armaments and to the failed military campaign in the Dardanelles. A coalition government was formed but that fell mainly because of the Somme Campaign, where Britain suffered 57,000 casualties on the first day alone, 1st July 1916. The "Welsh Wizard", David Lloyd George came to the forefront and became the first Welsh-speaking Prime Minister. He led a coalition government and with it came a change of war policy.

"Lloyd George immediately set about transforming the British war effort, taking firm control of both military and domestic policy. In the first 235 days of existence, the War Cabinet met 200 times. Its creation marked the transition to a state of total war – the idea that every man, woman and child should play his or her part in the war effort." (History of the United Kingdom During World War I) By 1916, Britain was on a "Total War Footing", with London exercising direct control over everything.

Social issues also took their toll on everyday life in Wales during the War. Lloyd George told a Bangor audience in February 1915: "Drink is doing more damage in the war than all the German submarines put together." Laws were introduced to weaken the strength of beer; to reduce opening hours and restrict the sale of spirits. Many scams appeared to circumvent these restrictions. Drunkenness and rowdy behaviour was a feature of towns throughout the United Kingdom. With the decline in moral standards, sexual diseases were on the increase.

Women in Cardiff faced a curfew "to prevent drinking and other evils among women". An order under the Defence of the Realm prohibited "certain women" from being out of doors between 7pm and 8am. All women were banned from licensed premises between 7pm and 6am. Breaking these laws meant a prison sentence. There was a big drive during the war years to "clean up the streets" and working class women were held responsible for the moral collapse in the nation. (Workhouse Tales, 2015)

Smoking also increased during these years. Whereas pre-1914 it had been a predominantly male habit, during the war it became common for many women, especially young girls, to smoke. Spending on tobacco increased during the second year of the war by over £4million!

Another disturbing aspect of life in Wales during the First World War was the treatment handed out by Welsh people to non-Welsh citizens. In Aberystwyth, a German professor, who was anti-Kaiser, was literally hounded out of the town by street protests. Mobs would go looking for German workers to expel. The UK became a sanctuary for Belgian people and many came to live in Wales, but there were disturbances in Milford Haven involving Belgian refugees. There was also trouble between the locals in Pembroke Dock and American navy personnel. (Arts and Humanities Research Council Website)

Wales had a Prisoner of War camp at Frongoch near Bala, in North Wales. After housing some German prisoners of war in early 1915, it was used in 1916 to hold insurgents after the 1916 Easter Rising in Dublin. Some of the rebels were executed but 1,863 of the rank and file Irish republicans found themselves incarcerated in the old whiskey distillery at Frongoch. One commentator said, "Ironically, the British brought together the cream of a generation of revolutionary nationalists and allowed them, in the camp at Frongoch, to map out tactics for the future." (Carradice, 2010)

Interestingly, it was observed that "more than anywhere else in the UK mums in the South Wales valleys liked to name their children after WW1 battles." Babies were named Arras, Loos, Dardanelles and Somme. One of the most popular was Verdun. Verdun was one of the bloodiest of the First World War and it lasted ten months, with around 976,000 soldiers injured and around 300,000 killed. The legendary Welsh actor, Richard Burton, had an elder brother born in 1916 who was called Verdun. (Williamson, 2016)

The Apostolic Church in Wales adopted a policy of helping the poor and needy. Before any tithes were sent to the central finance office, each local assembly deducted one percent for a local poor fund. D.P. Williams believed that the poor had first claim upon the tithes that the local church collected. The officers of each local church then had the responsibility of distributing help as needs became known. An example of this was the assembly in Penygroes, the village where D.P. Williams lived. Acting on a prophetic word, the monies that the local church had in reserve were used to clear all the debts that the local believers had accumulated due to the poverty they were experiencing.

Later, in 1925, with Wales suffering severe hardships because of the general strike, each local assembly was instructed to retain three shillings in every pound for the local poor fund and were at liberty to help any who were suffering.

THE POST 1918 YEARS

Following the suffering of the war years, our early pioneers faced many challenges as they sought to preach the Gospel and encourage people to find purpose and new life in Christ.

Prior to 1914, Wales had been a country in transition. People had been concerned about issues like unemployment, industrial oppression, fairer working conditions and adequate housing. In regards to faith, there was a drifting away, as there was in other European cultures. Biblical criticism and the theory of evolution were the doctrines of the day. But what changes came as a result of the First World War?

REALIGNMENT OF THE POLITICAL SCENE IN WALES

Jessica Flynn writes "The First World War may be considered a significant watershed in the history of Wales, for the following reasons. Politically, notwithstanding the rise of Lloyd George, the war marked the end of the hegemony of the Liberal party in Wales. In 1906 Wales had returned 35 out of 36 MPs sitting on the Liberal benches in the House of Commons (the other was Labour's Keir Hardie). But by the General Election of 1922 half of all Welsh MPs were socialists, and the Liberal party never regained its Victorian and Edwardian predominance". (Flynn, 2014)

John Davies, in his article, *The Legacy of WW1* states, "The war undermined allegiance to the Liberal Party and destroyed the optimism characteristic of pre-war Welsh society. Welsh nationality, so robust at the turn of the century, became something which needed to be defended and cosseted". (Davies J.)

A CHANGING SOCIAL AND ECONOMIC SCENE

It was to have been "the war to end all wars" and there was a determination to make Britain fit for the returning heroes. Interestingly, some of these returning heroes, who had fought to preserve British democracy, were not entitled to vote. This posed a dilemma for the politicians and The Representation of the People Act was passed in 1918. This act of Parliament gave all males who were over the age of twenty-one and who were resident householders, the right to vote. It also gave the vote to women over the age of thirty who met some minimum property qualifications.

In making the land fit for its heroes, physical and material things became the priority and spiritually many were disillusioned. Nonconformist and Anglican ministers had played a major role in recruitment for the war. Biblical language was used to encourage individuals to sign up. The churches had identified themselves with the imperialistic cause. However, as the war progressed and the toll of dead and injured increased, many questioned where God was amongst the untold suffering that was experienced on the battlefields and with the families back home.

INVASION OF OTHER DOGMAS

Into this vacuum came both Labour and Communistic dogma. These creeds were already present in Wales, but with the credibility of the Liberal party shattered by forced conscription in 1916, these alternative political philosophies had a ready audience. Both offered an alternative world-view where Jesus was not Lord and God was non-existent. Both offered a way of doing things that cut God and faith out of the picture.

Kenneth Morgan writes, "In 1917 the valleys were seething again with class bitterness. A massive new encouragement came in Russia with the February revolution, followed by that in October. It aroused immense enthusiasm amongst Welsh miners, railwaymen, and steelworkers. Soldiers' and Workers' Councils appeared in the Rhondda on the model of Petrograd. Maerdy was renamed 'little Moscow'; the red flag flew at pitheads." (Morgan K. O., 1981)

John Davies quotes from a local Welsh newspaper: "There was no place outside of Russia where the Revolution has caused greater joy than... in Merthyr Tydfil" proclaimed the Merthyr Pioneer, and the miners of Ammanford sang: 'Workers of the Vale of Amman/ Echo Russia's mighty thrust." (Davies J., 1993) Some mining representatives met in Swansea on 29th July 1917 to discuss the soviet system but the conference was broken up by the army.

The introduction of the Welfare State made healthcare and benefits more accessible for those experiencing ill health or poverty. Davies writes, "...the war greatly stimulated the growth of the welfare state. The Ministry of Pensions was established in 1916, mainly to assist the wounded and the widowed; schemes were developed to safeguard the interests of wives and children and to increase the number covered by National Insurance. In the field of education, H.A.L. Fisher's act of 1918 raised the school leaving age to fourteen." (Davies, J., 1993)

The "Total War" concept of Government control that existed during the war seemed to be carried over into the post war years. Boards were established for shipping, engineering, shipbuilding and agriculture. "The Ministry of Munitions became a pioneer in introducing powerful new physical controls upon production and supply, prices and profits" (Morgan K. O., 1981)

A CHANGING SOCIAL AND ECONOMIC

Flynn states: "Economically the war also represented a climacteric, after which heavy industry in Wales went into a prolonged quarter-century of decline. The coal industry, for example, had reached peak production figures of 57m tons in 1913, and the workforce was at its largest immediately after the war when 271,500 men were employed in the South Wales coalfield."

She continues, "But the 1920s and 1930s saw the industry go into a slump, exacerbated by the economic downturn of the Wall Street Crash and Great Depression. Whereas tens of thousands of migrants had flocked to Wales from England in pursuit of economic opportunities from the early 1890s onwards, the flow was reversed in the inter-war decades in what has been termed by the Rhondda writer, Gwyn Thomas, as 'the black death on wheels', significant out-migration from the Welsh valleys to London, to the new industrial towns of the Thames valley and to the West Midlands."

In conclusion she states: "Overall the war brought to a shuddering halt the buoyancy, optimism and self-confidence characteristic of Edwardian Wales and replaced it with a society anxious over its prospects and uncertain as to which of its national characteristics (language, religiosity, social cohesion, aptitude for rugby football) would be sufficiently resilient to retain validity in a world in flux." (Flynn, 2014)

A LOSS OF CONFIDENCE IN NONCONFORMIST DENOMINATIONS

Davies comments, "The war had a profound impact upon the countryside, striking the final blow which destroyed the estates of the landed gentry. Organised religion, a dominant feature of Victorian and Edwardian Wales, went into rapid decline, partly because of the cynicism caused by the activities of clerical recruiters". (Davies J. , The Legacy of WWI)

One of the four main nonconformist denominations, the Calvinistic Methodists, after various discussions, came to the conclusion that their procedures and structures were outdated and unsuitable to meet the needs of the times. These discussions were included in a report.

D. Densil Morgan writes, "There was no doubt in the minds of the report's authors that the nation was facing a crisis of faith which only a renewal of experiential Christianity founded on a credible doctrinal base could hope to resolve. The reasons for the present malaise were faced honestly: that religion was becoming peripheral to the interests and aspirations of the rising generation; that urbanization and modernization were making Christian convictions seem obsolete; that the current post-war craze for entertainment, amusement and pleasure was playing havoc with the seriousness of purpose which used to characterize Nonconformity at its most thoughtful". The report also mentioned how education was now the great hope for individual betterment and that social reform was being promoted as the saviour for mankind. It did also include this challenge, "Our forefathers made heaven, hell and judgement very real to their listeners; it is our task to make the transcendent reality of the spiritual world equally real." (Morgan D. D., 2011)

AN ANTAGONISTIC INDUSTRIAL WORKFORCE IN THE VALLEYS

In the summer of 1916, there was a miners' strike in the South Wales coalfield. It was provoked by the demand to produce more coal with no increase in pay. The BBC History of Wales website tells us, "The enormous increase in coal industry profits was not being passed on to the miners, who naturally wished to have their share. Over two hundred thousand miners in Britain refused to be intimidated by the Munitions of War Act that made striking a criminal offence." (BBC History Website)

In South Wales, the importance of coal to the British war effort cannot be underestimated and this made the miners confident of victory in their fight with the coal owners. Lloyd George himself came to Cardiff to meet the miners, assuring them that the owners would honour the agreement between the government and the Miners' Federation.

However, the outcome was that in November 1917 the government took control of the Welsh mines. (This control was later extended to include all the British coalfields.) The Welsh miners, inspired by the outbreak of the Russian Revolution and the news that in Russia workers' councils were being set up, determined to continue striking. (BBC History Website)

Kenneth O. Morgan comments, "In no part of the British Isles was the contrast between pre- and post-war conditions more pronounced." (Morgan K. O., 1981) Wales was not the same place after World War I and into this situation came our forefathers with the message of the four-fold Gospel and a vision of a Church beyond any national or ethnic boundaries. The time was right for such a move from God.

Worsfold wrote, "...the Apostolic Church in Wales did not arise in a vacuum, nor were the economic conditions prevailing allowed to impede the spiritual and numerical development of the secessionists. There was no lurching or even zigzagging from the course they were now on. It was progress all the way. Difficulties were seen as an opportunity to overcome." (Worsfold J. E., 1991)

I do feel at times that we play the "post-modern card" too much in regard to our approach to Church today. We forget that Jesus did not live in a "Christian country" but in a land that was occupied by a foreign army, where there were social and political strata, a land where conditions were generally unfavourable to the preaching of the Gospel. Our forefathers faced many challenges in the world of the early twentieth century, but they faced them all and proved that the LORD is LORD indeed.

CHAPTER TWO
THE BIG PICTURE

> *"...this is what was spoken of through the prophet Joel; 'And it shall be in the last days,' God says, 'That I will pour forth of My Spirit on all mankind; and your sons and your daughters shall prophesy...'"* Acts 2:16-17

The Apostolic Church in Wales came into existence on 8th January 1916 because of a split in a Pentecostal denomination called the Apostolic Faith Church (AFC). The leader of this group, whose base was in Bournemouth, was Pastor William Hutchinson. The Welsh pastors and overseers of the AFC were called to a meeting by Pastor Hutchinson on that date. The meeting was held in the Ammanford church, in South Wales.

The truth was that William Hutchinson was claiming infallibility and declaring that he had total authority over all matters concerning the AFC. One who was present at that meeting reported: "Pastor Hutchinson spoke for three and a half hours and said that he had come there as the Chief Apostle. No-one else was to open his mouth, neither prophet nor interpreter, nor anyone else, as he alone had the authority over everything at that time". (Weeks, 2003)

This meeting brought to a head various concerns and discussions that had already taken place amongst the Welsh leaders concerning both policy and authority within the AFC. As a result, on the 8th January 1916, nineteen Welsh Apostolic Faith churches broke away from Hutchinson and formed the Apostolic Church in Wales. The breakaway group came under the leadership of Pastor Daniel Powell Williams. Some of the Apostolic Faith churches in Wales, such as Swansea and Mountain Ash, did not join the new breakaway group.

In 1933 D.P. Williams wrote this about the separation: "Our connection with the late Pastor W.O. Hutchinson (he had died in 1928) had existed for a number of years, but terminated because of several things which were detrimental to our views, such as Church government and Church property, as well as other matters, which it would not be advisable in such a brief memoir as this to enumerate."

Various writers on the AFC split have suggested reasons for the divide, such as: the Welsh group couldn't handle English control (but some Welsh churches did not leave the AFC); there were feelings of jealousy and rivalry between the different leaders within the AFC; and further, that Welsh nationalist pride was the cause of the split.

Pastor Jonathan Black, in his *Apostolic Theology* blog writes, "In fact, the accusation of Welsh national sentiment… just doesn't make sense. Within a month of the split, the Williams brothers had gone to England to minister with people there who had also come out of the AFC. So the parting of the ways wasn't only confined to

Wales, and the Welsh ministers were concerned for the well-being of their English brethren. In March 1916 – only two months after the split – a convention was held in Penygroes with English and Scottish preachers. In fact, during that convention Robert Jardine, an Englishman, was called, through several prophets, to the apostleship, and ordained by D.P. Williams and Thomas Jones (the Apostolic Church's only two apostles at the time). Therefore, the very first apostle ordained in the Apostolic Church after the break with Bournemouth was an Englishman working in England!" (Black, Why What Happened in 1916 Happened, 2016)

The important question is this: did The Apostolic Church in Wales come into existence in 1916 because some men had differences over organisation and "other matters", which D.P. Williams did not explain, or was there something bigger taking place? Was God using the frailties of men to bring something of His purpose to birth?

The 20th Century saw God doing a work of restoration across the Body of Christ. I remember first hearing this truth when listening to Pastor Teddy Howells, a past President of The Apostolic Church in the United Kingdom, but it is a view of church history that many other Christian leaders share.

The early Church, by revelation from God the Holy Spirit, preached, taught and lived by certain truths. Four of these key truths were: salvation by faith alone (Acts 16:30-31); water baptism by immersion (Acts 8:38-39); the baptism of the Holy Spirit with an evidential sign (Acts 2:1-4) and the headship ministries of Jesus Christ (Eph 4:11-13).

John, the last of the twelve original apostles, died in 100 A.D. and in subsequent centuries there was a gradual dilution and partial disappearance of these truths that had been so prominent in the Early Church. I say partial, because from my reading of Church history, there was always a remnant or a prophetic group who continued to hold to and experience New Testament Christianity.

"Revival", as Dr. Martin Lloyd–Jones defines it, is "a return to Pentecost". (Lloyd-Jones, 1987) For the church today our hope for revival should not be based on an Old Testament model but on what happened on the Day of Pentecost, and revival should bring in its wake a recovery of Apostolic Christianity. Arthur Wallis, in his article *Restoration of the Church*, gives this summary: "In all the great spiritual movements through the years, the Lord has been seeking to recover lost truth and bring His people back to original Apostolic Christianity." (Wallis)

This is a vast subject which can only be touched upon here, but let me provide a few snapshots of how the Lord has worked in past centuries to recover Apostolic Christianity.

14th Century - Restoring the importance of God's Word:

John Wycliffe produced an English translation of the Bible, making God's Word available to ordinary people in their own language. Arthur Wallis writes, "This was God's first strategic move to bring back His Church to New Testament faith and practice." (Wallis)

15th Century – Restoring a focus on the Great Commission:

The Lollards, a group of itinerant preachers, went out from place to place preaching the Gospel of Jesus Christ.

16th Century – Restoring the truth of justification by faith:

Martin Luther's Ninety-five Theses, challenging the use of indulgences and papal pardons for the forgiveness of sins, provided the spark that ignited the Reformation. "The glorious Reformation broke over Europe, bringing into clear light the great truth of justification by faith. People began to understand the genius of the Gospel of God's grace which had so long been obscured by a doctrine of salvation by works," to quote Arthur Wallis once more. It also witnessed the restoration to the Body of Christ of the truth of water baptism by immersion. Those who preached and practised this truth - the Baptists, Mennonites and Anabaptists suffered much persecution.

20th Century

- Restoring the baptism of the Holy Spirit with the sign of speaking in new languages
- Restoring the revelation of the eternal purpose of God
- Restoring the ministry of apostle and prophet

As we examine the context into which the Apostolic Church was born in the early 20th Century, we will consider the restoration of each of these three truths in turn.

THE BAPTISM OF THE HOLY SPIRIT WITH THE SIGN OF SPEAKING IN NEW LANGUAGES

In his book, *Word and Spirit Together*, David Pawson gives specific examples from centuries subsequent to A.D.100 of people experiencing Spirit baptism with signs following. This is his assessment: "While the incidence varies enormously, we have seen enough to demonstrate continuity through the last two thousand years." (Pawson, 1998)

D.P. Williams quotes some specific examples of this: Irenaeus, Bishop of Lyons from A.D. 177 to 202, records, "We have many brethren in the churches, having many prophetical gifts, and by the Spirit speaking in all kinds of languages." St. Chrysostum, A.D. 347 – 407, states, "Whoever was baptised in Apostolic days, straightway spoke in tongues; one spoke in Persian, another Roman and other languages, but more abundant than all endowments was the gift of tongues." (Williams D. P., 1931)

A further example is David, a 6th century Welshman, who was later to become the patron saint of Wales. David was chosen to be bishop, and wished to be consecrated in the holy city of Jerusalem. He set off on foot for the pilgrimage, accompanied by some monks, one of whom kept a journal of their travels. This journal relates how they had only travelled as far as Gaul (France) when, "ye holy father, David, was baptised in ye Holy Ghost and spake in tongues as in ye days of ye apostles." (Pawson, 1998)

In the 12th century Hildegard of Bingen is reputed to have spoken and sung in tongues. Her spiritual songs were referred to by contemporaries as "concerts in the Spirit."

In the 14th century, the Moravians are recorded as speaking in new languages and in the 17th century, the early Quakers made mention of speaking in new languages in their meetings.

A further example from the 19th century concerns the Holiness Movement, which thrived in both America and Great Britain. Michael Harper writes in his book, *As at the Beginning*, about the 19th Century Holiness Movement, "Men such as Charles Finney, D.L. Moody and R.A. Torrey had great influence on both sides of the Atlantic and constantly taught a further experience for Christians, which they called 'Baptism in the Spirit'. From time to time, too, speaking in tongues took place in the meetings." (Harper, 1974)

It is evident from Church history that the key truths of 1st Century Apostolic Christianity were not totally lost, but became increasingly sidelined and clouded with superstition by the established church over the centuries.

So what did God restore to His Church in 1900 and what was new about what happened at that time?

Michael Harper explains, "What was new was the linking of speaking in tongues with the experience of the baptism in the Holy Spirit. It was this that sparked off the Pentecostal revival." (Harper, 1974) Until 1900, the expression "baptism in the Spirit" was generally used to describe an experience of sanctification which was subsequent to conversion. It was an expression particularly used in the Holiness Movement to describe the experience of a "clean heart" before God. The Holiness Movement emerged from 19th century Methodism and a fuller account can be found in William Kay's book, *Pentecostals in Britain* (Kay, 2000).

We can trace this new understanding and experience of the work of the Holy Spirit back to a Bible School in Topeka, Kansas, USA. The students had been asked to search the Scriptures and find what the biblical evidence was for the baptism in the Holy Spirit. As a result they came to the unanimous opinion that speaking in tongues was the evidence. On 31st December 1900, hands were laid on one of these students, Agnes Ozman, and she spoke in new languages.

I don't intend to recount the full story of how this experience spread from Kansas in the early years of the 20th century, but spread it did. It travelled as far as Azusa Street in Los Angeles; two missions in India; Chile, Norway, Sweden, Korea, Great Britain and beyond. From this small beginning in Kansas, the growth of Pentecostalism is an amazing story. It has been described as "the most under-reported story of our time." It has been said that Pentecostalism is the great religious success story of the 20th Century, and surely it continues to be the greatest success story of the 21st Century.

Some have called it, and sadly still call it, a work of Satan. Others said it would not last and that it was a human counterfeit. Well, it has lasted and continues to spread. Pentecostalism is the fastest growing stream of Christianity in the world. In the United Kingdom, Pentecostals are the third largest religious grouping behind Anglicans and Catholics. In the world, Pentecostals are the second largest religious grouping behind Catholics. We are all aware of the weird and the crazy that can be associated with Pentecostalism but, as Robert Morris (a well-known author and Pentecostal leader) has said, "people who are weird with the Holy Spirit were weird before they received the Holy Spirit: they're just weird people."

The early Pentecostal believers often faced ostracism from other Christians and vehement criticism, especially from the Evangelical leaders. Derek Prince in his book, *Who is the Holy Spirit*, writes, "When the baptism and the gifts of the Spirit first impacted the Church in the early years of the twentieth century, it was neither fashionable nor popular to be labelled 'Pentecostal'. There was a stigma attached to it. There was a price to be paid... Their experience was not cheap." (Prince, 1998)

I pastor an Apostolic Church in Northern Ireland and stories are told of our beginnings in County Armagh in the early 1920s, when Christians from other denominations would come to our open air water baptisms and throw clumps of earth and grass at our forefathers. Of course, this persecution was not only because they believed in the fullness of the Holy Spirit, but also because they practised water baptism by immersion.

Despite opposition, Pentecostalism has continued to grow and flourish. William Kay writes, "The Pentecostal and Charismatic Movement is one of the wonders of the twentieth century." (Kay, 2000) It is a wonder because it is a work of God.

Donald Gee in his book, *The Pentecostal Movement*, makes this comment: "The Pentecostal Movement does not owe its origin to any outstanding personality or religious leader, but was a spontaneous revival appearing simultaneously in various parts of the world." (Gee, 2010)

As regards Great Britain, there are two specific events we must mention: the 1904 Revival in Wales and the 1907 Revival in Sunderland.

THE WELSH REVIVAL

The founder of the Apostolic Church, Daniel Powell Williams was saved during the Revival. There has been much debate about whether the Welsh Revival was Pentecostal in the way we would now define the word. Without doubt there were Pentecostal aspects to the Revival.

My perspective is this: if you ask for the Holy Spirit, you will receive the Holy Spirit. It is certainly true that during the Welsh Revival people were encouraged, even instructed, to pray for the Holy Spirit to come. Jesus said in Luke 11:12-13: *Now suppose one of you fathers is asked by his son for a fish; he will not give him a snake instead of a fish, will he? Or if he is asked for an egg, he will not give him a scorpion, will he? If you then, being evil, know how to give good gifts to your children, how much more will your heavenly Father give the Holy Spirit to those who ask Him?*

D.P. Williams gives this account of the Welsh Revival: "In the year 1904, the great outpouring of the Holy Spirit in many places in Wales was above description. The manifestation of the Power was beyond human management... The weeping for mercy, the holy laughter, ecstasy of joy, the fire descending, burning its way to the hearts of men and women with sanctity and glory, were manifestations still cherished and longed for in greater power. Many were heard speaking in tongues and prophesying. So great was the visitation in Penygroes[1] and the districts that nights were spent in the churches. Many witnessed to God's healing power in their bodies." (Williams D. P., 1931)

Frank Hodges, who was based in Hereford and became one of the early pioneers of The Apostolic Church, testified, "I was really desperate for the baptism of the Spirit, and hungry in my heart; I thought I would go down to Wales for the blessing... Arriving at Gorseinon, I went to a little house close to the home of Evan Roberts[2] ... In this house one night we were singing hymns. There I saw for the first time a person baptised in the Spirit. A young man began to speak; and I knew he could not say the things he did unless God was there... And the Lord began to analyse things for

---

1   Birthplace of D.P. Williams and initial location of the Apostolic Church headquarters
2   Renowned leader of the Welsh Revival

me: 'Is it light?' asked the Lord. 'Wonderful light,' I replied. 'Is this Glory?' 'Wonderful glory.' 'What spirit can it be then?' 'It is God absolutely,' I said. I got a wonderful baptism in the Spirit. I had a Welsh tongue, and I spoke in Welsh." (Riches of Grace, 1962)

In Penygroes, the village D. P. Williams came from, the group known as "the Children of the Revival" certainly moved into Pentecostal practices and experiences in the years following 1904. Noel Gibbard in his book, *Fire on the Altar*, writes about an occasion when Evan Roberts visited a woman in Penygroes: "Evan Roberts visited Sarah Jones, a believer who exercised many of the spiritual gifts, including prophesying, healing and speaking in tongues. One source says that she first spoke in tongues during the Revival, but another claims it was early 1906." (Gibbard, 2006)

THE REVIVAL IN SUNDERLAND

The second event is the 1907 Revival in Sunderland, in the north-east of England. The leader there was a man called Alexander Boddy, a Church of England vicar, who invited Thomas Barratt from Norway to his church in Sunderland. Barratt was British-born, but moved to Norway at an early age and later became a pastor in the Methodist Episcopal Church. He was in New York to raise funds for the work in Norway. Stirred by a magazine giving details of the Revival that was taking place in Azusa Street, Los Angeles, he made contact with the leaders there. Barratt himself received the baptism in the Holy Spirit, with speaking in new languages, in New York on 15th November 1906. Returning home, he became the founder of the Pentecostal movement in Norway.

The Rev. Alexander Boddy heard about the spiritual awakening in Norway and visited Barratt at the beginning of March 1907. Boddy had previously invited Evan Roberts to come to his parish in the North-East of England but instead he visited the Revival in Wales for himself. In comparing the two Revivals Boddy wrote, "My four days in Oslo can never be forgotten. I stood with Evan

Roberts in Tonypandy, but have never witnessed such scenes as those in Norway." (Kay, 2000)

In 1907, there was opposition in the press and in some evangelical groupings in Great Britain towards this "new" biblical exposition of the baptism in the Holy Spirit with the evidence of speaking in tongues. The Keswick Movement, The Pentecostal Mission, Dr. Oswald Chambers, Jessie Penn-Lewis, Rev. Campbell Morgan, Rev. F.B. Meyer, and Rev. Graham Scroggie were some of the key evangelical organisations and Christian leaders of the day to join this camp. However, Alexander Boddy, undismayed by the anti- Pentecostal stance taken by many, invited Barratt to his church, All Saints, in Sunderland.

Barratt arrived by boat in Newcastle on 31st August 1907. Michael Harper writes, "No time apparently was lost, and the same evening a prayer meeting was held in the vestry of the church. The next day Barratt preached in the church at the evening service. There was an after meeting which continued in very un-Anglican fashion until 4 a.m., and the first three members of All Saints' were filled with the Holy Spirit as on the Day of Pentecost, 'speaking in other tongues as the Spirit gave them utterance.'" Barratt stayed in Sunderland until the middle of October and the national headlines were, "Staid Unemotional Matrons Taken Home to Bed o' Night 'Drunk' with Ecstatic Joy"; "Strange Revivalist Scenes – Vicar's Child Talks Chinese". (Harper, 1974)

This Revival in Sunderland, and the subsequent yearly Pentecost Conventions, became a focal point for men and women who would eventually be key leaders in the Pentecostal groupings that formed in the UK post 1907. Amongst them were the Jeffreys brothers, the Carter brothers, Donald Gee, Smith Wigglesworth and Cecil Polhill.

I have highlighted two very important events in the spiritual history of Great Britain in the 20th Century – the Welsh Revival and the Sunderland Revival. I have no doubt that both were inspired and set in motion by God in order to restore an Acts 2 experience of the baptism of the Holy Spirit to the Body of Christ in Great Britain. They were also the means by which God made strategic connections between people who were to be key players in the early development of the Pentecostal churches in the United Kingdom.

David Allen in his book, *There is a River*, tells us that D.P. Williams, along with other future Pentecostal leaders in Great Britain, "had their first unforgettable tastes of Pentecost" in Sunderland (Allen, 2004). Although I have found no evidence that Williams went to the Sunderland conventions, we are certain that he saw them as key in the Revival fires being stirred again after the 1904 Welsh Revival, and some from Penygroes did find their way there.

William Hutchinson visited Penygroes in 1906 and had a vision of "three balls of fire above his head, the first of which he believed symbolised the gift of tongues" (Kay, 2000). In 1908, he attended one of the Sunderland Conventions and was filled with the Holy Spirit. He opened the first Pentecostal church in Great Britain in November 1908. In 1910, D.P. Williams met with Hutchinson at a meeting in Penygroes and spent a number of years ministering with Hutchinson in the Apostolic Faith Church.

A Welsh minister, by the name of Rev. Clark, went to Hawick in Scotland to conduct revival meetings in 1908. This minister had received "a special anointing of power from God" during the Welsh Revival. One of the sermons he preached was "Have you received the Holy Spirit since ye believed?" In the congregation was a farm worker called Andrew Turnbull. In his biography, written by his son Tom, we are told, "My father realised at once that this was the experience he needed. Obeying the minister's injunction, he tarried until he was endued with power from on high." (Turnbull, 1965)

Andrew Turnbull received a remarkable gift of tongues. It was so remarkable that at the Sunderland Convention in 1913, the course of tongues he gave at one of the meetings was identified by a missionary from Africa, as an African language. The missionary confirmed that the English interpretation was exact. Turnbull, and the "Burning Bush" assembly which he was leading in Glasgow, joined the Apostolic Church in 1919. Something of his story will be told in a later chapter.

There is one further connection which I must draw attention to because it has an international dimension. In August 1908 Thomas Barratt, on his way back from India, stopped off in Denmark. During his stay Anna Larssen, a famous actress, was converted and later filled with the Holy Spirit. Anna married Sigurd Bjorner in 1912 and together they formed the Danish Pentecostal Movement. It was this couple who brought the Apostolic Church to Denmark in 1923, having visited the Apostolic National Convention in Penygroes. It was also through them that initial links were made with Italy.

THE REVELATION OF THE ETERNAL PURPOSE OF GOD

We have looked at the restoration of the truth of the baptism of the Holy Spirit with the sign of speaking in new languages. Let us now turn to the second truth that God was restoring in the 20th Century – the truth of the revelation of the eternal purpose of God.

Having spent some time researching old Apostolic Church publications for this book, the one thing that has struck me time and time again in reading about the lives and ministry of our early leaders is this – they knew that they were in partnership with the LORD and that they were involved in something that was ETERNAL. God had revealed to them something of which the Apostle Paul speaks in Eph 3:9-11: *"...the mystery which for ages has been hidden in God... so that the manifold wisdom of God might now be made known through the church... this was in accordance with the eternal purpose which He carried out in Christ Jesus our Lord."*

Gordon Weeks, Apostolic Church apostle and historian, makes this observation: "One can only marvel at the faith and vision of men and women who saw beyond the smallness of their circumstances and were in tune with 'the eternal purpose', affecting the nations in every continent." (Weeks, 2003)

D.P. Williams gave this explanation regarding the strategic times in which he was living and ministering, "... never since the days of the former Church have the gifts and prophetical ministry been so world-wide as in recent years. The operations of the Holy Spirit have spread all over the earth in the same manner as in the former days, and that for a specific sign and purpose, before the coming of the Lord, and to prepare His people ready, and as a prophetic testimony of the coming Kingdom, when everything will be subject to His rule. Therefore, it is very important that we should grasp the governmental aspect of the divine agency of the Holy Spirit in the Body of Christ... so that every function may find its place in the Body and ministry of the Church." (Williams D. P., 1931)

William Rowe, an early leader in the Apostolic Church, wrote, "'The Eternal Purpose': This is the most distinctive feature of Apostolic faith and purpose... What does the name 'Apostolic' mean? The Greek word is translated 'messenger' as well as 'Apostle' in the New Testament... The Apostolic Church is a Messenger Church. It was specially called into being to bear a message; and that message is the Eternal Purpose of God (Ephesians 3:11). Some folk think erroneously that our main objective is to declare that there are apostles and prophets today. That is not the Apostolic Vision; that is incidental, though important. Salvation is the door; Holiness is the way; Pentecost is the power; the Eternal Purpose is the goal." (Riches of Grace, 1962)

Our early fathers had a purpose in mind for the Church which was rather more visionary than many church mission statements we see today. I fully appreciate that the language and the abundance of words which they often used will not cut any ice as we present church to our congregations in the 21st Century. However, that purpose which they saw clearly and the understanding which they had, of what God desires both to demonstrate and reveal through His Church, has not changed.

Warren Jones, a past national leader of the UK Apostolic Church, prepared a study a number of years ago on the eternal purpose of God. In it he states, "Modern Christianity is taken up with the NOW. God's purpose is for ETERNITY. We need to ask how ETERNITY relates to NOW." (Jones)

Perhaps, in the past, our grasp of truth as a Fellowship disengaged us from our communities and the wider Body of Christ. Having the courage to ask how eternity relates to now and seek an answer will give us an eternal dimension to our purpose for living and our mission into the world. The one thing it will certainly do is make us Christ-centred.

THE RESTORATION OF THE MINISTRY OF APOSTLE AND PROPHET

This is the third restoration truth of the 20th Century. At the time of the formation of the Apostolic Church in Wales in 1916, there were no more than four recognised apostles in the whole of Great Britain and few recognised prophets. Now, some one hundred years later, many ministers, in many and various denominations or non-denominational networks, carry the designation of apostle or prophet.

After the 1st Century A.D. Church history makes only occasional mention of the ministries of apostle and prophet. However, in the 19th Century, The Catholic Apostolic Church sprang up, led by

Edward Irving, and one distinctive truth which it promoted was the restoration of these two ministries to the Church.

In 1908, William Hutchinson established the first Apostolic Faith Church in Bournemouth and, from this base, the first Pentecostal denomination in Great Britain was birthed. It was also the first group in the 20th Century to preach and practice the twin ministries of apostle and prophet. D.P. Williams was ordained as an apostle in the AFC in 1914 and his brother, Jones Williams, had been recognised as a prophet in February 1913. Thomas Jones and his son Omri, who were also part of the group which broke away from the AFC, had similarly been ordained with them as apostle and prophet respectively.

It was at AFC conventions that D.P. Williams would have first heard prophetic directions concerning the calling of men as apostles and prophets, and, also experienced the first ordination of an apostle – Hutchinson himself in August 1913. D.P. would also have encountered for the first time Bible teaching on the headship ministries of Jesus and their function in the Body of Christ. This was his testimony after hearing Musgrave Reade teach on the Body of Christ at an AFC convention in 1913: "I have had wonderful revelations since I have been at this conference, wonderful revelations of the work of God and the way the Lord wants to manifest Himself in His Body." (Williams, 1931)

For the Apostolic Church in Wales, these dual ministries were considered as "two wheels of the chariot". They turned together. The wisdom and judgement of the apostle co-operate with the revelation that comes through the ministry of the prophet. "For our fathers these gifts of men were the evidence that 'God dwells in the Body of Christ by His Spirit'; they were present to protect the Church from 'the craftiness and deceit of men'; they operated for 'the perfection of the Church, for the work of the ministry and the edifying of the Body'; and 'for unity of Spirit, faith, knowledge and love' (Eph 4:12-16)." (Davies & Yeoman, 2008)

D.P. Williams related this story at the 1937 Apostolic Convention, Penygroes, and it illustrates these twin headship gifts in operation bringing revelation and wisdom. It was discovered that some of the members in the local Penygroes assembly were in debt. The assembly had already been directed that they were not to hold open-air meetings but to stay in the church. Times were hard and there was widespread poverty. The assembly received this prophecy: "Bring your bills to the table." This was done and then a further prophecy was given: "Owe no man anything." The local church had a building fund at the time with over £50.00 saved. D.P. Williams continues, "Therefore, out of the storehouse the debts were paid. Every grocer was paid. All was clear and now we were commanded into the open-air to witness for Him seeing we had now dealt honourably with our neighbours."

This truth of the ministry of apostles and prophets was preached and practiced by early Apostolic pioneers. They were ridiculed for their dependency on the prophetic word, even by other Pentecostal groups in the UK and overseas. They were criticised and mocked for allowing the prophets to call people into international, national and local offices. However, at the 1937 Apostolic Convention, Pastor D.P. Williams said, "The secret of our unity in the Apostolic Church is that God speaks in the church. It is His voice that has united us. It is His voice that keeps us together." James Worsfold, Apostolic Church historian comments, "Williams' statement... indicated the beginning of a new understanding being born in him, an understanding which would prepare him to receive what came to be known as the 'Apostolic Vision.'" (Worsfold J. E., 1991)

But the Apostolic Church was not only about the apostle and the prophet. D.P. Williams used the hand as an illustration to show both the distinctiveness of each of the five headship ministries of Ephesians 4:11, but also the unity that existed between the gifts as they operated together in the Body of Christ. He wrote, "The thumb represents the apostles, with its grip and strength to clasp and grasp... the prophetic function, represented by the index finger, next to the thumb, always supports, and is at the command of the thumb in handling and writing. Being the index finger to point the way, it will symbolise the prophetic office. The third (long) finger (evangelist) reaches forth in front of others, as a pioneer preaching the Gospel to the world, gathering unto the apostles those that shall be saved... Then the third and little finger represent the pastor and teacher to shepherd, feed and guide the flock of God, preparing it ready for the Kingdom and the throne unto which they are all called, the whole presbytery of five offices assisting each other in their oversight of the assemblies." (Williams, 1931)

Perhaps rather wordy and over-elaborate but, if there is one thing that we can say about our forefathers, it is this – they had a vision which was world-wide and they had a method of fulfilling it which proved fruitful. In the chapters that follow, I trust that the stories of some of our early pioneers will demonstrate what that vision and method accomplished in Great Britain and far beyond in many nations of the world.

The birth of The Apostolic Church in Wales in 1916 was part of God's purpose of restoring to His Church truths that He first revealed in the early church. In previous centuries God restored to the Church the truth of justification by faith and the priesthood of all believers. In the 20th Century He was restoring to His Body the truths of the baptism of the Holy Spirit with the speaking of new languages, an understanding of the eternal purpose of God, and the ministries of apostle and prophet.

T.N. Turnbull describes how our fathers saw themselves: "The Apostolic Church is a body of believers who joyfully dare to stand for first century Christianity, its faith, its practices and its government." (T.N.Turnbull, 1959)

The life stories that follow will reflect how these truths of restoration were evidenced in ministry around the world by a confidence in the full Gospel, a dependency on the Holy Spirit, an obedience to prophetic guidance, a victorious faith and an eternal perspective.

CHAPTER THREE
DANIEL POWELL WILLIAMS

*"...and upon this rock I will build My church,
and the gates of Hades will not overpower it."*
Matthew 16:18

There have been a number of books written on the life and ministry of Daniel Powell Williams. However, we could not exclude him from this volume for two reasons. Firstly, because his example of faith and godliness was an inspiration to all who knew and loved him, and secondly because his impact on the early Apostolic Church, both nationally and internationally, was immeasurable.

HIS EARLY LIFE

Daniel Powell Williams was born on the morning of 5th May 1882, in a simple Welsh cottage in the small village of Penygroes, near Ammanford, South Wales. He was not a healthy baby and during those early months the prospect of a long life held no certainty. It was a Welsh speaking family and he was the second child of nine sons and three daughters born to Esther and William Williams. Granville Johnson, late apostle and missionary of the Apostolic Church, relates, in an article in the *Riches of Grace,* May 1982, an incident that happened when Daniel was four years of age: "William, being a strict "Chapel" man, lifted his young son up on one of the seats in the Chapel to recite. On hearing young Daniel's recitation, Mr. Bowen, the minister, said, 'Here is a lad with enough cheek to make a preacher.' Little did he realise that twenty years later he would be giving Daniel a call into the Congregational ministry." (Johnson, 1982)

But what kind of person was Dan, as he was known locally, before coming to faith in Jesus Christ? We do know that when he was only ten years old, his father went blind and Dan, to help the family financially, went to work in the local coal mine for one shilling per day. James Worsfold, provides this further insight into his young life before his mighty conversion during the Welsh Revival: "During his youth Williams (Daniel Powell) struggled with a dual nature which manifested itself in outbursts of uncontrollable temper… He believed he had inherited this angry disposition from his grandfather… In later years he was moved to testify in one of his preached messages that in his younger days he experienced hysterical fits of rage that would lead him to tear everything up. After his conversion he prayed, 'Lord, I have a devil in me. Please will You take it out of me.' This was Daniel's testimony later in life: 'I marvel at what I am. I do not find the old demonic power dominating me. Jesus has performed such a mighty work in my life. By the grace of God it is a long time since I lost my temper.'" (Worsfold, 1991)

This highlights a truth that I have discovered in researching the lives of many of the men included in this book - they were men who knew and understood what they had been without Christ and they knew and understood how great their salvation was through the Lord Jesus Christ.

HIS CONVERSION

As a young man of twenty-two years of age, Dan Williams was born again on Christmas Day 1904. It was a transforming experience. The Welsh Revival had broken out in September 1904 in a village called Loughor, South Wales, approximately twelve miles from Penygroes. The Revival spread and Dan's first contact with this move of God was in a meeting in Ammanford, a small town near Penygroes, during November 1904.

His initial opinion of what he saw and heard was this: "This is all nonsense. Nobody knows that he is saved." He was persuaded to stay a little longer in the meeting and the Holy Spirit started to convict Dan of his sin. When he left the meeting the influence of the Holy Spirit continued in his life. In his book, Gordon Weeks, Apostolic Church historian, writes, "Now great waves of religious emotion swept over him and he was continually confessing his sins to friends and relations." (Weeks, 2003)

On Christmas Day 1904 Dan went to Loughor, with his brother-in- law and a friend, to hear Evan Roberts, the renowned preacher of the Welsh Revival. It was the afternoon meeting and he asked Evan Roberts to pray for him. Roberts laid his hands on Dan and he started to weep and then cried out, "There is no hope for me. My sins are too great!"

In the words of Gordon Weeks, this is what happened next: "He became unconscious of all around him and this awful experience was followed by the calmness of heaven filling his soul. The fire began to burn in his heart and, regaining consciousness, he found himself with a few friends in the darkened room. As he lay on the floor a girl sang, 'The gates of heaven are open wide: I see a sea of blood...' As she sang he saw a vision of Christ on the Cross. Blood flowed from the Saviour's body, blood that bathed a sinner's head making the flesh as white as wool. It was revealed to him that this was himself made white in the blood of the Lamb. Enraptured he exclaimed, 'I have seen Him, I have found Him.' It is no wonder that he always claimed that Christmas Day as the day of his salvation." (Weeks, 2003)

It is important to understand that it was the depth of this powerful conversion experience that laid the solid foundation for all that was to follow in D.P. Williams' life and ministry. In researching the lives of many of the early Apostolic Church fathers, a common thread has emerged – they each had a profound encounter with God at the time of their conversion. Their Christian lives began with a deep conviction of sin and an experience of a mighty deliverance from God which continued to shape and impact all that lay ahead, propelling them across land and sea to tell others of Jesus.

Of course, the same can be said of many other Christians, both great and small, throughout history. But what of the Church today? Might it be that today, there is not always such a deep conviction of sin in the hearts of men and women, nor such a sense of a mighty deliverance from God at the time of conversion, to lay that deep foundation of a heart wholly committed to being a living witness for Jesus – a heart willing to go anywhere and do anything, whatever the cost, to make Him known to others and to see His Church built up? We cannot but read about the lives of D.P. Williams and these other early church fathers without being challenged in our own hearts.

The Apostle Paul speaks of this kind of godly conviction and sorrow producing "repentance leading to salvation, not to be regretted; but the sorrow of the world produces death." (2 Corinthians 7:10) It is this thought that Charles Spurgeon takes up and expresses in his own words:

"A spiritual experience which is thoroughly flavoured with a deep and bitter sense of sin is of great value to him that hath it. It is terrible in the drinking, but it is most wholesome in the bowels."

"Stripping comes before clothing; digging out the foundation is the first thing in building and a thorough sense of sin is one of the earliest works of grace in the heart." (Spurgeon, 2004)

What impact did this conversion encounter with God have on D.P. Williams? Granville Johnson's article continues, "For the next forty-three years Daniel continually looked for opportunities to tell others about the saving power of Jesus Christ" (Johnson, 1982).

Bryn Thomas, Apostolic Church pastor and historian, writes, "Following the experience in Loughor, Williams gave himself wholeheartedly to developing a deeper spiritual understanding and relationship with God." (Thomas, 2016)

The God who saved him, now became the God whom he was going to seek with his whole heart, for the rest of his life. Again this depth of experience challenges us regarding the all too commonly heard, present-day invitation to come to Christ because "God loves you, has a plan for your life and can help you with your problems." All of this is undoubtedly true, but it fails to mention the need for repentance and the sacrificial call of the Gospel, which D.P. Williams and so many of his colleagues responded to – a call to turn from sin, die to self and follow Jesus through the grave of baptism into resurrection life.

THE CALL OF GOD

Through his conversion experience, I believe God, who had great spiritual things in store for D.P. Williams, was getting his heart right for him to "serve the purpose of God in his generation." In their biography, *Born in the Fire,*, Davies and Yeoman say this of his passion for the Lord following his conversion: "…Daniel's heart beat strong with love for the Lord. A consuming desire to seek and save the lost possessed him. He was resolved at all costs to stand for and to be loyal to his Saviour, for Christianity had become to him a religion of fire. He resolved that the neighbourhood should know what it really meant to receive the pardon and mercy of God. The covenant was made, and once made, should never be broken." (Davies & Yeoman, 2008)

The Biblical principal of Jeremiah 29:13 began to bear fruit in Dan's life -*"you will seek Me and find Me, when you search for Me with all your heart."* He certainly had a new heart toward God, but what happened next? How did God fulfil this promise?

Dan had by this time married Elizabeth Harries, from Llandeilo, and before long he saw his family come to salvation. He also commenced prayer meetings in the coal mine where he worked, resulting in many of his colleagues coming to faith in the Lord Jesus Christ. It was there, in the depths of the earth that he had another powerful encounter with the Lord – an experience that brought him face to face with the will of God for his life.

Dan himself wrote, "During the first months of my conversion, I was leading colliers to the Lord underground and wherever I found sinners wanting Jesus (for I would go on my knees with the Bible open, and lead them to see the light of Calvary). One Friday afternoon I heard a voice speaking to me underground, when the sweat was streaming down my face, hammering the coal with a pick at the coal face at the Emlyn Colliery, Penygroes. The voice asked my soul, 'Are you willing to give your home life, your wife and your two little children, to me, and leave this place, and go out in my name, to preach the love that I have shown towards you, and given to you?' I did not know what to say. It was as if I was between heaven and earth, sobbing, crying and broken-hearted. But I told the Lord, 'I cannot earn my living, if you will not leave me alone.' I had my wife and children, and wanted to live honestly and honourably. I had built a little house to live in, after I got married, and now Jesus wanted to have me with all I had. The hand of the Lord was so heavy that I begged Him to take His hand away, or take me out, and give me grace to preach to the world. I said to the Lord, 'Now, if you want me, Lord, to be a minister, and to go out to the world to preach the Gospel of the cross, you tell the minister and the deacons of the Church. I am not going to force myself at all. You must tell them, Lord, and I am giving you two weeks' notice, and in two weeks' time I want you to let that minister tell me, or I am giving up; I cannot go on in the spiritual and the natural all the time.'" (Davies & Yeoman, 2008)

The minister of the Welsh Congregational Chapel that Dan attended was still Rev. William Bowen -the same minister who, when Dan was four years of age, had said on hearing him recite in the chapel, "Here is a lad with enough cheek to make a preacher." After laying the fleece out before the Lord, Dan was in high expectation but, then he continues the story in his own words: "Every time I met the minister, I was expecting him to say something… but on Thursday night, before the two weeks had passed, I met him on the road. It was dark, and he called to me, 'Is that you Daniel? I am coming with you to the meeting; and I have got a secret to tell you tonight.' My heart began to beat in my breast. The Lord said to me, 'He is going to ask you tonight to be a minister.' Like Moses, Dan's reply was 'How can I?' The Rev. Bowen replied, 'Oh, my boy, the Lord has saved you and has blessed you so much in the Revival that He will be sure to form you to be a minister.'" (Davies & Yeoman, 2008)

The matter was put before the congregation and D.P. Williams was duly ordained. On Thursday 1st February 1906, he preached his first sermon. His text was Matthew 16:18 (AV): *Upon this rock I will build My church, and the gates of hell shall not prevail against it.*

In his article, Granville Johnson writes, "For the next six years Daniel preached in over 80 chapels this message of the Gospel. Much of the Revival fire had gone out of the churches, but the work of the Holy Spirit was taking a different direction, towards a Bible-based church ministry and growth." (Johnson, 1982)

Within thirteen months of Dan's conversion, God was developing his heart to hear from Him and also to respond in the way that God desired - with obedience. Thank God for His written Word and the way God uses His book to speak to us and challenge us. But, let us never forget, God also wants us to experience Him in the depths of our being. Some call such experiences as D.P. Williams had "crisis experiences", but that very word "crisis" can leave us with a wrong impression of these encounters with the Lord. Though maybe not frequent, they are surely normal, because we are in a relationship with the Lord God. In fact, they are absolutely vital to the ongoing developing of our hearts. Such experiences from the Lord can only serve to deepen our willingness to respond to His call in our life and strengthen our desire to receive from Him and Him alone, making us more effective ambassadors for the Lord Jesus Christ.

HIS SPIRIT BAPTISM

While the Welsh Revival was not Pentecostal in the sense that we would define it today, during the Revival there were manifestations such as we would read of in Acts 2 and I Corinthians:12. D.P. Williams wrote about the experience of Pentecost coming to Penygroes during the Revival: "The burning heat of the Divine presence would sometimes be so intense as to engender a desire to flee away... Homes were changed, people of various stations in life were regenerated, we witnessed the sublime manifestations of the Holy Spirit with tongues of fire."

Although, in general terms, the influence of the Welsh Revival on the people of Wales was beginning to decrease there were pockets in Wales where an Acts 2 baptism of the Holy Spirit was being experienced. These manifestations of the Spirit continued to be evidenced in Wales after 1906. A thirst had been birthed in many for more of God. These "Children of the Revival", as they were called, met in little groups and held "cottage meetings". Missions were started and churches were eventually established because the Revival had created a desire for more of God.

The Azusa Street Revival in Los Angeles, California, in 1906 re-established a Spirit baptism that was evidenced by the speaking of new languages. This brought a new surge and hunger for God and a fresh Holy Spirit visitation came to Wales and the United Kingdom, in the immediate years following the 1904-05 Revival. One eyewitness said this of the post-revival experience: "Many were filled with the Holy Ghost and the sign of speaking in tongues followed. Some thought this was going to be a great blessing to the Welsh valleys, but, to the consternation of many hearts, it brought division."

D.P. Williams' home village of Penygroes was one of those where the baptism in the Holy Spirit with signs following was evidenced. In an earlier chapter, I referred to Sarah Jones of Penygroes, "who exercised many of the spiritual gifts..." One source says that she first spoke in tongues during the Revival, but another claims it was early in 1906. As far as Penygroes was concerned, however, 1906 was still a time of Revival. There was an Acts 2 group meeting in a home in the village and Dan Williams certainly would have been aware of it.

Remembering the earlier chapter, "The Big Picture", the point which we need to emphasise is this: the Lord was restoring in these early years of the twentieth century, both in the United Kingdom and in the world at large, the biblical truth of the baptism in the Holy Spirit with the sign of speaking in tongues. In Wales this was happening through the various cottage meetings that came into existence following the Revival. Meanwhile in Scotland, in Kilsyth in 1908, a group of believers at the Westport Hall experienced the baptism in the Holy Spirit, with signs following. Similarly, in England, the Rev. Alexander Boddy and his Anglican Church in Sunderland experienced an outpouring of the Holy Spirit in 1907, and members of the Evangelistic Hall in Penygroes are known to have paid a visit there.

At this time in his life, Dan was facing a very busy schedule, working in the local mine, caring for his wife and a growing young family, studying God's Word and preparing sermons. He did not have the money to go to college so, according to his biography, "he worked unsparingly in private meditation and reading of appropriate books that opened his understanding in the various fields of pastoral and theological needs."(Davies & Yeoman, 2008) Remember also that, in order to fulfil his preaching engagements, he had to walk many miles, either going the whole way on foot or walking to a railway station to catch a train.

This busy schedule resulted in D.P. having something of a mental breakdown. In his own words: "Engagements in abundance were forthcoming, but they did not continue long before a collapse occurred, resulting in a period of four months indisposition... A gentleman from a considerable distance was led to take me away for five weeks' holiday..." (Davies & Yeoman, 2008) He went to the seaside town of Aberaeron, on the west coast of Wales, to recuperate. It was there that he met a group of Spirit filled believers who were speaking with new tongues. The leader was a man called William Phillips, whom he had never met before, but this meeting in 1909 proved to be a "God appointment".

As a result, Dan was filled with the Holy Spirit and spoke in new languages. He had joined this group of believers as they climbed a hill overlooking Cardigan Bay. This is how William

Phillips described what happened next: "Here they knelt, prayed and praised. As they were praising God, Daniel fell flat on his face, weeping, sobbing and groaning. He resembled a worm trying to get a place to hide in the earth. Those who were present agreed that it was a sight that they would never forget. Ecstasy overwhelmed his soul and he spoke with tongues as the Holy Spirit gave him utterance. He had studied for the ministry but he still required the power of the Holy Spirit." (Phillips, 1936)

Furthermore, this link with William Phillips developed into a friendship and, in time, they were to become ministerial colleagues in the Apostolic Church. D.P. actually ordained him in 1916. William Phillips became a remarkable leader in the Apostolic Church and pioneered churches in Northern Ireland.

How William Phillips came to be in Aberaeron in 1909 is in itself an amazing story. He had previously been living in America. One day, while drinking in a hotel in Cleveland, Ohio, he heard the voice of God calling, "William." This experience changed his life. He came back to Wales as a converted man, and opened a mission in Aberaeron, was subsequently baptised in water and then received the fullness of the Holy Spirit with the gift of speaking in new languages. It was at this time that Dan came to convalesce in Aberaeron. This was not coincidence, but God was at work, not only for the now but also for the future. William Phillips, accompanied by Evan Jones, became the first missionary that the Apostolic Church in Wales sent overseas, after its inception in January 1916.

THE EXPERIENCE OF THE PROPHETIC

As the "Children of the Revival" in Penygroes experienced this new wave of the Holy Spirit, the members of their house group, who had continued to meet after the 1904-05 Revival, formed themselves into a church in August 1907 and called themselves

"The Evangelistic Church." They remained an independent, non-denominational house group under the leadership of Mr. Eben Griffiths. In February 1910, they moved from a house into their own church building, which became known as "The Evangelistic Hall." James Worsfold tells us that D.P. Williams was present for the opening service, and appears in the photograph taken to mark the occasion. (Worsfold, 1991)

D.P. wrote, "...from time to time, I visited this place, but without any intention of linking myself to them, as my object was to continue the career of an ordained minister. I soon discovered, however, that my life was being planned by the predestined will of God towards a dispensational movement...The outstanding feature of this new movement was the baptism and fullness of the Holy Ghost with signs following, together with divine healing."

It was in the Evangelistic Hall that Daniel, sometime in 1910, heard directive prophecy for the first time and it concerned himself: "It is I, the Lord thy God, that have led thee, my young servant, into this place. In a mysterious way have I brought thee here, for My purposes concerning thee are great, and shall be marvellous in the eyes of many. My hand have I laid upon thee for a work hitherto not revealed unto thee. Chosen art thou by the Lord thy God to gather My sheep, for, verily, scattered they are on the mountains of Israel. I hear their bleating, saith the Lord. But I will gather them, and thou shalt shepherd them. There shall be one fold, but many flocks. If thou wilt obey My voice I will send thee unto them. The performance of My word shall be sure concerning thee if thou wilt hearken to the word that I have spoken unto thee this day, saith the Lord."

This was his response: "It was incontrovertibly and unmistakably the voice of God, searching, profound and divine, so much so that I fell prostrate on my face in deep contrition and brokenness of heart...The revelation was beyond doubt or question.

The overwhelming influence of the predicting word was so drastic that all my future plans were broken, my prospects, seemingly, hampered, my hopes and desires consequently shattered...These utterances seemed so mystifying that, on the one hand, they appeared impossible. As I lay in dire contrition, a deep conviction possessed my soul in regard to baptism by immersion. And whilst thus meditating, the word of the Lord came again: "And on the morrow thou shalt be buried with thy Lord." The next day, Dan Williams was baptised in water. Baptism by immersion was not practiced in the Welsh Congregational Church, so his obedience demonstrates how deeply this first experience of the prophetic had impacted him.

I want to stop here and just plant a thought. I fully appreciate that we must have a solid biblical theology in our lives. I understand the New Testament pattern, as laid out in the epistles, that behaviour comes out of belief but, while seeking to have a biblical belief system, let us also renew our commitment to have full-on experiences with God. You and I are in relationship with the Lord God, through the Lord Jesus Christ, in the power of the Holy Spirit, and that means we are to experience him. The old song put it like this – "He walks with me and He talks with me." The evidence of my relationship with the Lord is not just belief, but experiences, through which He writes his signature across my life. In regard to the life of D.P. Williams, the thing that convinced him of the validity of the prophetic was not a belief, but a personal experience of an encounter with God in that Evangelistic Hall in Penygroes. It was this that spoke into his heart and impacted his life.

Worsfold wrote this regarding D.P.'s first experience of the prophetic: "We in the Apostolic Church today have good cause to thank God that Williams accepted this initial word of prophecy and allowed it to provide a new motivation and direction for his life." (Worsfold, 1991)

Soon after this occurred in 1910, Daniel heard another directive prophecy in the Evangelistic Hall, when the leader of The Apostolic Faith Church (AFC), William Oliver Hutchinson, and his assistant, James Dennis visited Penygroes. It is, once again, James Worsfold who takes up the story, telling us that this visit "was prompted by a prophetic word given through a recognised prophetess living in London.

While in a home praying for a sick child, to the surprise of those present, a prophetic word came through Dennis which said, among other things, that 'the hour had come for the Lord to make known His choice in relation to the shepherd of His people'. Instructions were given that hands be laid upon Williams, separating him to the ministry, and that the occasion was to be celebrated with the observance of the Lord's Supper. The prophetic word found a response in Williams as well as in those present". (Worsfold, 1991)

While those in the home accepted this call upon D.P., not all the members of the Evangelistic Hall were so open and welcoming. The matter was not pressed any further but, eventually, through other prophetic words in this local church in Penygroes, he was asked to become their leader. D.P. Williams was beginning to experience both the worth and the fulfilment of the prophetic in his life.

THE INFLUENCE OF WILLIAM HUTCHISON

D.P. Williams first met William Hutchinson in 1910 in Penygroes. The regard that they both had for each other following their first meeting is confirmed by this fact - when D.P. was finally recognised as the leader at the Evangelistic Hall, he wrote to Hutchinson about his appointment and the letter was published in the AFC magazine, *Showers of Blessing*, in February 1911. Hutchinson wrote: "Further News from Wales. We rejoice to hear the glorious news that comes from Penygroes. Our beloved Brother Dan Williams has been placed as overseer to the assembly. Since then God has mightily blessed the place and souls are being saved, sanctified and baptised in the Holy Ghost." (Hutchinson, 1911)

D.P. Williams spent the years 1910 – 1915 in ministry with Hutchinson and the AFC. These years have been, to some extent, glossed over in previous Apostolic Church historical accounts. However, it was an important, formative time in his life and also for the ministry that God had for him after he parted company with the Apostolic Faith Church in January 1916.

William Hutchinson promoted and practiced a biblical Pentecostal model for local church, recognising the full complement of Christ-given ministries as per Ephesians 4:11. He was a recognised apostle himself, who believed and followed prophetic direction. He had a vision for world mission, sending missionaries first of all to South Africa, and he taught and practised the truth of "body ministry" within the AFC congregations.

So, from that first contact in 1910, Daniel was introduced to and became involved in the beliefs and practices that William Hutchinson promoted in his ministry. What impact did this have on his life?

It was during this period with Hutchinson that D.P. Williams was recognized as an apostle and brought into full-time ministry. He experienced the dynamic of the prophetic in the Apostolic Faith Church and saw the word of the Lord coming to pass. In time he was appointed superintendent of the AFC churches in Wales and travelled with Hutchinson throughout the United Kingdom. During his ministry with the AFC, he came into contact with many Pentecostal missions and groups.

His brother was recognised as a prophet within the

denomination and it was there, with Hutchinson, that Dan sharpened his understanding of the importance of the prophetic channel and prophetic content. He developed and published a set of beliefs for the Apostolic Faith churches in Wales and it was there he came under ministry regarding the Body of Christ.

It was also during these years, on 11th October 1911, that Daniel and Elizabeth's eldest daughter, Olwen, died. She was only seven years of age. Sadly, they had already lost a baby girl, Esther Maria, prior to Olwen's death. The Lord God had been and was continuing to shape his heart through trials and sorrows of many kinds. Pastor James Brooke, a colleague from the Apostolic Faith Church, wrote this account in the denomination's magazine, *Showers of Blessing*:

"Beloved, it was wonderful to see Brother Dan and his wife. Just before the coffin was closed down, they came, and over the body of their first-born they adored and worshipped their Lord and praised Him amid their tears. Beloved, it melted me down. I wept quietly. To me it was quite as much a miracle as if the dead had been raised. No rebellion... By the time we reached the burying ground fully 250 people had gathered. After the little coffin had been lowered there was a deep silence...Then Dan, in a clear voice, started singing: 'He died of a broken heart for me. He died of a broken heart. Oh wondrous love, it was for me, He died of a broken heart.' The Spirit of God seemed to lay hold upon those gathered, and like a mighty sound, it must have been heard all over the village. It seemed to lift us away from the time to another scene, where the God and Father of our Lord Jesus Christ gazed upon Him who gave Himself up for us all."

The minister concluded his report with these words: "What stood out, beloved, above everything else was the wonderful grace that was given to Pastor and Mrs. Williams. I have never seen anything like it myself before. Hallelujah! What a Saviour! God bless you all." (Brooke, 1911)

The whole story of that day is truly amazing. A full account can be found in *The Origins of the Apostolic Church in Great Britain* (Worsfold, 1991).

These five years that D.P. Williams spent in ministry with William Hutchinson, within the AFC network, were undoubtedly significant in the developing of the man and of the purpose that God had for him. Hutchinson and Pastor Dan became close friends and colleagues in these years and perhaps Hutchinson's role as mentor to him has not been fully acknowledged in previous works on the history of the Apostolic Church.

In later years, D.P. himself did acknowledge the blessing that the Welsh churches had known when they were in relationship with Hutchinson and the AFC. In a 1933 publication, he added this comment when writing about the separation: "...It is just to mention, however, that a great blessing was derived through his (Hutchinson's) instrumentality at the commencement of the work. The time came when the Lord desired us to sever this connection in January 1916..." (Williams, 1933)

As mentioned in the previous chapter, D.P. Williams and a number of Welsh colleagues and churches broke away from the Apostolic Faith Church in January 1916, because of Hutchinson's increasingly unscriptural doctrinal stance. He had begun to regard himself as the "Chief Apostle" and to consider his authority superior to that even of scripture, denying other apostles and prophets the right to disagree with him.

WHAT HAPPENED AFTER JANUARY 1916?

The height and width of any building is determined by its foundation. I want to suggest this – the years following D.P. Williams' conversion in December 1904 and up until January 1916 were foundational in his life. In these years he faced many personal, spiritual and ministerial trials, but he was a man readied by God to take on the challenge of carrying the message of restoration around the world. What he accomplished in God, in the years from 1916 until his death in February 1947, was undoubtedly remarkable. Some of what God outworked through him will become evident as we look at the lives of other pioneers who ministered with Pastor Dan from 1916 – 1947, but I do want to relate here some events and incidents in the life of this man and his ministry.

Great sorrow once again visited his home on May 23rd 1918 when his wife Elizabeth died. She had shared his faith and upheld him through many trials, but now he found himself alone with seven young children. Later that year he married Mabel Thomas, from Porthcawl, who stood faithfully beside him in raising the children and in fulfilling the call of God upon his life.

On one particular night in 1919, Dan went to see his brother, Jones Williams, who lived about two miles away in Penygoes. He often went to Jones' home to discuss the work of the church and spend time together in prayer. However, at that time, there was opposition in the village to the Apostolic Church. Chapel people claimed it was "of the devil."

The moment he stepped outside his brother's house to return home, a man suddenly appeared and stood beside him. Pastor Dan started to walk and the man walked with him. Part of the journey included passing a colliery on one side and open fields on the other, but the man never left him. When he finally arrived at his own front door, the man who had accompanied him suddenly disappeared. Pastor Dan was home safe and the Lord had provided angelic protection from unseen dangers.

It was also in 1919 that D.P. Williams received two prophetic words from his brother, Jones: "Journey – journey, you must, and I will gather together" and, "The hour has come when I am sending you, My servant, into this valley; and inasmuch as you have found obedience in your heart, you shall find that I will work in very truth in a manner that will cause the enemy to be stirred." Following the direction of these two prophecies, he moved to Pontypridd, sixty miles from Penygroes, and became pastor of the Apostolic assembly there. Gordon Weeks writes, "They (the Pontypridd church) had gone through a time of great difficulties, but with coming of the Pastor, the crisis was over, the church found its balance and new members were added." (Weeks, 2003)

1919 proved to be a significant year for the Apostolic Church in Wales. In that year a group of churches in the Hereford area, also known as "The Apostolic Church" and led by a Pastor Frank Hodges, joined forces with D. P. Williams and his colleagues, as did the Burning Bush Church, led by Pastor Andrew Turnbull in Glasgow. Two years later, a further defining moment took place for the future of the Apostolic Church as a whole.

A man, by the name of Herbert Chanter, from Bradford, attended the 1921 Christmas Convention in Pontypridd. He was involved in the leadership of a Pentecostal group, based in Bradford, which had other assemblies in Kent, London, Bedford and the north of England. He came to Pontypridd with a prophetic promise in his heart. The Bradford group had been told that the Lord intended Bradford to be the hub of a wheel, "the spokes of which would extend in all directions throughout the world." (It was this prophetic word that also spoke of "belting the globe" with the Gospel).

Herbert Chanter writes, "In the summer of 1921 this question was continually with me; 'Why are we not a united Apostolic Church?'" During the Pontypridd convention, he received prophetic guidance and returned to Bradford to report what he had experienced. The following year, at the Easter Convention in Bradford, a miracle from God occurred. The Williams brothers from Wales and Pastor Frank Hodges, with two elders from Hereford, appeared there unexpectedly. There was no prior arrangement. They all said that they had come to Bradford by prophetic direction. Pastor Chanter recalls, "This coming together, without premeditation, was so remarkable that we could only say that it was the Lord; there must be some purpose in which we were all concerned." (Weeks, 2003)

The outcome was this – Herbert Chanter, and the churches he led, finding that they shared a common vision, also joined forces with D.P. Williams, Frank Hodges and Andrew Turnbull and their churches in Wales, England, Scotland, and Northern Ireland and together they became known as "The Apostolic Church". A doctrinal statement was agreed; an administrative structure was put in place and a Missionary Council, with representatives from Scotland, England and Wales, was established with its headquarters in Bradford. D.P. Williams was chosen as the President of the Council. Gordon Weeks records, "The meeting was adamant in the total rejection of any thought of a 'Chief Apostle'. The president was the Chairman and in no way pre-eminent! They remembered January 1916 too well!" (Weeks, 2003)

D.P. Williams was not only a man of vision, faith and power, but also a man of wisdom and grace, as can be seem from the following brief incident in his life. He served as the pastor of the Skewen Apostolic Assembly, near Neath, between the years 1924 – 1929. Ben Noot, later to become an Apostolic pastor himself, was attending that assembly then and recalled how D.P. dealt with one particular challenge:

"At that time he was the innocent victim of some slanderous letters. These were filled with vindictive, malicious hatred, for no cause whatever, from the pen of some misguided and deluded person. It was characteristic of the Pastor, however, that, after showing one just received to a near friend in his study late one night, and on being asked what he was going to do about it, he simply put it in the fire, saying, 'That's what we'll do! Let us pray for the poor fellow!' immediately turning word into action and pouring out strong cryings for the deliverance of the person in question, and a plea for his forgiveness." (Noot, 1936)

In the same article, Ben Noot makes this comment, "The results of his pastorate in Skewen are with us today. Several of the young men, who are now themselves in the ministry, are the product of his unremitting toil." Who were these young men? Let me mention a few of their names: Cyril Rosser who went to Nigeria; Alf Greenaway who went to New Zealand and Australia; Ben Noot who went to Canada; James Eynon who went to New Zealand; Tom Roberts who went to France and his brother Owen, who served the Lord in the United Kingdom. During D.P. William's time in Skewen, an assembly was opened in Port Talbot, the seeds for an assembly in Neath were planted, a cottage meeting was opened in Resolven and links were confirmed with a group in Kenfig Hill, near Bridgend. We need to remember that, while he was untiringly involved in church planting and pastoral care in South Wales, he was also untiringly committed to his role as National and International Leader of the Apostolic Church.

The story is told of how, on another occasion, D.P. was with some helpers at a cottage meeting in Resolven, near Neath, South Wales. There were some young men from the village in the meeting. The power of God was clearly present and, through the laying on of hands, these young men had fallen to the ground. There was a woman there, Minnie Davies, who, on witnessing Pastor Dan and the helpers laying hands on others, ran out of the meeting shouting to her husband, "Come Henry, these men have Jesus Christ in their finger tips." (Apostolic Herald, 1936). Minnie and Henry had a daughter called May, who later, with her husband George Williams from Pontardawe, served the Lord in full-time ministry in Nigeria and in the United Kingdom.

In D.P. Williams' biography there is a chapter entitled "Missionary Journeys", which includes this summary: "In the year 1922, Pastor Dan, with various Apostolic teams, began a series of missionary journeys that would take him to thirty or more countries over a period of twenty-four years." By 1929, it is estimated that he had travelled some 50,000 miles and preached to twenty-one different nationalities. At the 1944 Penygroes International Apostolic Convention, towards the end of his life, he was preparing for a visit to the USA and Canada and estimated that, counting all his land and sea journeys, he had travelled not far short of three hundred thousand miles! His subsequent trip to North America proved to be his last missionary journey. What highlights can we mention of these many travels?

On a 1922 trip to the USA, with three other pastors from the UK, the car in which they were travelling missed a sharp turn in the road and somersaulted twice into a field, leaving the four pastors underneath the car. There were minor injuries, but they proved the Lord in a safe deliverance.

While he was preaching on a visit to Denmark in January 1924, a man faced him with his fists raised. Speaking English, the man denounced him as a deceiver. Pastor Dan remained quiet and unmoved, despite this threatening behaviour, and the man just turned on his heels and left the building. The church service continued.

On a 1927 visit to Italy fifty-six people were saved and two deacons and two elders were ordained. At a convention in Paris in November 1930, an elder, two deacons and two deaconesses were ordained, twenty-five people were converted, nine people were baptised in water and many people were healed and filled with the Holy Spirit.

In 1931, Pastor Dan travelled to Nigeria with two colleagues.

In Lagos, it was reported that over four hundred people were converted and over eight hundred people were healed or baptised in the Holy Spirit. The Lagos press headline read, "Never before has Lagos witnessed such scenes as those which are now daily taking place in this Revival and Divine Healing Crusade." When the UK Pastors left Nigeria there were almost two thousand people present to bid them farewell at the harbour. As a result of this one visit, the Apostolic Church family worldwide had fourteen thousand new members in Nigeria.

On a 1935 trip to Scandinavia, Pastor Dan preached in Denmark, Norway, Sweden, Estonia, Latvia and Poland. While in Latvia, he spoke at a meeting attended by four-hundred and fifty Russian Christians. In a meeting in Norway he spoke to seven hundred people and in Latvia, he preached to a congregation of one thousand five hundred people.

These are merely snapshots of the man and his ministry, but it is clear that, in all his travels and his missionary service, God used D. P. Williams in a remarkable way. He was an instrument in God's hand, to further that prophetic promise given in 1921 – the promise of "belting the globe" with the Gospel.

In the meantime, what had been happening in the United Kingdom? By the end of 1926, there were forty assemblies in Scotland alone, with two thousand members. In a report that Pastor Dan gave in 1933, he mentioned that there were ninety assemblies in Wales.

THE FINAL SCENE

D.P. Williams experienced personal trials, sorrows and challenges of many kinds throughout his life. He knew what it was to face opposition and to be ridiculed in his ministry; all through his ministerial life he suffered the effects of a serious mining accident; he knew the physical demands of obeying God's will; he knew what it was to be separated from family for weeks and months at a time; he knew the challenge of living sacrificially and walking by faith. To have looked at all these things humanly would have been overwhelming, but D.P. had a heart that God had made right!

Not least amongst his sorrows were the deaths of several close family members, three of whom have been mentioned already – his daughters, Esther and Olwen, and his first wife, Elizabeth. Further heartache came on August 22nd 1924, with the death of his thirteen year old son, Moelwen, who with his last breath cried, "Hallelujah!" At the close of D.P. Williams' life, more family sorrow was to come. In one week in 1947, the Williams family were devastated by the death of a daughter on Monday 10th February and by the death of Pastor Dan himself, on Thursday 13th February.

D.P. and his second wife, Mabel, had returned early from a mission trip to North America. The trip had begun with sadness because, on arriving in Canada in April 1945, they were informed that his brother, Jones Williams, who had been so close to him throughout his years of ministry, had died. Let Pastor Dan continue the story: "Eleven months had passed since our coming when suddenly a cloud came over our lives with news from home. Mair, our daughter, was preparing to join us in Canada when she contracted tuberculosis. She was just twenty-one years old... Naturally speaking, it would have been very easy to collect our things together and make for home, but we had been sent by the word of the Lord and nothing but the voice of the Spirit would release us."

Pastor Dan, his wife, and the colleagues with them sought the Lord in prayer. News was received that Mair was better and so they made their way to the USA. Again, word came, via a cable to Toronto, that Mair was very ill and the request was to come home immediately. Again, prayer was made and a word from the Lord was sought. Pastor Eynon, who was with them, prophesied, "I want you to understand that I have seen desires in you to abide in this land, but I have ordained that your bones shall rest in the soil of your birthplace. The end of your responsibility should be where you commenced."

Miraculously a voyage home was found for them at short notice. Pastor Dan, who had been seriously ill during the months he was away, became ill again on the voyage home. He was in fact ordered to bed, but the one thing that both he and Mabel held to was the "word" that had been given to them by Pastor Eynon. They arrived back in the UK early in November 1946 and, coming to Penygroes, they found Mair sitting up in bed, crying with joy that her father and mother were back home.

They had returned at a time when the whole country was suffering one of the severest winters on record and Pastor Dan himself was taken ill again. Mabel Williams wrote in her diary of the dilemma she faced, with her husband confined to bed in one room and their daughter confined to bed in another, "Often times it was difficult to know which room needed the most attention… It was pathetic to hear them passing messages to each other, until both had lost the energy to communicate. I then had to be the one to convey them." (Davies & Yeoman, 2008)

Pastor Dan's last message to Mair was, "Tell her today that to be with Christ is far better."

Mair replied to her mother, "O Mamma, I am too young to die. I am willing to die for the Lord, but I haven't yet lived for Him." Mabel wrote, "Then she closed her eyes and said, 'Lord, Thy will be done.' For weeks she went through an awful conflict wondering why the Lord did not answer prayer to heal her, when so many were praying for her. But one night the Lord gave her that verse

'Delight thyself also in the Lord, and He will give thee the desire of thine heart.' Then He asked her, 'Are you willing for My will to be your only desire?' She answered, 'Yes, Lord!' After that we would repeatedly hear her saying, 'Lord, Thy will be done!'"

Mair organised the hymns for her funeral and a few days before she died she testified to the doctors and invited them to come to her funeral. She told some of the neighbours that she wanted to see them in heaven. Mabel writes, "Her deathbed scene will not easily be forgotten. Many were her sayings as she wished us all goodbye, with a parting message to each, dividing up her little belongings, many of which she treasured and were of sentimental value. Then she said, 'I would like you all to be missionaries – but just where you are. Will you now kiss me goodbye.' Then she called, 'Dada, dada, goodbye! I am going soon.' He answered faintly, 'Goodbye my child!'" Mabel had collapsed three days earlier, so she was not with her daughter when she died on the 10th February, but Mair's last words were "The Lord answers prayer. Jesus, Jesus, Jesus!" (Davies & Yeoman, 2008)

Mabel writes, "...when I was told that my husband was grieving I crept back quietly to his side, and promised him that I would not leave him again. On February 13th, in the early morning, we noticed a change in him and sent for the doctor. When he came he asked me if I would go into another room, as he did not want me to see him passing. His last words were, 'I shall be satisfied when I awake, with his likeness. Leave me now to God and to peace.' A few hours later they brought me the news that he had passed on. I turned to the Lord and I thanked him for the 29 happy years that we had had together."

Mabel was led to open her Bible at the passage Hosea 2:16: *It shall be at that day... thou shalt call me 'Ishi'*. She writes, "'Then, Lord,' I said, 'I shall not know widowhood.' My heart leaped for joy as I realised that my Maker would be my husband."

HIS LEGACY

D.P. Williams was a great man. He stands on a par with all the great leaders of the Pentecostal movements in the United Kingdom in the early twentieth century. James Worsfold, who had researched twentieth century Pentecostal History very thoroughly, expressed this opinion of Pastor Dan and his brother, Pastor Jones Williams: "History should see the brothers Daniel Powell Williams and William Jones Williams not only among the good, but among the great." (Worsfold, 1991)

In truth, D.P. Williams has not always received the acknowledgement due to him by writers of UK Pentecostal history, although, Keith Malcolmson in his book, *Pentecostal Pioneers Remembered*, has gone some way to rectifying that failure. He writes this: "It is a wonder to read this testimony of a Welsh speaking preacher, from an obscure village in Wales, being raised up of God to pioneer and establish churches across many nations. Just as the Lord anointed His servant David, while looking after his father's flocks of sheep, to go forth as King of Israel, so also He anointed the humble Dan to go forth belting the globe with the Gospel." (Malcolmson, 2008)

Pastor George Jeffreys, of the Bible Pattern Church Fellowship, said this when he heard of Pastor Dan's death in 1947, "Well! A great man, a great leader has been called home. A great loss has been sustained by the Church of God in the world today."

Ken Weller, in his essay, *A Critical Analysis of the Apostolic Church's (United Kingdom) Understanding and Use of Prophecy and Prophets* (Weller, 2005), helps us to appreciate something of the prophetic legacy that D.P. Williams left. His teaching on prophetical gifts and callings was not accepted by other Pentecostal groups and it went against Hutchinson's teaching on the prophetic.

Hutchinson claimed infallibility for prophecy, setting it on a par with Scripture. Pastor Dan, however, never made such a claim. He taught that there were three distinct parts to the prophetic in the New Testament Church: a spirit of prophecy, a gift of prophecy and the office of the "set" prophet. Each distinctive had its own operation and purpose but they were all empowered by the Holy Spirit under the Headship of Jesus Christ. But infallibility was never claimed because those used prophetically were recognised as fallible, human channels and prophetic words were to be tested and judged by Scripture.

In regard to his biblical understanding of the prophetic, D.P. Williams has certainly left a legacy for future generations. It was an understanding that cost him ridicule and criticism, but an understanding that can both inform and inspire us as we seek greater measures of the prophetic for our own lives. His teachings on the subject are to be found in his book, *The Prophetical Ministry in the Church* (D.P.Williams, 1931). He made this statement in the treatise: "If we are called as an Apostolic Church to witness for something above another, we witness the unassailable truth that we are a standing Body that is an evidence of the existence and value of the prophetic ministry." (D.P.Williams, 1931)

His appreciation and confidence in prophecy had not come instantly: "When prophecy began, after the 1904-05 Revival, I asked myself if I could trust it or would it be seen to be a rotten bridge. At the beginning I walked dubiously on the bridge, but there came the moment, after having proved the prophecy, that I could have jumped on the bridge! It was not rotten but safe." (D.P.Williams, 1931) D.P. Williams lived and ministered according to the word of the Lord. He had very able prophets alongside him, one being his own natural brother, but it was under Pastor Dan's apostleship that the ministry of the prophet both developed and matured and became the force that it was. (Worsfold, 1991)

Rick Joyner, in his book on the Welsh Revival called *The World Aflame*, comments, "Pastors D.P. and W.J. Williams (Jones Williams), founders of the Apostolic Church in Europe, were both converted during the Welsh Revival. These men carried the fire of their conversions until their deaths. They impacted much of the church in Europe and started a worldwide movement devoted to returning to apostolic church government that continues today." (Joyner, 1993)

Jonathan Black, an Apostolic pastor, writes, "What started with a small number of Welsh churches a century ago, has spread far beyond Wales and that handful of assemblies, through the preaching of the Gospel. Today the Apostolic Church has over 15 million members around the world, in 100 countries." (Black, 2016)

However, D.P. Williams' legacy was not only global - for many with whom he came in contact it was personal and individual and impacted whole families for future generations. He never lost his zeal for the Gospel or his love of leading others to Christ. In his own words, while speaking at a Salvation Army Help Brigade in Copenhagen, he said this: "I had the privilege to travel the nations and I have seen hundreds and even thousands of souls coming to Jesus ..."

What more can be said of D.P. Williams, apostle and visionary leader, pioneer, church planter and winner of souls, poet, missionary, theologian, faithful servant of God and man of faith, who lived courageously in the power of the Holy Spirit ? His son Ion sums up his father's life in this way, "He had eyes to see the supernatural, a heart to feel the supernatural, and boldness to declare the supernatural ... his mind was awed by a sense of divine things."

CHAPTER FOUR
ANDREW TURNBULL

> "Truly, truly, I say to you, he who believes in Me, the works that I do, he will do also; and greater works than these he will do; because I go to the Father."
>
> John 14:12

D.P. Williams first heard of Andrew Turnbull when he received a letter from a former colleague in 1916. Robert Jardine wrote, "I have met a man of God in Glasgow; there are signs and mighty deeds done through him in the name of Jesus!" (Worsfold J. E., 1991)

However, it transpires that Andrew Turnbull and the Burning Bush Fellowship in Glasgow had already heard about "a group of Pentecostal believers in Wales, who were convinced of the efficacy of directive prophecy." Gordon Weeks writes, "A prophecy was given (in the Burning Bush) saying that the Lord was going to bring them a further step in His perfect will by sending them two of His servants from the south. This was confirmed by a vision given to a lady of telegraph poles and wires running from Glasgow to a point in South Wales, along which messages were being sent both ways. Another vision was of two rivers joining together. Pastor Turnbull wrote and invited the brethren from Penygroes to visit Glasgow. In Penygroes prophecy had been given directing that Pastors D.P. and W.J. Williams should go to Glasgow so the invitation was accepted and they travelled to Scotland." (Weeks, 2003)

That visit took place in 1918 and in 1919 the Williams brothers returned to Glasgow. As a result of their ministry on these occasions, the Burning Bush joined the Apostolic Church in Wales.

In later years both Andrew Turnbull and his fellow pastor, John MacPherson, looked back on these visits of the Williams brothers and the decision for their churches to unite: "Up to this stage in the history of our assembly not very many had been converted, but from the day the church was set in order the Lord began to bare His arm in salvation. Scarcely a week passed without souls being saved, baptised in water and filled with the Holy Spirit; as many as 108 and 109 being baptised in water in two successive years. God told us that many sparks would fly out from the fire which He had kindled and that they would ignite and lighten many places in Scotland, and this has been abundantly fulfilled before our eyes, for there are now 48 assemblies in Scotland." (Mac Pherson, 1933)

A very close friendship developed between D.P. Williams and Andrew Turnbull and, in subsequent years, they travelled and ministered together both in the UK and overseas.

EARLY YEARS AND CONVERSION

Andrew was born on 11th March 1871, the eighth child of James and Agnes. Four further children were to follow. James Turnbull was a ploughman and the family lived in a small cottage on a farm near Kelso, in the borders of Scotland. Because of illness, Andrew attended school for only four years, but he learned how to plough the land and groom horses. In 1883, when he was twelve years old, his brother Thomas died of consumption. Thomas was a Christian and died singing the chorus, "Safe in the arms of Jesus." Tom Turnbull, in his book, *Apostle Andrew,* recounts how Thomas' death had a deep impact on his father. (Turnbull, 1965)

When Andrew was fifteen years old the family moved to a nearby farm, called Rutherford, where his father found employment. Tom Turnbull describes how this brought Andrew into contact with new friends and his life began to change for the worse: "Under their influence, he began to drink and adopted other vices. The first evening he arrived home drunk his mother burst into tears, but even that failed to bring him to his senses. He smoked a foot-long pipe, attended dances and had started to swear. But he was soon to consider his evil ways."

Andrew's mother died on 4th December 1892 and, overcome with grief, he came under deep conviction of sin. His son writes, "His enjoyment of the world's pleasures was on the wane. He wondered anxiously at times whether he was to blame for his mother's premature death. Often he heard again her cry of hurt and disappointment when she knew he had begun to drink, and he would break down, sobbing openly. Afterwards he began to pray, doing so at every opportunity, pouring out his soul to God for deliverance from sin and pleading for salvation." (Turnbull, 1965)

A few weeks later he began to attend a mission in a nearby church and, on 10th February 1893, he was converted. As he was making his way home late one night, he was considering his spiritual condition when the lines of a song came into his mind: "Only trust Him, only trust Him, only trust Him now!"

Ian MacPherson[3] in his book, *Ploughman's Progress, A Study of Andrew Turnbull,* explains what happened next: "Three times he repeated the refrain. Then, all at once, as he was passing the old stack-yard gate, a creature, whom he instinctively recognised as the Devil, appeared to him at a distance of about twenty yards along the road. It was in the shape of a large pig, and in the half light it gleamed phosphorescent, the colour of brimstone. Such a sight in such circumstances might well be calculated to create fright even in the most courageous of men. But Andrew stood his ground. In the name of Jesus he resisted the enemy and in a moment or two the apparition vanished. Then almost immediately, Andrew felt himself surrounded by a flock of snowy sheep whose glowing fleeces sparkled in the darkness. And presently one of the sheep, twice as large as the rest, looked up into his face, emitting a bleat of recognition. It was the Lamb of God, whose blood had been shed for his sins. It was the Saviour for whom he had so long been looking. The sheep, however, were not earthly: they were heavenly. Andrew looked at them with wonder, and, as he looked he was transfigured by their radiance. Tears of joy burst from his eyes. 'Now, Lord, I know I am Thine,' he exclaimed. And his burden rolled away forever." (MacPherson, 1936)

In his conversion we can identify seeds that were to develop and bear fruit in his later ministry: he heard and recognised the voice of God; he learned the reality of the Gospel through conviction of sin and deliverance; he had an encounter with the Devil, but proved that the name of Jesus had power to overcome him.

PREPARATION FOR MINISTRY

Andrew became a very enthusiastic Christian, with a passion for the Gospel. He wore a tie with the words "ALL FOR JESUS" on the knot and many thought he had become a religious fanatic.

---

[3] Late Apostolic pastor, apostle and teacher and son of the aforementioned Pastor John MacPherson from the Burning Bush, Glasgow.

The change in his life was evident and he was courageous in telling others about the Lord. He became involved with the Faith Mission Evangelists, spreading the Gospel in Kelso and the neighbouring villages, and saw many come to Christ. During one mission his father, three sisters, a brother and a cousin were among the converts.

In December 1895 Andrew married Jean Simpson, the daughter of the farm steward at Rutherford. She was a country girl and farm worker who had been converted around the same time as Andrew. With no home of their own, they spent the first five months of their married life living with their respective families until, on 30th May 1896, they moved into their own home near Yetholm, a village eight miles south-east of Kelso.

For six years Andrew worked as a ploughman, bringing in meagre wages to support his wife and growing family. However, in 1902 they moved to Hawick, another town in the Scottish Borders, where Andrew worked as a carter for ten years. In those years his family continued to grow until they had four sons and a daughter. A second daughter had died in infancy. Every morning and evening Andrew led his children in family worship.

He attended the local Baptist Church in Hawick and there he was grounded in the Word of God and was baptised in water. He became involved with the local Railway Mission and, as part of a local team, he sang and preached the Gospel throughout the Scottish Borders. Tom Turnbull writes, "During the last three years of his connection with this Mission he was its chairman, and he was regarded by his fellow-workers to be an excellent leader of meetings. Every week he preached in the open air - a work in which he delighted."

His son continues, "Although Andrew was very happy in the Baptist Church and the Railway Mission in Hawick, he felt he had not reached the peak of his spiritual experience. More was required in his spiritual life, and his expectations were soon realised." In 1908, the Rev. Fred Clark, a Welsh minister, came to the Railway Mission in Hawick to conduct Revival meetings. He had experienced the power of the Holy Spirit during the Welsh Revival and God used him to bring Andrew Turnbull into an experience of Pentecost. In one of the services he preached on the scripture: "Have ye received the Holy Spirit since ye believed?" and Andrew recognised that he needed the baptism in the Holy Spirit.

"On Sunday, 18th February 1908", Tom writes, "father attended a prayer meeting for the special campaign being held in the Railway Mission. Twelve men were on their knees fervently beseeching God to save souls. It was then that the power of the Holy Spirit overshadowed and filled my father, and he spoke in tongues as the Spirit gave him utterance, doing so for a long time." (Turnbull, 1965)

This experience brought Andrew into conflict with both the local Baptist Church and the Railway Mission. Former friends separated from him, refusing to believe that his experience of the Holy Spirit was from God. He was forced to resign the positions he held in the Baptist Church and the Railway Mission. The story is told that when some Christian leaders in Hawick came to visit Andrew to advise him about this "baptism", his wife was heard to say to them, "I know nothing about what my husband has received, but one thing I can say - he was a good husband before, but has been a better one since!"

Towards the end of 1908, and in response to this opposition, Andrew established a Pentecostal Assembly in Hawick. Under his leadership it grew in numbers and developed in Pentecostal experience. He was the only one who could preach so he had to study God's Word constantly to prepare sermons.

Around this time Andrew also experienced the power of God to heal. His son, Tom, suffered as a child from bouts of croup and, on one particular occasion, became very ill, struggling for breath. At the time, Andrew was in the house with a friend. Instead of calling for the doctor, they both got down on their knees and prayed for Tom. The child was miraculously healed and never suffered from croup again.

In 1912, Andrew, Jean and their five children moved to Portobello, a seaside town near Edinburgh. Andrew had received the offer of a job there and, after seeking God's will, accepted the position and moved away from the Borders. There was no Pentecostal church in the town. Andrew urged his employer, another Spirit filled Christian named Mr. Ferguson, to start such a church. After a time, Mr. Ferguson opened his own home for meetings. Pentecostal leaders, such as William Hutchinson, visited the group and brought prophetic direction. This resulted in Mr. Ferguson being called as the pastor and Andrew Turnbull as the presiding elder.

When the church grew and became too big for Mr. Ferguson's house a hall was built. Many people were drawn there by the remarkable healings that were taking place. This is one of the examples that Tom Turnbull records: "An Edinburgh lady stricken with consumption had been given up by her doctors. Hearing that Andrew Turnbull was being used by prayer to God to effect divine healing, she attended the services. My father prayed for her, laid hands on her and, according to James 5:14, anointed her with oil. Immediately, she afterwards said, it was as if fire was running all through her body and she was healed instantly. Professor Philips of the Royal Infirmary, Edinburgh, aware of her condition, was astonished to find that she was perfectly free from the disease."

Tom also recalls an incident when his father was healed: "Catching a chill while bathing in the sea, he began to decline physically, growing thinner and thinner. Many who knew him believed he was dying. One night, while he was in bed awake, his wife laid her hands on him in her sleep. In the same instant he was healed. From that day he grew stronger, soon being fully restored to normal health." (Turnbull, 1965)

It was while the family were living in Portobello that every one of the Turnbull children, Tom, James, Andrew, Alice and Richard, were converted and filled with the Holy Spirit. Some received spiritual gifts and Tom began to prophesy. Gordon Weeks describes an incident in 1915: "In Portobello a prophecy was given by Thomas (Tom) Turnbull, aged twelve and a half: 'I would have My servant go to a large city in the West of Scotland. He is to rent a large house conducting services in one of the rooms. A large spiritual fire will be lit in the West of Scotland, and sparks will fly out, and ignite, and commence many assemblies in Scotland.'" (Weeks, 2003)

Mr. Ferguson and others told Andrew that he would be foolish to act on such a prophecy. He was forty-three years of age, earning a good wage for the first time in his life, and the family were living rent free in a large house. This was a great challenge. It would mean that he, and his two older sons, would have to find employment and the family would need a new home.

Pastor Joshua McCabe, who became a colleague of Andrew after the family moved, gave an insight into how this directive word from one so young was handled and how God confirmed the word to Andrew Turnbull: "...Andrew knew the prophecy was beyond the intellectual ability of his son but could not yet understand that God was using Thomas (Tom) to direct him in a way he had not gone before. He confessed to being disturbed in spirit and God told him one night through Tom that he would give him a sign that He was with him and guiding him. The two youngest children in the family were asleep in bed. Andrew was instructed to wake them up and bring them into the fellowship meeting being conducted in the living room. 'Lay your hands on them and I will fill them with My Spirit and speak through them immediately.'" (McCabe, Pioneer of Faith) Andrew followed the command and that night Alice, aged eight, and Andrew, aged six, were both filled with the Holy Spirit and spoke in new languages as on the day of Pentecost.

In consequence, Andrew Turnbull accepted the revelation about going to the West of Scotland. After much searching for family accommodation in various towns, he leased a house in Armadale Street, Dennistoun, in the east-end of Glasgow. Richard, the eldest son, found employment for himself and his brother James at the Singer sewing machine factory in Clydebank. In Tom's biography of his father he writes, "In July 1915, acting in obedience to prophetical ministry, Andrew Turnbull left his employment at Portobello and moved to Glasgow in order to open a church there. He came to the city as a foreigner. The house in Armadale Street had six rooms, one of which was large enough for the holding of services. It also contained a bath that could be used for water baptism. In the furniture van that brought them to Glasgow, my father and mother, Andrew and Alice sat on a sofa at the back of it. As they went through the towns they sang:

> 'Oh, for showers on the thirsty land,
> Oh, for a mighty Revival.
> Oh, for a sanctified, fearless band,
> Ready to hail its arrival.'"
> (Turnbull, 1965)

The church in their home started with the Turnbull family, a school teacher called Miss Howard and a few other Christians from around Glasgow. Andrew was the pastor and did all the preaching and the gifts of the Holy Spirit were in evidence in the meetings. This was the third church he had planted since being filled with the Holy Spirit in 1908.

It was a challenge for Andrew to think of becoming a full-time minister. While in Portobello, the prophetic word was that he would eventually leave secular employment and serve the Lord full-time. However, the only income that the family had was what Richard and James were earning, together with some help from Miss Howard. Andrew found a job but was reprimanded by the Lord that he had not acted in accordance with the will of God. The family were told that the Lord would meet all their needs, and so He did.

Tom writes, "On one occasion my parents needed fifteen shillings to make up the rent, which had to be paid the next day. Mother was in tears, but father prayed about his need. Even as he was praying God was prompting a Christian lady in Glasgow to send him a pound. Time after time God answered prayer in this way in those early years in Glasgow. Sometimes five pounds would come by post at a time when it was most needed." (Turnbull, 1965)

The church grew and, as in Portobello, divine healing was a prominent part of the ministry. Andrew was also becoming known in Pentecostal circles. In 1916 he shared a mission in the North-East of England with Smith Wigglesworth. Andrew had met him previously at the Portobello assembly. Wigglesworth was a well-known Pentecostal evangelist whom God used, throughout his ministry, in many healings and miracles. The week's mission was so successful that Pastor Turnbull was invited to stay for a further fortnight. He asked his son Tom, who was only fourteen years of age, to join him for this follow-up mission and the gifts of the Holy Spirit were demonstrated in healings and deliverances.

The fellowship soon outgrew the room in Dennistoun and so, in 1916, they moved to a hall on Port Dundas Road, Glasgow. A sign saying "The Burning Bush Assembly" was put over the entrance. The church experienced much opposition but Pastor Andrew, encouraged by prophetic guidance, just kept following the path along which he believed God was leading him. Two years later larger premises were once again required and the "Burning Bush" moved to 104, Renfrew Street in the centre of Glasgow. This hall had seating for two hundred and fifty people.

From this new base, open-air meetings were commenced at various locations in the city including Bridgeton Cross, Bain Square and Phoenix Park. Tom writes, "In some places great opposition was experienced, and particularly from men who had had too much to drink. One man attacked the Pastor with an iron bar." (Turnbull, 1965)

Joshua McCabe gives this account of hearing Andrew Turnbull preach at one such meeting: "Before I knew him I heard him speaking at a T junction in Glasgow. On a Saturday evening I heard his stentorian voice preaching, 'God is love and He so loved the sinners of Glasgow that He gave His Son to die for them on the Cross of Calvary.' He pleaded with his audience, 5 or 6 rows deep around a band of people standing shoulder to shoulder in an open-air ring. There must have been at least 30 of them around the preacher. I found out later that this was one of Andrew's techniques to keep interrupters from breaking up the open-air service. If anyone tried to get into the ring the workers pressed shoulder to shoulder and kept them out."

He continues, "Pressing forward to listen, we saw this tall, well-dressed gentleman with fairish red hair, blue eyes that seemed to look right into your soul, fair complexion and such a kind and arresting look in his face. He spoke so clearly for 10 or 12 minutes, putting God's way of salvation so clearly and plainly before the audience. His talk was followed by a solo, from a young lass about 20 years old who sang, 'What will you do with Jesus, what shall your answer be?' Between the verses Andrew pressed the crowd of listeners to instant decision for Christ. I was a passer-by. Little did I think that Andrew Turnbull would influence my life, that he would become my father in God and help me, out of the wealth of his experience, to become a servant of Christ. I was already a believer."

McCabe joined the Burning Bush assembly, which had recently united with the Apostolic Church of Wales, some fifteen months after this open-air meeting. His family were already members of the assembly and he joined them when he was put out of a Christian fellowship for being baptised with the Holy Spirit and speaking in tongues. Speaking of Andrew Turnbull, he writes, "He received me into his fellowship and several years later, as a full-time pastor, I had the privilege of being his 'assistant' in the opening up of Apostolic Churches in Bo'ness, Aberdeen, Hawick and Carlisle, in the north of England. I owe so much to Andrew." (McCabe, Pioneer of Faith)

MINISTRY AT HOME AND ABROAD

A 1933 Apostolic Report states: "During the ten years the Church met at Renfrew Street, the hall, which accommodated about 250, had at different times come near the point of being overcrowded, but the Lord always came and relieved the situation by hiving off a part of the congregation and opening up other assemblies in the city for these members and also by sending overseers and elders to various places in Scotland to take charge of new assemblies."

In time, as the Burning Bush continued to grow, it moved again to new premises in North Frederick Street in the centre of Glasgow. Until 1919 it was an independent Pentecostal church, led by Andrew Turnbull and a small team of elders, but, when the Williams brothers paid their second visit to Glasgow that year, it became part of the Apostolic Church. On that occasion Andrew was ordained by Pastor D.P. Williams as a pastor in the Body of Christ. The following year, at the Apostolic International Convention in Penygroes, he was recognised as an apostle. Again, prophetic guidance lay behind these callings.

Although there were many challenges and difficulties, wonderful things were happening at the Burning Bush. Tom Turnbull explains that his father's preaching was not so much theological or doctrinal, but evangelical, exhortative and practical and God confirmed it with signs following. He inspired others with his zeal for the Lord. From 1920-1927 over a hundred people were baptised each year, sometimes many more. There were frequent, open-air meetings in the city, with unbelievers often kneeling on the pavement to accept Christ. In the church services God's power was demonstrated in salvation, healing and deliverance.

Under Andrew Turnbull's ministry the Apostolic work in Scotland began to develop numerically and spiritually, not only in Glasgow, but throughout many parts of the country. His son writes, "Pastor Turnbull held many campaigns in various places, and as a result assemblies were founded in them. Eventually between 50 and 60 assemblies were established during his ministry. Large numbers of Christians from other churches received the baptism in the Holy Spirit with signs following, and some of them joined the Apostolic Church... He preached in many countries, but it was in his beloved Scotland that he made his most sustained efforts... For some years he was away from home for nine months of each year... Six months of this absence he spent preaching in Scotland... Always he made many friends, and always he made fresh members for the church... Soon assemblies extended from Carlisle in the south to the Orkney Islands in the north... In thirteen years he saw the membership expand in Scotland from a mere 30 to some 1,600." (Turnbull, 1965)

Andrew Turnbull would have been the first to say that this work did not grow solely by his efforts. Many able ministers, apostles and prophets were raised up to help pioneer and consolidate the work, including his own four sons. Cathcart, McCabe, Larkins, Gardiner and Dickson were just a few of the pastors that laboured with him and were later sent forth from the Burning Bush to minister far away in other lands.

Turnbull also held missions throughout England and Wales and in 1920 he travelled to Belfast where there was, even at that time, political unrest. He went with a team of Welsh Apostolic pastors to hold a two-week mission. On the final night thirty-five people were converted and, as a result, an Apostolic Church was opened in Belfast and eighty-seven people were taken into membership.

By 1922 two other Pentecostal groups from Hereford and Bradford had amalgamated with the Welsh and Scottish regions of the Apostolic Church and a Missionary Council was established, with its headquarters in Bradford. Andrew Turnbull was appointed vice-president and in this role he visited various countries: North America in 1922; Denmark in 1926; Italy in 1930; and France and West Africa in 1931.

Wherever he travelled people were saved, healed and delivered. In Grosseto, in Italy, forty-two were saved and many healed: "A woman who had been unable to walk without aid for eleven years, walked several times around the hall after the Pastor had laid hands on her. An elderly man with a dislocated arm bound in a sling and causing him much pain, asked for deliverance. Within minutes he removed the bandage, shouting, 'I am healed!' and waving his arm. All pain was gone, never to return."

In 1931 Andrew Turnbull accompanied D.P. Williams and Jones Williams to West Africa, where they witnessed Revival with hundreds saved, healed and baptised in the Holy Spirit. As a result of this visit many Nigerian churches embraced the Apostolic doctrine and vision, with a total of 14,000 Pentecostal Christians joining the Apostolic Church. (Turnbull, 1965)

GREATER WORKS

The chapter began with these words of Jesus: "Truly, truly, I say to you, he who believes in Me, the works that I do, he will do also; and greater works than these he will do; because I go to the Father." John 14:12

Andrew Turnbull was a man who saw this promise fulfilled in his life. However, let us remember that this is a promise for every believer in Jesus Christ, regardless of title, office, background, education, age or theological persuasion. Andrew Turnbull began life as a humble ploughman, with little education and few prospects in life, but even before he was ordained as a pastor he witnessed God's power at work through him in a mighty way. His impact for the Kingdom of God touched the lives of thousands of people, not only in his native Scotland, but far beyond.

Andrew Turnbull is evidence of what God can do with a life wholeheartedly surrendered to Him. He undoubtedly learned to walk by faith and move in the supernatural power of the Holy Spirit. We will examine just a few of the main characteristics of his remarkable ministry:

THE SUPERNATURAL GIFTS OF THE HOLY SPIRIT

Soon after he was filled with the Holy Spirit, Andrew received the gift of tongues. His son Tom relates what happened on one occasion when he was travelling in a railway compartment which was occupied by several Africans: "He felt prompted to speak, but hesitated to do so. Unable to restrain himself, he finally spoke words in a foreign language. Immediately one of the Africans began to weep, saying: 'Massa, you speak in my language, and what you have said touches my heart.'" (Turnbull, 1965)

Joshua McCabe, in his tribute to Andrew Turnbull, states, "Seven times in Andrew's ministry his speaking in tongues was recognised by people as their language. Two Africans and a missionary to Africa recognised a message from God to them when Andrew spoke to them under the anointing of the Spirit." (McCabe, Pioneer of Faith)

CONFIRMATION OF THE WORD WITH SIGNS FOLLOWING

Andrew Turnbull certainly knew the experience of the Lord working with him, just like the original twelve apostles in Mark 16:20: *"And they went out and preached everywhere, while the Lord worked with them, and confirmed the word by the signs that followed."*

Tom Turnbull gives an account of some wonderful miracles that occurred during his father's ministry: "A serious accident, which partially dislocated the spine and set up inflammation, caused Miss Leadbetter, Orkney, to lie in bed for months. Afterwards she was able to crawl about, but suffered from intense pain from time to time. The several doctors who examined her said they could do nothing for her. She wrote, 'Pastor Turnbull prayed for me and laid hands on me. Immediately fire went through my body and all pain vanished. This happened many years go, and I have never had any pain in my spine since. Jesus Christ healed me!'"

Turnbull continues, "One outstanding miracle was that of Mrs. Spiers from Chapelhall. After an illness, she passed away in her home, and the doctor, after examining her, signed the death certificate. While she was still alive, Pastor Turnbull was sent for, only to be told on arriving at her home that she was dead. He asked to see the corpse. Entering the death chamber, he took her hand and, under inspiration, spoke a few words in tongues. She replied to him at once in the same manner. Afterwards she lived for over forty years, keeping the death certificate to prove to people that she had died and was alive again." (Turnbull, 1965)

THE AUTHORITY OF THE NAME OF JESUS

During Andrew Turnbull's ministry there were many examples of deliverance from the demonic by the authority of the name of Jesus. His son recalls, "He prayed fervently for a person possessed by demons, and then would say, 'In the name of Jesus I command thee, thou evil spirit, to come out.' The demons would cry out and even address him. Sometimes the possessed person would cry aloud, fall to the floor and froth at the mouth, convulsed, as the demon departed. Amazing scenes of this nature were often witnessed in the churches where he ministered. He had the gift of discerning the presence of evil spirits." (Turnbull, 1965)

Pastor Cecil Ireson tells this story about Andrew Turnbull: "In 1930 we invited the Pastor to hold a series of evangelical services in Kennington, and I do so remember one Sunday afternoon service, when the Pastor called those in need to come out. Many responded, and the pastor, though dealing with complete strangers, started at the end of the line, and looking at a young man for a brief second or two, said, 'Come out of him, you foul spirit, in the name of Jesus.' The young man slumped to the floor, and began foaming at the mouth immediately: in a word he was possessed by demons, and these were discerned and discharged by the might of that glorious name 'Jesus.'" (Ireson, 1970)

The following story is from a visit that Pastors D.P. Williams and A. Turnbull made to Denmark in April 1926: "In the Apostolic Church in Hillerod, the leader had great sorrow in that one of his children, a dear boy of 10, was demon-possessed; he could not refrain from stealing, lying and swearing. The father had tried by fair means and by force to deal with him, but to no effect. The lad was so audacious that he stole from his father's pocket when getting a drubbing. The poor father felt it impossible to go on as leader in the assembly, having such a wicked son. Arriving at the house we talked with the boy, who immediately confessed how he was. Pastor Turnbull seated him on his knees, kissed him and talked kindly to him – and then we prayed to Jesus for him, and while we were praying the boy himself shouted: 'Go, Devil!' Later on he told his father that when the brethren prayed and laid hands on him, then the demon went out. It is now a month ago, and the boy is completely changed – the evil spirit has left him and his is free! Is it not marvellous? Jesus is indeed, the same yesterday, today and forever." (Turnbull, 1965)

OBEDIENCE TO THE SPOKEN WORD OF THE LORD

From his early days as a Christian, Andrew Turnbull learned to recognise God's voice and its importance in his life. He valued direction from prophetic ministry and moved in faith to obey it despite the sacrifices and the risks involved, as we saw earlier when his young son prophesied a move to the west of Scotland in 1915. God honoured his faith and his belief in the prophetic word and this was evidenced by the rapid expansion of the work under his ministry.

Pastor D.P. William paid this tribute to him: "What do you think made Andrew great? ...It was his faith in the spoken word of God that brought him pre-eminence. Let Pastor Turnbull but hear His voice, and he would go through fire and water. He had no time to analyse it by human logic. It was not by logical reason that he knew the voice of God, but by supernatural instinct, by divine intuition. He believed God! He knew God! He feared immensely. Let the work in Scotland and elsewhere speak. Cities, towns and villages prove this among us." (Riches of Grace, 1937)

THE OLD WARRIOR

Andrew Turnbull was a shepherd who cared for his sheep, visiting them, welcoming them into his home, teaching them, correcting them and counselling them. The Bible was the only book he read, carrying it always with him and opening it at every opportunity. His deep compassion was seen particularly with those that were suffering. As he prayed for the sick or those that needed deliverance, he would shed tears over them. He had time for those who came to him or sought his help and he listened to them all with love.

The Lord also honoured Andrew's family. The financial support that the two oldest boys gave to their parents when the family moved to Glasgow was exemplary. All four sons became full-time ministers in the Apostolic Church. His daughter, Alice, married Tom Harper, who was an overseer in the Glasgow area.

In his later years Andrew was known affectionately as the "Old Warrior". From 1933 his health began to decline and he died on 23rd June 1937, at the age of sixty-six. On his death bed Andrew Turnbull's last words to Tom, his son, were, "Always follow your father's God."

Over five hundred people attended his funeral, with many travelling long distances. Pastor D.P. Williams gave the address and also wrote a poem in honour of his friend. He called it "The Old Warrior":

"I place this medal on thy breast,
My tribute bring my friend;
Take thy repose in tranquil rest,
With joy that has no end.

Thou warrior of the host of God,
Defender of the lentil field,
See! Through thy stand and righteous rod,
Great stores the future yield.

Christ, Who has been my Sun by day,
Will be my Star at night;
On my deep rest shall shine alway
His everlasting Light!"

CHAPTER FIVE
CECIL C. IRESON

"...he is a chosen vessel of Mine, to bear My name before the Gentiles... For I will show him how many things he must suffer for My name's sake."
Acts 9:15-16

Cecil Ireson was the initial inspiration for this present volume. Pat and I were in Sicily in June 2013, staying with Pastor and Mrs. Samuele Scandurra, when I noticed a book on their shelf entitled, "My Life and Thought". It was the autobiography of Pastor Cecil C. Ireson. When I started to read it, I couldn't put it down.

There were things about the story that amazed me and I wondered, "How many more men have there been in the Apostolic Church whose lives would be just as challenging as that of Cecil Ireson?" The book you are now reading, is the result of seeking to answer my own question.

C.C. Ireson's autobiography was published in 1970, some four years after his death. In the foreword, Ian MacPherson, paid this tribute to Pastor Ireson: "For close on a quarter of a century, I have cherished for the man himself a high respect and warm personal affection. In him I have found a combination of strength and gentleness, firmness and fatherliness, candour and courtesy, which appeals to me irresistibly."

Concerning the autobiography itself, he writes, "Pastor Ireson unfolds for us the story of his heart." Undoubtedly something of that heart is revealed in the words of Ireson's dedication at the beginning of his book: "This book is dedicated to the Glory of God, and to the sacrifice and service of my helpmeet, Kathleen, who stood so loyally by Arthur and Ruth while I was away those years in the Far East." (Ireson, 1970)

THE GOD WHO SAVES FROM SIN

In 1896 Cecil Ireson was born in Leicester of "humble parents", as he himself says. In 1912 he was born again of the Spirit of God: "As a young lad of 16, five days after my birthday in the City of Leicester, in the Midlands of England, I was converted to God from idols. I do not mean that I was heathen in the sense of bowing down to wood and stone: but I am saying that I was converted to God from idols; and in the reality of that experience God led me on."

He had been invited to attend a mission led by Frederick and Arthur Wood of the Young Life Campaigners. "It was here," he relates, "in a public hall hired for the occasion, that I saw my need of saving grace, centred in the Person of our Lord Jesus Christ." He was converted and became a follower of Jesus Christ and worshipped at a Wesleyan Methodist Church.

It was in this church that his love for the Bible and a desire to study it was birthed. No doubt the methodical way that the Methodists used to both teach and study the Scriptures had an impact on him. He writes, "I was now saved and seeking to be led of God, who had become so real to me." (Ireson, 1970) His expectation at this time was just to be part of a local church and follow a career in engineering.

The thrill of his conversion experience in 1916 never left him. Many years later, in August 1938, Cecil Ireson was speaking at the Apostolic Church International Convention in Wales, prior to setting off for China. In his testimony he specifically mentions the night of his conversion when he saw "the Bleeding Lamb of Calvary", and his exhortation to the congregation was, "Oh, let us be witnesses for Him."

THE GOD WHO FILLS WITH THE HOLY SPIRIT

The Wesleyan Methodists did not teach an Acts 2:3-4 demonstration of the Holy Spirit, but they certainly taught about an experience of the Spirit. As a Christian group they talked about a "second blessing" and believed that this blessing was separate from the experience of conversion. Some commentators would even go so far as to suggest that the Methodists were the parents of twentieth century Pentecostalism. But this "second work of grace", as it was also called, was about "being holy." The Wesleyan Methodists taught that there was a moment in a Christian's life when they were made holy and those attending their churches were taught to seek this experience and "get the victory" over sin.

This is the teaching that Cecil Ireson would have received in the midweek Bible classes. He would have heard people asking, "Have you got the victory?" meaning, "Have you been baptised in the Holy Spirit?" or "Have you been made holy?" It is significant that the Wesleyan Methodists were taught to seek and expect God to work powerfully in their lives and this was an important truth for him to learn early in his walk with God.

Apparently Cecil was challenged about the baptism in the Holy Spirit within a year of his conversion. Let him tell in his own words what happened when he received "the second blessing." It certainly wasn't according to Wesleyan Methodist teaching: "I was in an open-air as a young man of 17; after finishing the little message that I had, a lady faced me and said, 'I will never rest until you are baptised with the Holy Spirit fire.' I knew not what she meant..." However, he responded to this challenge from the Lord.

The story continues: "After a Sunday morning service in the year 1913, I came out of the House of God, making my way home for lunch. Entering the house, and being alone that day, I had a strong urge to seek the face of God in prayer. I engaged myself thus, kneeling down and pouring out my heart in praise to God, when suddenly, and unexpectedly, the Holy Spirit fell upon me, 'as on us at the beginning', to use words of Scripture. Thus I was baptised with the Holy Spirit, and that with signs following. Who could adequately describe the glory and the ecstasy, as one received such divine invasion? Indeed I hardly knew myself, for though I had read Acts 2, 4, 10 and 19, I had little idea of the full purpose and power of being thus filled with God. Later, I found others with a like experience, though 'Pentecost', so called, was not so widespread as it is today." (Ireson, 1970)

Many years later, in 1937, Cecil Ireson had the privilege of meeting the woman who had challenged him all those years beforehand about the baptism of the Holy Spirit with fire. He recalls: "I remember knocking at her door; and she came, and looked at me; and wondered who I was. Ultimately I told her. I cannot tell you the hallowed hour which followed as I wept with her in the presence of God; and how together we thanked Him for His definite Hand of predestination, which singled me out and brought me to that experience, so young in life." (Ireson, 1970)

It is clear from this account that the experiences from God that he had received some twenty years previous were still real for him. The years had not dulled the impact of salvation or of the filling of the Holy Spirit. He still had a heart of gratitude for the people God had sent into his life with the message of the Gospel and the challenge of being filled with the Holy Spirit. Most of all he had a heart of gratitude for the Lord Himself, who had graciously come into his life at a young age.

When I read of someone's experiences of the Holy Spirit it stirs me inside to both ask and expect repeated infillings of the Holy Spirit, with "signs following." Thank God for the prophecy of Joel, which the Apostle Peter quoted in Acts 2:17: *"And it shall be in the last days"*, *God says*, *"that I will pour forth of My Spirit on all mankind..."*

So, within the first year of Cecil Ireson's Christian life, he had experienced two central Gospel truths – firstly that Jesus is Saviour and secondly that Jesus is the Baptiser in the Holy Spirit.

THE GOD WHO HEALS THE SICK

The following year, in 1913, Cecil Ireson experienced another central Gospel truth – Jesus is the Healer. He was suffering from heart trouble and writes that he was scarcely able to get his breath. This condition did improve a little after some time spent in bed, but, as the threat of war loomed, he failed a medical for the Fleet Air Arm. At this point he asked the Lord to heal him, though at that time he had heard nothing of divine healing.

Continuing the story in his own words he recalls: "In those days of difficult breathing, I was directed by the Holy Spirit to *Psalm 91:14-16 'Because he hath set his love upon me, therefore will I deliver him: I will set him on high, because he hath known my name. He shall call upon me, and I will answer him...'* God said 'He shall call upon Me,' and that is what I did." (Ireson, 1970) The

Lord answered and he was miraculously healed. Through this experience, Cecil proved Jesus to be his Healer as well as Saviour and Baptiser in the Holy Spirit. This truth became a vital part of the message that in years to come he was to preach and practice, both in the United Kingdom and overseas.

The following accounts are extracts from his autobiography:

"I was asked, some twenty years ago, to visit and pray for the daughter of one of our faithful deaconesses, whose child, around 12/14 years, was spitting blood! I found her lying on the settee, looking so ill and deathlike. We prayed together, asking God to undertake for the girl. Subsequently she was taken by her mother to the hospital again, and they pronounced her free of tuberculosis. The mother, in acquainting me of the news, first laughed and then cried as she was emotionally moved in her gratitude to God. I saw this daughter, May, of Sister Perry, of the Kennington Assembly, a week or so ago, she being in the service, and happily married with three children.

"I remember some thirty-five years or more ago being asked to accompany Pastor W.H. Lewis to pray for a sister who had St. Vitus' Dance, such being a nervous disease causing irregular and involuntary movements of the limbs or face, medically known I believe as 'chorea'. This trouble had developed into something very distressing indeed. She was not able to keep her head still for a moment, but was constantly jerking her head in all directions. We prayed for her, anointing her with oil in the Name of the Lord, but seemingly nothing happened. However, the following morning, which was a Sunday, the trouble miraculously ceased, for nothing short of a miracle could have brought this about. The sister subsequently told us that she had contemplated taking her life by reason of the affliction, but the Lord undertook. Praise be to God!"

He cites these, and other incidents, as just a few of the many miracles of healing he witnessed throughout his ministry. In the *Riches of Grace,* November 1936 a further example appears:

"*Wonderful answer to Prayer* – Brother E.J. JONES, writes, 'Without doubt the Lord is blessing the Barking Church. On May 16th, 1936, I met with a cycle accident at Cold Norton, cutting my face and right hand; also severely spraining the ligaments of the wrist of the left hand, causing much pain and swelling, which kept me awake at night. On Sunday, May 17th, I attended the evening service, after which I was anointed and prayed for by Pastor C. Ireson, after which the pain ceased, and I was soon able to use the hand again. The Great Physician Heals today!'" (Riches of Grace, 1936)

THE GOD WHO PREPARES PEOPLE FOR SERVICE

So far, we have traced how God, through experience, had been laying down in Cecil Ireson's life Gospel truths that would be foundational to his ministry. However, he was still unaware that, through it all, the Lord was preparing him for future service and the many challenges that lay ahead. This is what he wrote, "I little dreamed in my early teens that I would ever be called upon one day to leave such a city for other places across the world…"

How had God been preparing him for the work that He had for him? He had met with the Lord personally, been saved and filled with the Holy Spirit and healed in the name of Jesus. He had proved the power of prayer; he had learned to distinguish the voice of the Holy Spirit and he knew that the Bible was the living Word of God.

Through all these encounters and through his continuing to seek God, a call to preach was certainly being birthed in his heart and his character was being shaped for His God-given mission and service.

THE GOD WHO WORKS OUT HIS PURPOSE

Cecil Ireson left Leicester in 1916 and spent two years in Lincoln. In 1918 he moved to Glasgow, working there till the Armistice was signed in November of that year. There is no record that he ever came across Pastor Andrew Turnbull from the Burning Bush in Glasgow, who featured in an earlier chapter.

While Cecil was in Glasgow he worked at a shipyard. He writes, "Each day I entered that shipyard in Dalmuir, winding my way in and out of the ships in course of construction, little did I realise that one day I would go around the world, and have the privilege of seeing so much." (Ireson, 1970)

At the end of the First World War he moved from Glasgow to London, where his parents were then living. He felt God lead him to an Open Brethren assembly where he not only met and married Kathleen, his life's partner, but he also learned much truth on the Person of Christ. It was there that two particular things happened which would give more direction to his life.

Firstly, in 1922, Cecil started to have strong convictions about the will of God for his life and, after sitting down to count the cost, he committed himself wholly to seek and follow God's purpose.

Secondly, in 1926, he came into contact with an Apostolic Church for the first time. Cecil and Kathleen had by this time already left the Open Brethren assembly and had been visiting various other churches in the London area. For a short time they had attended an Elim Church in Clapham, where they sat under the ministry of Pastor George Jeffreys. Cecil doesn't actually tell how he made contact with the Apostolic Church but, in the early part of 1926, the Lord linked him with Pastor William Lewis, who had commenced a work in Acre Lane, Brixton. Before the end of

1926, Cecil Ireson was appointed the overseer of this new church plant.

There had been a concern for some time amongst the leadership of the Apostolic Church about the progress of the London churches. The work was being covered by Pastor Hector Chanter, who was based in Bradford, and he had made an appeal to Pastor D.P. Williams in October 1923: "What do you think about London being properly set in working order; they are floundering about not knowing how to have the perfect mind of the Lord?"

As a result, in February 1926, William Lewis, a recognised apostle, had been sent to London to oversee three existing Apostolic churches in Peckham, Dulwich and Hammersmith. While covering these churches, he also opened this new church plant in Brixton.

This was not all just a coincidence. Cecil Ireson had come to London initially because his parents had moved to the city, but it was in London he found his future wife, who would be a great support to him in the ministry in the years to come; he became more aware and committed to the calling God had on his life and he discovered the church group through which God was going to use him.

Regarding 1926 and how God's purpose unfolded at this stage of his life, he wrote, "I was now a member, and an officer of the Church known as 'Apostolic', and with over forty-two years of fellowship therein to this time of writing, feel so thankful that God thus led me, and enlightened my eyes to see the things I have seen, and for the grace of God given to me to sacrifice and to serve Him as I have sought." (Ireson, 1970)

THE GOD WHO SENDS HIS SERVANTS ON MISSION

In 1934, Cecil Ireson was recognised as an apostle by the Apostolic Church and suddenly God's plan for his life began to open up in a new way.

By 1937 he was a member of the Apostolic Church National Council and was also serving on the Apostolic Church Missionary Committee. He was in business and still living in London but in early 1937 he was called into full-time ministry and was sent to Barnsley in Yorkshire.

Concerning this call to Barnsley, he explains, "...in the year 1937, in May, the Lord called me to leave business and to come to Barnsley, Yorks., and become a salaried minister of the Church. I may say that in the previous December I went to Bradford, still working in business, and still feeling the revelation opening, deepening, and unfolding, and in the quiet of my own spirit, as I left Bradford, in December, 1936... I lifted my heart heavenward and in my spirit said, 'O God , if You are going to call me out into the ministry, let me come to Yorkshire!'"

But in July 1937, just two months after the call to Barnsley, Cecil was asked by the Apostolic Church Council to go instead to China to superintend the missionary work in the north. London to Barnsley was one thing –but Barnsley to China! In fact, another colleague had been approached previously, but he had declined the call. Cecil continued to pastor the church in Barnsley until he left for China at the end of the following year.

This call to China did not come as a total surprise to him. Speaking at the 1938 Apostolic International Convention three months prior to setting sail, he recalled, "I had a strange fear of China and when the call came for me for that land... I rose to give expression that I had the fear of China and of being called to such a land. I may say that when the word came I found myself in Gethsemane... there was the will of God facing me on the one hand, and my own human will on the other hand. However, I can say that God gave me victory, and has given rest to my spirit. Praise His Name!"

Reflecting on his twenty-six years as a Christian he continued, "I commenced the journey at the Cross of Calvary, and as I am looking back there are definite landmarks in my experience that have brought me to this hour."

One such landmark was this: "Pastor W.H. Lewis gave me a book once (he may have forgotten it), entitled 'A Thousand Miles of Miracle in China'; that to me was not incidental or trivial and of no consequence."

The theme running through Cecil Ireson's testimony at this 1938 International Convention was this – "The Life of Sacrifice." He asked the congregation this question, "How can we follow Jesus unless we leave all? He knew the challenges he was facing – "China with its fightings; China with its floods; China that has foes...", but he was very firm in his belief – "China is calling... I have a call."

The Japanese Army had invaded China in 1937 and, before the end of that year, they had occupied Lin Cheng, a town in the north, not far from Peking, were the Apostolic mission was based. Sad to say, the Japanese used the Apostolic Church building there to carry out executions. Ling Cheng was almost on the frontline between Free China and the occupied areas.

Fully aware of the volatile situation that prevailed there and the sacrifice it would entail to leave his wife and two children behind, Cecil Ireson obeyed the call and set off for China on 4th November 1938, to take up the role of superintendent of the Apostolic work there.

The plan was that Mrs. Ireson and their daughter, Ruth, would come to China some two years later. Cecil wrote this about the parting: "Needless to add, the parting from my wife and family was painful to say the least, though there was a sense in which I had passed through my Gethsemane months before."

He arrived at Lin Cheng on Saturday 25th February 1939. "It had taken me almost four months to complete my journey," he writes, "having to use three ships, two of which I had to wait for considerably. Then trains, rickshaws, and a bullock cart, for that was how I completed the last few miles with my heavy trunks piled high, for I had responded to a call and to a need, and had gone there to stay." (Ireson, 1970)

Pastor Hector Gardiner, an Australian Apostolic missionary, had gone to meet Pastor Ireson and travelled back with him to Lin Cheng, where he was greeted by the rest of the team. He describes the scene: "I was met outside the walled village of Lin Cheng by Sister Pedersen and the Bible women and evangelists, together with many of the Apostolics of our Mission. They came out to greet me with banners with Chinese characters thereon. They were words of welcome to the new 'Mu-shih,' which means 'Pastor.'"

Pastor Ireson writes, "The day after our arrival we had our first Sunday morning service. This was announced by the ringing of a bell... About three hundred gathered together and after many words of welcome by the six native evangelists as well as Miss Dagny Pedersen (a Danish Apostolic missionary) and Mrs. Gardiner, I had the unspeakable joy of conveying my heart to them through the able interpretation of Pastor Hector Gardiner."

On 1st March 1939, Cecil Ireson, accompanied by Dagny Pedersen and Hector Gardiner, went on his first tour of the stations. Some of these stations had congregations of up to a hundred people and, at the first station he witnessed fourteen Chinese people coming to Christ.

It was on this mission trip that he also experienced for the first time the Chinese "kang" - a bed made of bricks. Additional challenges came in the form of travelling by bicycle on rutted paths and being stopped and questioned by Chinese guerrillas. The report he wrote of this first mission trip ended with these words: "I thank God once again for my call to this needy land, looking daily to Him for the necessary grace to be of service in this land." (Ireson, 1970)

In the March/April 1939 *Apostolic Herald*, Pastor Gardiner's report of the military situation in Lin Cheng reveals some of the dangers they were facing. The Japanese had launched attacks from Lin Cheng against villages in the area. He writes, "Some of our Christians had been made to act as guides and after getting word I went... to effect their release." (Apostolic Herald, 1939)

The Chinese had attacked the Japanese garrison in the town; aeroplanes had been flying overhead and bombing the Chinese positions around the town and Japanese reinforcements had arrived to relieve the besieged troops, but the outlying mission stations were also under threat. In order to reach them the missionaries had to travel by bicycle.

His report continues, "The greatest hardship for our Christians (Chinese) during these times is that they are under orders from the Chinese command to evacuate their homes and district on the approach of the Japanese forces. The idea being that no Chinese will render assistance to the enemy in any particular direction. Having outstations in these areas, you can imagine the difficulty of keeping things going and it necessitates continual running backwards and forwards according to which place is in danger. The fact that we have been able to continue keeping these places open right through the war period testifies to the way in which God is blessing and overruling.

"...we were working under great difficulties, for the Japanese soldiers were in our village, being on guard on the gates as we went in and out. Then a few miles from the walled village, we had seven or eight outstations, all in Free China, not conquered by the invaders. Thus each time we rode out on our cycles, accompanied by our seven native evangelists, we were under suspicion. We would ride out... and after some distance, we would see a Chinese soldier on his horse scanning the horizon, looking for the enemy. We would alight from our cycles, and placing them down on the earth, we would walk up to the soldier fully armed, bowing after the Chinese fashion, explaining the purpose of our journey. Being satisfied with our explanation, we would ultimately reach our destination. Then after a day or two we would return home..." (Apostolic Herald, 1939)

"Home" was within a compound of buildings surrounded by a wall in Lin Cheng. Pastor Ireson and the other the missionaries, together with the Chinese evangelists and their wives, "lived within this compound, surrounded by a high wall, one side being the wall of the village. Each night the Japanese soldiers would ride out to the surrounding villages, bringing in men and women to be shot!"

After an initial period working with the missionary team in Lin Cheng and the outlying mission stations, Pastor Ireson went to Peking for three months "to commence studying Mandarin in a language school, where no English was either known or used by the Chinese teachers." Before eventually leaving China he was able to read much of the Gospel of John in Mandarin and could converse a little with the people.

It was while he was in Peking that something happened that would change the world. Cecil Ireson writes: "The declaration of war (World War II) was made on September 3rd 1939. I heard it in Peking, Northern China, being on that day in a German missionary home. It was Hitler's voice I heard that day upon the radio."

When he returned to Lin Cheng, things were still difficult. "Trying to make contact once a month with Peking, for the purpose of obtaining money and stores of various kinds, became very trying, especially for me with an English passport... The railway from Peking to the nearest station to us was run entirely by the Japanese military, and no one could possibly travel without a pass issued by them. As soon as I would appear on the small railway station to go to Peking, I would be suddenly confronted by a Japanese soldier with a bayonet. After reading my pass, and seeing I was English, he would exclaim in a grunt 'English no good, no good.'"

The other missionaries advised Cecil to leave Lin Cheng for a period of time, not only because they feared for his life but also because there was a threat that the Japanese would close the mission down because of an Englishman's presence there.

He first went to Peking and then "was directed by the Church in Australia to go to Japan, where we had missionaries, and where I was needed to undertake a specific work." The supervision of the missionary work in China had been transferred from the UK to the Australian Apostolic Missionary Board on 1st October 1939.

In the January 1940 issue of the *Apostolic Herald*, there is an article by Pastor Ireson entitled *"Fighting! Fears! Flooding! Fevers!"* These were four foes with which the Chinese people were well acquainted.

The fighting was serious, but floods were also a major issue for China. He wrote, "Almost every year she suffers from floods, this year being the worst experienced for over twenty years. Railway tracks, bridges... literally washed away." Actually, a wall at the compound had also been swept away.

What about "Fevers"? "A ride in a rickshaw, or to sit in a dirty

Chinese room is all that is required to be bitten and, alas, infected by typhus," he relates. (Apostolic Herald, 1940)

Finally fears – "Fears of banditry." Wherever you travelled there was a risk of being set upon, even "for a very few dollars", by bandits, whose brutality knew no bounds.

The article would have taken sometime to arrive in the UK but at the time of writing, Pastor Ireson was staying with a Salvation Army Officer in Peking and from there he moved on to Japan, arriving in Kobe, on 17th January 1940. Reading some Apostolic Missionary Board minutes from that year, we are told that Pastor Ireson undertook "personal work among our missionaries and with Pastor Coote" in Japan. We do know that there had been some personality clashes in recent times among the missionaries and there was an ongoing issue. There were also some serious doctrinal questions to be faced there and, in addition, the financial pressures were increasing due to the war.

Leonard Coote and family were from the UK and had gone to Japan independent of the UK Apostolic Church to start a mission there. In time a link was made with the Apostolic Church in Australia. To support Pastor Coote, and to establish Apostolic Churches in Japan, both the Australian and New Zealand Apostolic Churches had sent missionaries there from 1936. By time Cecil Ireson arrived, the Australian and New Zealand churches had seven missionaries in the country, not including the Cootes.

Cecil Ireson arrived back in Lin Cheng at the end of 1940. Hector Gardiner wrote, "On the 7th December we had the joy of welcoming our beloved Pastor Ireson back into our midst at Lin Cheng. This was something that we had hoped for, but hardly expected to come to pass; not only did we rejoice, but the Chinese brethren were delighted once again to renew fellowship with Pastor 'Love,' as he is known to them. His Chinese name has for its meaning 'Love.'"

THE GOD WHO DELIVERS HIS SERVANTS FROM THE ENEMY

On his return Cecil Ireson recalls, "Passing through the gate into the village, I was immediately reported to the head commanding officer by the guard, and meeting him, I was asked my nationality, etc. On being told I was English, and after our asking whether relations between the Japanese and the British were less strained than formerly, he replied, 'The British are our enemies. There is only one thing we do with our enemies and that is shoot them.' I was then given ten days to quit the station."

And in ten days, he did leave Lin Cheng. Hector Gardiner, in an article in the July 1941 *Apostolic Herald,* gives an account of Pastor Ireson's last days at the Mission, from which it is clear that he was much loved by the Chinese Christians in Lin Cheng, although he had spent but little time there since February 1939.

He writes, "On the Thursday of the final week the Chinese brethren invited him, along with us, to a real Chinese meal... A real happy time of fellowship ensued that broke down all racial barriers, accompanied by laughter and happy conversation. On his last day, Pastor Ireson, in real Chinese manner, invited the Evangelists and the workers to a return meal, this being the only practical way of showing his gratefulness for their tokens of love." (Apostolic Herald, 1941) A banner with the words "Ching shen ai Jen", which means, "To Honour God is to love men", was presented to him as a gift.

Various meetings were held during those ten days, both for the Chinese and the missionaries on the compound, with Cecil Ireson preaching and teaching from God's Word.

Gordon Weeks tells what happened in one of these meetings:

"Just before he left he received a clear message of comfort and assurance when an illiterate Chinese girl gave a message 'in tongues' which was in perfect English." (Weeks, 2003)

As the other missionaries bade him farewell, Hector Gardiner describes their feelings: "Monday afternoon the Evangelists, Miss Pedersen, Brother Newland and I escorted Pastor Ireson to the station some fifteen miles away. Just at dusk he boarded the train for Peking. As we turned to go home even the weather seemed in sympathy with the fullness of our hearts, for heavy sleet and a strong head wind made our return trip miserable on our bikes in the darkness." (Apostolic Herald, 1941)

On leaving Lin Cheng, Pastor Ireson made his way to Australia, via Japan. Arriving in Australia, he spent fourteen weeks visiting Apostolic churches in the country, lecturing on China and ministering in various centres. In May 1941 he moved on to New Zealand. He writes, "How well I remember looking out through the porthole of my cabin each morning, to see one of the Australian naval battleships escorting us over... for the seas were submarine infested." He spent a further fourteen weeks visiting Apostolic churches on both the North and South Islands of New Zealand. He finally left Wellington, on Sunday 31st August 1941, for the long journey home to the Britain.

The journey took seven weeks and was very dangerous. The ship did not have a naval escort as it crossed the Pacific Ocean. "I was twenty days in the Pacific Ocean before reaching the Panama Canal... On entering the canal the American marines took over, while planes swept over our heads... After going through the canal, our ship headed for Halifax, Nova Scotia, and after being four days in that port, we joined a convoy of 55 ships, to make the hazardous journey of 2,365 miles to Glasgow. Destroyers guarded us across the Atlantic, whilst we dropped depth charges from time to time, owing to enemy submarines. Then for those fourteen days and nights we were entirely blacked out, as indeed we had been since leaving New Zealand." (Ireson, 1970)

Pastor Ireson arrived back in the United Kingdom on Saturday 18th October 1941. He had not seen his wife and children for three years, and, during his absence they had been subjected to much bombing in London.

He wrote of his departure from Lin Cheng: "Those who have judged me for coming out would do well to think again, for I was ordered out by the 'powers that be.' Then I was advised by those with whom I co-worked to leave, lest the work be jeopardised. Cables were accordingly despatched and replies received, all I fear without understanding. Who could assess the true position, but those on the spot, ten thousand miles away, especially so when all revealing letters were censored by the Japanese authorities in Peking who controlled all the postal services?" What lay behind these comments?

Cecil Ireson was interviewed by the Apostolic Church Mission Board shortly after his return to Britain in October 1941. The interview notes reveal the friction that had existed between him and the Board since October 1940, at which time he had asked to come home because of the situation that was developing in China. Meanwhile his wife and children were living in London and the situation was also deteriorating there with the commencement of the Nazi bombing of the city on 7th September 1940. On 21st October, 1940, the decision of the Board had been that Pastor Ireson had been called to go to China as an apostle and that he still had work to do, but, on the 29th October 1941, the Board agreed to rescind that previous minute.

The minutes of the interview indicate that Cecil Ireson was "the last Britisher" to leave Hopei Province; that the only China Inland Missionaries left in the whole of North China, except Peking, were

German and Danes; further, that within a month of Pastor Ireson leaving, all the women missionaries, beside Dagny Pedersen, had left the province; and, finally, that Mrs. Gardiner had had to flee to Peking and then travel on to Australia, once it was discovered that she was British born.

However, there was one pastor who did not escape the situation. In December 1940, Pastor Aubrey Newland and his wife, who were missionaries from Australia, had transferred from Japan to Lin Cheng to help the work. Before leaving he had arranged for the repatriation of all the Apostolic missionaries in Japan. He came to Lin Cheng to work with Dagny Pedersen and Hector Gardiner. It appears that Pastor Gardiner had left on furlough, to join his wife in Australia, but Aubrey Newland was eventually arrested by the Japanese and was interned at Shanghai until the end of the war.

Pastor J.B. Clyne, a colleague of Cecil Ireson, remembered his return: "I well remember sitting in a Finance Committee in Glasgow in 1941, when one of the office staff called me to the outer office to say that a gentleman was at the enquiry asking for me. Great was my surprise to find Pastor Ireson awaiting me. His ship had come in convoy to the Clyde. The Committee gave him a warm welcome before he made his journey southward to London and home." (Riches of Grace, 1966)

In these dangerous years, Cecil Ireson had travelled thousands of miles alone. He didn't have a Barnabas or a Timothy alongside him, but he gives glory to God for His grace and strength and protection: "God forbid that I should unduly speak of the hazards encountered - the anxieties experienced - the fears within - the fightings without - the perils and the privations both on land and on sea. Let me rather magnify the greatness, the goodness, and the grace of God, who thus preserved me, provided for me, and caused me to praise His great and wonderful name." (Ireson, 1970)

Miss Dagny Pedersen returned to Denmark in 1949, after some thirty eight years of service in China. The Gardiners left on furlough in 1942, but were unable to return to Lin Cheng in 1943. The Communists had taken control of the north and the area was closed to all missionaries. Hector had buried his first wife, Viola and her son, Junior Berg, in China.

Cecil Ireson had left China in 1941 with a heavy heart: "I... left the Far East... I left there all my dreams... with my fellow missionaries out... having gone back to Australia, I saw little hope of those dreams taking shape." He had gone to China with every intention of staying. Plans were in place for his wife and daughter to join him in a few years, but unforeseen events intervened. As he later wrote, "...one cannot fully understand God's providences."

THE GOD WHO CALLS HIS SERVANTS HOME

On returning to the United Kingdom, Cecil Ireson took his place again on the staff of the UK Apostolic Church. He went on to minister in Plymouth, London, Hereford, Bradford and Penygroes. Britain was not yet a safe haven and, during their time in Plymouth and in London, he and his family continued to experience the bombing raids of the Second World War. "One terrible night (in Plymouth)," he recalls, "we suffered the loss of ceilings, doors and windows, together with most of our china etc." During his years of ministry, he also fulfilled various national appointments in the church until his retirement in 1962.

Recalling nearly forty years of ministry, he wrote: "Thus it is in the many years my ministry has involved preaching, praying, ordaining, dedicating, inducting, farewelling, receiving into fellowship, baptisms in water and teachings in the various fields of doctrine, devotion and dispensational settings. Speaking very humbly, I have seen some saved, secured, sanctified. Some again healed and uplifted in heart. Some returning to the Lord they had left, and some renewing their vows and getting the victory. All these have been far from casual, occasional, for surely, if God is present, if it is His Word we present, if the Holy Spirit is in us according to His promise, then every meeting has events, experiences, possibilities." (Ireson, 1970) The Lord called His servant home in 1966, at nearly seventy years of age.

In a tribute to him, Pastor J.B. Clyne wrote, "As a man and a brother Pastor Ireson was of equitable temperament, a genial personality, a good mixer and a faithful friend and fellow servant of Christ." (Riches of Grace, 1966) No doubt when he arrived at his heavenly home, he met with many to whom he had ministered during his time in China - people from the outlying mission stations and Lin Cheng who had suffered at the hands of the Chinese and the Japanese.

What can be said of Lin Cheng today? I contacted Asia Harvest and this is part of the reply I received:

"Lin Cheng today has a population of around 210,000 people. We estimate there are only about 1,300 Protestant Christians of any kind in Lin Cheng. One reason for this low number is because Hebei Province is renowned for being the most Catholic of all of China's provinces. In Lin Cheng we estimate there to be approximately 8,500 Catholics, giving the county a Catholic to Protestant ratio of about 7:1, which is very rare and extreme of all the locations in China that we have surveyed... Unfortunately due to the life-changing decades since they were in China, there will be no visible trace of the Apostolic mission today, and no Apostolic church as such, as it will be illegal in today's China... There is little doubt, however, that the spiritual seed that was sown by the Apostolic missionaries can still be seen today among the house church networks that function in the town and country."

CHAPTER SIX
JAMES MCKEOWN

"According to the grace of God which was given to me, like a wise master builder I laid a foundation..."
1 Corinthians 3:10

"A Giant in Ghana" is the title of a biography on the life of James McKeown, written by Christine Leonard and published in 1989. It well describes the measure of this man who came from humble origins yet accomplished so much through God. During fifty-three years of service in Ghana he saw 3,500 churches established and touched the lives of countless thousands. Without doubt, he was an apostle of faith and his life story continues to be an inspiration to many.

(N.B. Ghana was formerly known as the "Gold Coast" until it gained independence in 1957. As this chapter deals mostly with James McKeown's life pre-1957, it will be referred to here as the "Gold Coast".)

EARLY LIFE

James McKeown was born at Glenboig, a village near Glasgow, on September 12th 1900. His parents, who were from Northern Ireland originally, had moved to live in Scotland. James' brother, Adam, gives us this background in his autobiography, *A Man Named Adam*: "I do not have the exact date of my father and my mother's marriage, but it would be approximately 1896. After they were married they moved from Ireland to Scotland, where my father, a hardworking man, applied himself to labouring jobs, first in the brick works at Glenboig, and later in the iron works at Coatbridge. Mother operated a small community store and as they both worked and saved it was toward a goal, and that was to return to Ireland and buy a farm, for that was where my father's heart was." (McKeown, 1985)

While the family were in Scotland, James' parents came into the experience of Pentecost. They were strict Presbyterians. However, a man from their church visited the outpouring that was taking place at that time in Sunderland, under the ministry of the Rev. Alexander Boddy[4]. Christine Leonard takes up the story: "When the Glaswegian came back speaking in tongues all the Presbyterians went to hear him, but James remembers his mother begging her husband not to go anywhere near! This can have had no effect because James can still remember how horrified he felt the next day, 'Mother, he's speaking in tongues! He's disgraced us!' Worse was to come a few nights later. Father looked after the family so Mother could go to the meeting and receive this strange new gift." (Leonard, 1989)

Adam McKeown continues, "My father and mother were among the first to receive the baptism in the Holy Spirit with signs following. I was told that it was not an unusual sight on a Saturday

---

[4] See chapter 2

night, when customers would congregate in my mother's little shop, to see my father with open Bible in his hand, expounding the Word and the Way more clearly to eager listeners. All this had a profound effect on my father's life, so that when we moved back to Ireland in May 1912, our home at Tullynahinion became a centre of Pentecostal activity and a beacon light to wayfarers seeking the way."

James' father had bought a farm in Tullynahinion, near Portglenone and, together with his wife and seven children, settled down to farming in County Antrim. On Sunday mornings the family would attend services at 3rd Portglenone Presbyterian Church. They were members there and had their family pew near the front of the church, but on Sunday evenings, as Adam recalls, "People would come to our home for a meeting or a time of fellowship, and so for the remaining hours our home would become the scene of Pentecostal activity. It was not unusual for some of those meetings to last into the wee hours of the morning." (McKeown, 1985)

George Jeffreys and his group, The Elim Evangelistic Band, had started to pioneer in Northern Ireland, proclaiming the "full Gospel" message of Jesus as Saviour, Healer, Baptiser and Coming King. Jeffreys was a Welshman who was saved during the Welsh Revival and became the founder of the Elim Pentecostal Church. Together with his brother Stephen, he held many Gospel crusades in which God moved powerfully in salvation, healing and miracles.

George Jeffreys visited and ministered in the McKeown home. One of the earliest churches that Jeffreys planted in Northern Ireland was in Ballymena, the McKeown's local market town. Smith Wigglesworth was another Pentecostal pioneer to visit their farmhouse in County Antrim. Christine Leonard writes, "To the McKeown children these great men of God were familiar figures. Even if unconsciously, they absorbed a great deal from them. James retained detailed memories of the few sermons he heard Jeffreys preach and was to put them to good use in Africa. James' and George Jeffreys' preaching styles were remarkably similar – both had a power in their preaching which did not come from noise or emotionalism." (Leonard, 1989)

CONVERSION AND BAPTISM IN THE SPIRIT

James McKeown was converted in 1919, under the ministry of the Elim Evangelistic Band. The preacher was a Mr. Mercer and, in James' own words, this is what happened: "Mr. Mercer was a plain man, like myself, but there was something about him which appealed to me. I saw that he was real, and I set myself to listen to what he had to say. Lamentations 1:12 AV was his text: *'Is it nothing to you, all ye that pass by? Behold, and see if there be any sorrow like unto my sorrow.'* He also read the story of the crucifixion from Mark's Gospel and I thought I had never heard it read so well. He preached on the love and suffering of Jesus Christ. I then lost sight of the preacher and this Jesus that had been so far away in my thoughts before, became very near to me. His love touched me and as I followed Jesus closely by the Word that was preached, I was full of sympathy for Him and His cause. Seeing Him led forth by cruel soldiers and set at nought by all, I felt, if I had been there, the one who took upon himself to strike Jesus would have had to strike me, for I was wholly in love with Him. The Holy Spirit making the crucifixion real to me, I was deeply moved, when suddenly, I became aware that I was gripped by the Gospel. The tears were rolling down my cheeks but I thought I was too young to be converted." (Riches of Grace, 1936)

Although he walked out of that meeting unsaved, some two weeks later he stood in another meeting and testified that he had become a follower of Jesus Christ. He fell totally in love with Jesus and, as he said himself, "Later on, it was that same love that took me to Africa."

James began to seek the baptism of the Holy Spirit, but nothing was happening. Christine Leonard writes, "After some time he broke down and told the Lord that he had exercised all the faith he had. He said 'If I don't get the blessing tonight, I'm finished.' It was a strange, emptying experience, but the filling came. He felt fire come on his head and move down his body. In the end he just had to let go and ended practically throwing the bench, at which he had been kneeling, across the room and shouting 'Glory to Jesus.' Quiet as he was, he spoke with tongues 'more than ye all.'" (Leonard, 1989)

These two biblical experiences of conversion and baptism in the Holy Spirit had a tremendous effect upon James' life and they were central to the message that he later came to preach, with its focus on Christ crucified and the baptism of the Holy Spirit with signs following.

SOPHIA KENNOCK

Sophia, or "Phia" as James called her, was also from County Antrim. They married in the summer of 1927. She was a seamstress who had come to Christ through the work of the Faith Mission. This was an organisation which sent men and women, known as "Faith Mission Pilgrims", into rural areas to preach the Gospel.

In 1923 Sophia joined the Faith Mission Prayer Union and wanted to become a Faith Mission Pilgrim. She explains, "But the Lord had still something more for me: the glorious baptism of the Holy Ghost. There was much opposition against me going to these Holy Ghost believers, but I had caught a glimpse of 'saints on higher ground', so I was determined to scale the utmost height." (Riches of Grace, 1936)

She and James were baptised in water by George Jeffreys in Ballymena. It was during an Elim church service in Ballymena that the Lord spoke prophetically saying that some of those present would go to Africa. James remembered that prophecy years later when he was addressing 80,000 people in Accra: "How unlikely it had seemed at the time that any of them could fulfil it – they came from such humble backgrounds." (Leonard, 1989)

An Apostolic Church Convention Report of 1936 records something of Sophia McKeown's testimony of those early days: "I had very sweet times of fellowship with the saints in Elim, but the Lord was still leading me further out in His Will. The revelation of the Apostolic Church was then brought before me. I had been warned against it, but while spending a holiday in Belfast, I was invited to a convention, heard the Word of the Lord through a prophet for the first time; was convinced it was the Lord speaking… I knew my Lord was speaking in the Apostolic Church, and He had led me thus far. I received the right-hand of fellowship from Pastor D.P. Williams, and became a member of the Apostolic Church; that is almost eleven years ago. I have not regretted it. In His Will, He is still calling out to further service for Him. He has graciously privileged me to go with my husband to Africa, where I hope to still continue my service for Him." (Apostolic Church Convention Report, 1936)

MINISTRY IN SCOTLAND

James had moved to Glasgow to find work prior to marrying Sophia as jobs were few in Northern Ireland. On the day of their marriage in the summer of 1927, he returned to Glasgow with his new bride.

While James' early years had been spent with the Elim movement in Northern Ireland, in 1926 an Apostolic assembly opened in Portglenone, a village four miles from where the McKeown family lived. In fact, James Robinson, in his book *Pentecostal Origins: Early Pentecostalism in Ireland*, records that William McKeown, James' father, was instrumental in the establishment of this assembly. (Robinson, 2005)

We can assume from this that James and Sophia would have known something of the Apostolic Church before they left for Scotland. They would also have heard of the remarkable ministry of Andrew Turnbull, the Apostolic pastor of the Burning Bush Assembly in Glasgow, and it was this church that they began to attend.

Through Andrew Turnbull's ministry over seventy other assemblies were opened up in Scotland between 1922 and 1932. Under his leadership, the Burning Bush produced some notable men and women who took the Pentecostal message throughout the UK and around the world. Not least among them were Turnbull's four sons, Tom, Richard, Andrew and James. There were women, such as Deaconess Howard, who preached and ministered in evangelistic teams around the UK Then there were some of the men and their wives that are mentioned in other chapters of this book such as Pastors Dickson, Gardiner, McCabe, Cathcart who travelled to far off lands.

James and Sophia would have known many of these leaders from their time in the Burning Bush. The impact of Andrew Turnbull's apostleship on many lives was transformational. It imparted to James McKeown a depth, richness and power of ministry which was subsequently evidenced in the work God accomplished through him in the Gold Coast.

Andrew Turnbull had a love for Africa and its people. In fact a brother from Sierra Leone had lived with the Turnbulls in Glasgow during 1917-18. Turnbull went to Nigeria with D.P. and Jones Williams in 1931. As the McKeowns read and listened to the reports of this visit, they, no doubt, would have remembered the prophecy they had heard some years previous in Ballymena indicating that some of those present would minister for the Lord in Africa.

Though he was still young, James McKeown evidently had leadership qualities. His biography states, "Even before James became a member of the Apostolic Church in Glasgow, someone prophesied that he should be the elder presiding over the assembly. The other elders disagreed and James kept quiet – he did not want to be an elder." (Leonard, 1989) However, before long, he was ordained as an elder there and began to be given preaching engagements both within the Glasgow circle of churches and beyond. He enjoyed open-air evangelistic meetings and loved to give his testimony.

Pastor Andrew Turnbull left Glasgow for the North of England in January 1931 and Pastor Alex Gardiner took over the leadership of the Glasgow assembly. By then the congregation numbered approximately seven hundred. Around this time James was suspended from membership for six months because he disappeared to Canada without informing the church leaders. Work was short in Glasgow and he had seen notices advertising for workers for the harvest in Canada. He wasted no time and set sail the very afternoon of the day he applied!

James was unknown in Canada, but, at the end of the first Sunday service he attended there, the minister approached him and asked him to preach. "How do you know I'm a runaway from the Apostolics?" demanded James. He did preach and in fact was invited to lead the church while the pastor was away on an extended trip. They were willing to pay for Sophia to come and join him in Canada, so it was a tempting offer. However, as James prayed, he clearly heard God say, "No." He obeyed the Lord and returned to Glasgow and the Burning Bush, where there was no further mention of his suspension.

When he had arrived in Glasgow he was initially unsure about the issue of prophecy and, in particular, directive prophecy. He explained his approach to life and ministry at that time in these words: "sanctified common sense was my rule of guidance." His experience in Glasgow changed that. "After some time," he said, "I proved beyond a doubt that God was, indeed, speaking to His people through the gifts He had given to His Church. The word of God through prophecy called me forth, step by step, to public ministry, which was very severe on my reserved make-up, but grace was given to follow Him who was calling. My experience taught me not to be exercised about ambitious desires, but to love the Lord and shine where I am placed... What matters where on earth we dwell? It's Jesus that matters." (Riches of Grace, 1936) The centrality of Jesus remained a key part of the message he lived and preached in the Gold Coast throughout his long service there.

These years in the Apostolic Church in Glasgow were clearly instructive and formative ones for James and Sophia, preparing and equipping them for what lay ahead. They witnessed families, such as the Cathcarts and the McCabes, being sent out from the Burning Bush on overseas mission. They would have heard news back from them about how God was moving powerfully with signs following the preaching of the Word and of the many churches that were being established.

The constant, ground breaking evangelistic activities of the Apostolic Church in Scotland must also have influenced this couple: a tent had been purchased for campaigns, tracts were designed and printed for outreach and there was much open-air preaching. Undoubtedly, during these years, their fellowship with Andrew Turnbull, hearing him preach the Gospel and seeing him move in the power of the Holy Spirit, inspired them to believe God for great things in their own ministries.

In 1935, at the Glasgow New Year Convention, James was called to be an apostle. The *Apostolic Herald*, February 1935, reported: "It pleased the Lord during the Convention to reveal many callings for the 'Body', including three new apostles, namely, Overseer James McKeown, who is to be located in the Edinburgh Area..." (Apostolic Herald, 1935)

MINISTRY IN THE GOLD COAST

It appears that James McKeown did not immediately become a full-time pastor. For some reason, when the call to the Gold Coast came later in 1935, he was still working as a tram driver in Glasgow. James' first reaction was to refuse the missionary call, believing he had insufficient training for such a work. The leaders' reply was that they felt James had an adaptability that was vital for missionary work. Christine Leonard writes, "Having refused the call, 15 months went by until James awoke in the night to hear his wife crying. 'Whatever is the matter?' he asked. Sophia was pleading that they go as missionaries. 'What can you do when your wife is crying at your back every night?' asked James. 'I agreed to go and gave up my job as a tram driver in Glasgow.'"

Leaving Sophia behind to follow him some six months later, James set off for the Gold Coast on 24th February 1937 and arrived on 7th March. There was no man-made harbour in Accra so boats would anchor off the port and canoes would go out to bring the passengers and luggage ashore. James was met at the beach and was taken by car to Asamankese – "a hot, bumpy journey" of some ninety kilometres up country from Accra. He was the only white person in a town of five thousand Africans and accommodation was a rented apartment in a two storey building. The landlord was a Mr. Anyane Kwabena, who had three wives and twenty-six children. James' adaptability was to be tested from the very first day!

Only part of James McKeown's ministry in the Gold Coast was with the Apostolic Church, so we will look at it in three distinct sections:

March 1937 – May 1938
June 1938 – May 1953
May 1953 – October 1982

I am including a map which shows the area where he was ministering, but the road network in the 1930s would have been nowhere near as advanced as it appears here.

March 1937 – June 1938

Sophia joined her husband in the Gold Coast on 15th September 1937. In Asamankese the church was led by a man called Peter Anim. Pastor Anim had met D.P. Williams, his brother, Jones, and Andrew Turnbull when they visited West Africa in September 1931 and later he also met Pastor George Perfect. In 1935 Pastor Anim and his church had decided to affiliate with the Apostolic Church UK and changed their name from "The Faith Tabernacle" to "The Apostolic Church, Gold Coast". In 1936 an Apostolic pastor, Vivian Wellings, who was then resident in Nigeria, made a visit to them and recommended that they apply for a missionary from the UK Pastor James McKeown was the missionary apostle who was sent.

However, in May 1937, a doctrinal issue came to a head within the Apostolic Church, Gold Coast, when James McKeown became ill and was rushed to hospital. A Church of Pentecost publication gives us the background: "James McKeown, in May 1937 went down with malaria. With the assistance of the District Commissioner at Kibi, he was sent to the then European Hospital (Ridge Hospital), in Accra, where he received medication. Anim's group, with the Faith Tabernacle doctrine of no medication, was displeased that James was taking medicine. The disagreement on the use of medication called for a meeting of the leadership of the church at the 1937 Christmas Convention at Asamankese. A resolution, which stated that McKeown was a man without faith, was sent to Bradford[5]." (Asare-Duah, 2014)

---
5   The missionary headquarters of the UK Apostolic Church.

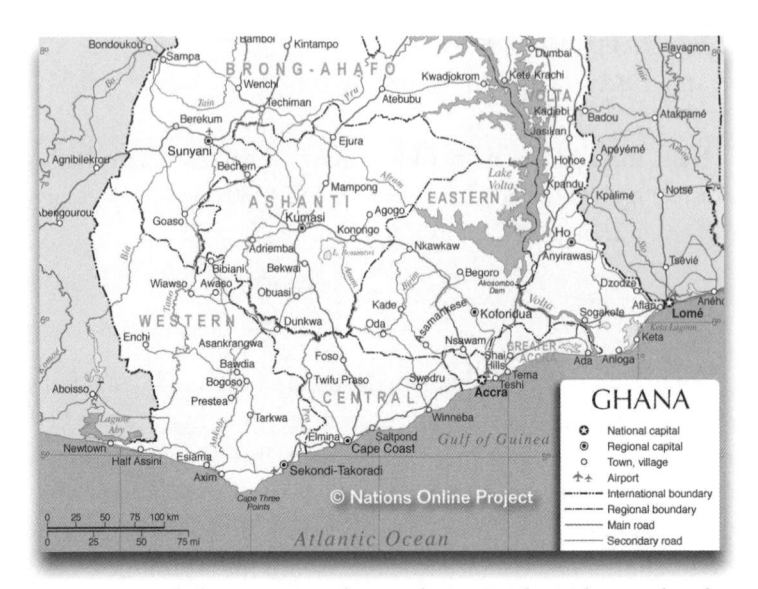

Anim and his group, from their Faith Tabernacle days, "believed Christians should look only to Jesus for healing; a doctor was the Devil. Anyone who took medicine would go to hell and was subject to the same church discipline as if they had been involved in sexual immorality or demon worship. Sores were not dressed. Wearing glasses was a sin – they said it was worshipping the god of sand (glass being made of sand)." (Leonard, 1989)

Between May and December the situation deteriorated. McKeown didn't agree with this perspective on faith. Christine Leonard writes, "Night after night James cried himself to sleep as he heard of Africans dying for the lack of simple and available medical care." He continued to preach and particularly challenged this extreme view of faith. When Sophia arrived in September, with typical understatement, he said, "I was glad to see her."

There were a number of different churches within Pastor Anim's group, but not all of them agreed with the Christmas 1937 resolution. At least four refused to sign the document and decided to throw their support behind Pastor James and Sophia McKeown. One of the churches that stood by the McKeowns was in the coastal town of Winneba.

By June 1938 the situation was such that the McKeown's moved, together with their native house girls, from Asamankese to Winneba. His biographer records, "They had no money, until a postal order for ten pounds arrived unexpectedly from Britain... With an uncertain future and £10.00 in hand, James and Phia moved to Winneba." The town was on the coast, about sixty-four kilometres from Asamankese. After fifteen months in the Gold Coast, it seemed he would have to start all over again.

June 1938 – May 1953

Winneba was not unknown to James McKeown as the church from Asamankese had worked there previously. In fact, James had walked from Asamankese to hold a mission in this coastal town and sixty people had come to Christ in the first meeting. Arriving now with all their possessions, James and Sophia rented part of a two-storey house in the suburbs of Winneba. They started to evangelise in the town and surrounding areas. A hall was hired for Sunday services and Sunday school and within a year the congregation had grown to two hundred.

An Apostolic Herald of 1939 tells how James was invited to visit a group, called "The Twelve Apostles Church", who lived on the western side of the Gold Coast. Their leader was Pastor John Naikaba and this group had received visions and prophecies over previous years that a white man would come and teach them.

James travelled on foot for seven days, arriving on 19th December to spend six weeks with them. During this mission 1,288 people accepted Christ as their Saviour and were baptised in water. Many signs followed the preaching of the Gospel. At times

Sophia accompanied her husband on treks into the bush. However, on this occasion she stayed at home as the location was too remote and the journey too difficult. So James returned to Winneba for a week to see Sophia and then went back to this group for another seven weeks. He said, "I appreciated my wife, poor Phia! How would you like to be married to a man like that? But I did not want to bring her to these places, far in the bush." (Leonard, 1989)

By 1939, as the Apostolic Church in Winneba continued to grow, another church had developed in Saltpond, some miles west along the coast. Sophia wrote back to Britain, "We have just had our first Easter Convention in Winneba, and it has far exceeded our expectations. The Convention commenced on Friday 7th April, continuing until Monday, 10th April. The theme of the Convention was "Vision." ...One pastor, one evangelist and one overseer were ordained... The gifts of the Holy Spirit were manifested..." (Leonard, 1989)

James and Sophia left the Gold Coast on 25th June 1939 to return home on furlough. During these first two years of missionary service they had proved God's faithfulness and provision through trials and hardships of many kinds: James' early months alone, facing serious illness; the relentless heat and threat of insects, snakes and other wildlife; understanding the culture of an unfamiliar land; the issues regarding healing in Asamankese; the need to regroup and start again in Winneba; weeks of separation when James was in the bush; times when there was no money, but God intervened; and the many miles travelled on foot, over difficult terrain, to see the Kingdom of God increase. They had won the hearts of the people they ministered to because they lived, worked and ate with them. They identified with the Africans, opening their home to them and cooking the same food that they cooked, which was unusual for foreign missionaries at that time.

By this time there were twenty-seven outstations established from Winneba and Saltpond. During their absence, the work was left in the care of Pastor Robert Kay, who had previous missionary experience in Nigeria.

As was customary with missionaries on furlough, James and Sophia were interviewed by the UK Apostolic Missionary Board in February 1940, prior to their return to the Gold Coast later that month. An extract from the minutes is included, paying tribute to them for their work and also recognising Sophia McKeown as a missionary in her own right:

When they returned to the Gold Coast in February 1940, Britain was at war with Germany. On the front page of the May 1940 Apostolic Herald there is a short report: "We give praise to God for the safe arrival in the Gold Coast of Pastor and Mrs. J. McKeown following their first period of furlough in the homeland. In a letter just to hand, the Pastor relates that the journey was not without incident: 'A few hours after we had left the convoy and most of the passengers had retired for the night, the alarm was sounded – all passengers on deck! Without any undue excitement all took up their positions in readiness to take to the boats if the need arose...' The Pastor states that, according to official reports, an enemy U-Boat was sighted and put out of action by a French destroyer." (Apostolic Herald, 1940)

Over time, other missionaries and their families joined the McKeowns in the Gold Coast -men like Pastors Charles Sercombe, Albert Seaborne, Stanley Hammond and James's own brother, Adam. In 1942 the Apostolic Church base was moved from Winneba to Cape Coast, a coastal town west of Saltpond. Previously, when James was on his way home from a trek, he had stopped at Cape Coast and it was there that he had heard the Lord say to him, "You are finished at Winneba." Christine Leonard writes, "He arrived home and he was telling Sophia that he thought they would soon be moving when there was a great noise and the end wall of their house fell down!" (Leonard, 1989) This confirmed their need to move.

Again they had little money, but soon James and Sophia found accommodation and used their new base in Cape Coast to spread out into bush areas with the Gospel. They remained there until 1948 when they made their final move to Accra. In each location, God, by the Holy Spirit, was working through this couple to build His Church.

The 1947 Apostolic Missionary Report gave this update on the work in the Gold Coast: "Today there are approximately one hundred Apostolic assemblies and stations in the country, many of them with large and enthusiastic congregations. Most of these stations have their own pastor or worker, and local government is exercised by elders exactly on the pattern in the homeland, and based on the scriptural plan for the New Testament Church." The report mentions a Christmas convention in Accra where the congregation was at least four and a half thousand. Services took place under a "mighty canopy specially erected, whilst hundreds were turned away! During the services, almost a hundred and fifty converts were made, scores baptised in the Holy Spirit, whilst over three hundred followed their Lord and Master through the waters of baptism." (Apostolic Missionary Report, 1947)

From the time he arrived in the Gold Coast in 1937 James McKeown had a plan for church growth. It was built around these five principles; a relationship with the Holy Spirit; the priority of evangelism; the absolute necessity of prayer; the discipline of financial giving and, above all, a passion for Jesus.

He trained people in these principles but, more importantly, he and Sophia lived them out in their own lives. Many Africans caught the vision and the passion that the McKeown's exemplified and they went on to do great things themselves for God.

May 1953 – October 1982

In May 1953 a Quadrennial Council of the Apostolic Church was held. This Council met every four years to discuss and decide upon policy for the world-wide Apostolic Church. James McKeown was present and had sent in an item for the agenda. Pastor Bryn Thomas records that McKeown "asked the Council to debate a pre-existing decision that UK (white) pastors were not subject to the authority of local (black) apostleship". (Thomas, 2016) This was an issue of discrimination that understandably troubled him. However, the main issue on the table at that year's Council was the "Latter Rain Movement".

The Latter Rain was a Pentecostal Revival that had started in Canada in 1948. Apostolic Publications from the 1940s and 1950s reflect a desire for revival to sweep through the church. There was a realisation among some that this Latter Rain move provided an opportunity for the Apostolic Church to recover something of the Holy Spirit life and power that it had known at its inception. It is important to understand that the Latter Rain was not a denomination, but a move of the Holy Spirit. As churches and pastors experienced this "new anointing" it challenged them about how and what they ministered. It also challenged church practice. There was a need for a "new wineskin", without so many rules and regulations, to allow the Holy Spirit to flow.

In the Penygroes Convention of August 1952 a prophetic word encouraged the leadership to accept this move of the Spirit and even to change the term they used for it: "speak not of it as 'Latter Rain', but I will give unto you a new term whereby you shall enter into what I call by the Spirit 'a new anointing.'" There was also this startling prophetic word: "You will not move one step further until you find the place of this anointing."

For some time Apostolic Latter Rain teams had held meetings in the UK, Nigeria and the Gold Coast. However, for the leadership of the UK Apostolic Church, there were other issues linked to accepting this move of God. Bryn Thomas writes, "There were a number of side issues that would have to be adopted if the AC were to accept Latter Rain totally. Looking at these issues with hindsight, they seem to be rather trivial, but for the General Executive of the time, they were major issues, such as ministers being paid according to the local church's ability to pay, rather than have a set salary..." (Thomas, 2016)

Gordon Weeks' account expresses further concerns: "The Latter Rain preachers began to insist on the abandoning of all denominational titles, organisation and structure. The vision of the Body of Christ was of totally independent local assemblies with teams of apostles and prophets travelling in evangelistic ministry throughout the world, but with no governmental or structured input into any assembly." (Weeks, 2003)

Within the 1953 Quadrennial Council opinions regarding the Latter Rain were divided. At the conclusion of the discussions all the men present were asked to reaffirm their belief in the tenets and the principles and practices as included in the Apostolic Church Constitution, which had been agreed in March 1937 (The Apostolic Church - Its Principles and Practices, 1937). Gordon Weeks records that, in response, James McKeown said that he felt unable to reaffirm. His decision was taken to be tantamount to his resignation from the Apostolic Church.

Furthermore, the Council required all pastors, elders, deacons and UK missionaries to reaffirm their allegiance to the Apostolic Church, its beliefs and constitution. The immediate result was that some pastors, officers and members in the UK, USA and Canada resigned from the Apostolic Church and some churches also left. In Nigeria four UK missionaries resigned. (Weeks, 2003)

Undoubtedly the long-term repercussions went much deeper. Bryn Thomas wrote, "The 1953 Council decision had such a devastating effect on the AC that it is difficult to fully quantify it even after more than 60 years."

James McKeown's resignation impacted greatly on the Apostolic Church Gold Coast. Byrn Thomas recorded: "On hearing the news that James McKeown had separated from the Apostolic Church they swung into action. They sent a cable to McKeown confirming their support for him. They opened their own bank accounts and renamed the fellowship, 'Gold Coast Apostolic Church.' The leaders of the UK Executive offered to attend a conciliation meeting, but the leaders of the Gold Coast Church refused. What followed was a bitter contest as individuals and assemblies were challenged with regard to their loyalties." (Thomas, 2016)

It is estimated that 100,000 people went over to this new denomination. It became known as "The Gold Coast Apostolic Church" and later, with the dawning of independence in 1957, it was renamed "Ghana Apostolic Church". Eventually, in August 1962, this new group became known as "The Church of Pentecost".

Pastor James McKeown returned to the Gold Coast in October 1953 to lead the Gold Coast Apostolic Church. The two groupings, the Apostolic Church Gold Coast (under the cover of the UK Apostolic Church) and the Gold Coast Apostolic Church drew up their battle-lines, and many conflicts resulted over money, property and people. For instance, on 12th July 1953, a court in Sekondi ruled that the Gold Coast Apostolic Church render account to the Apostolic Church Gold Coast.

Pastor Albert Seaborne and his wife were caught up in this conflict. The group which were against the resolution to withdraw from the UK Apostolic Church was led by Pastor David Tenobi. Because of the strife, he and his associates moved the Seabornes away from their place of residence to another town in the Gold Coast and found them new accommodation.

There were attempts to reconcile the two factions, both before and after James McKeown's return to the Gold Coast. A Church of Pentecost publication gives us this information: "James McKeown returned to the Gold Coast and a meeting was held between the Gold Coast Apostolic Church and the Bradford delegation together with Tenobi and Co. The two groups could not reconcile. Another meeting of James McKeown and his ministers, to which Tenobi was invited, was held on 15th October 1953. This also failed to yield the intended reconciliation." (Asare-Duah, 2014)

A delegation from Bradford met with those who wished to remain under the cover of the UK Apostolic Church. As a result, The Apostolic Church of the Gold Coast continued and made its base in Somanya, a town in the eastern region of the south Gold Coast. Pastor David Tenobi was their leader.

Some years later, in 1960, James McKeown faced a challenge of a different kind. While he was out of the country, a plot was put in place, by his deputy leader, to oust him. He was the subject of false rumours and brought before the civil courts of Ghana. It became a matter of national importance and the president of the country, Nkrumah, became involved. The disputes about property were resolved, the threat to expel James was withdrawn and a change of name for the denomination was decreed. From August 1962 the grouping that had been called "The Gold Coast Apostolic Church" and then, in 1957, "The Ghana Apostolic Church", now became known as "The Church of Pentecost".

Under the leadership of Pastor James McKeown, and with his wife Sophia by his side, this church experienced amazing growth not only in Ghana but in other countries in West Africa such as Nigeria, Cameroon, Liberia and Togo. Asare-Duah emphasises that McKeown's preaching centred on these truths: Jesus Christ and Him crucified; the baptism of the Holy Spirit and the power of God to change lives and bring holiness to the church. (Asare-Duah, 2014)

FINAL TRIBUTES

James retired to Northern Ireland in 1982, after nearly forty-five years on the field. Sadly Sophia died the following year. James died six years later, in 1989, and his funeral was held in Ballymena. However, he was not forgotten in Ghana, where 20,000 people attended his open air memorial service in Accra.

He was a man who, in his long years of service, not only established over 3,500 churches but also touched the hearts of countless thousands of people. *The Gallant Soldiers of The Church of Pentecost* (Asare-Duah, 2014) includes these two tributes to him:

"James McKeown's ministry was people-orientated. He always came down to the level of people, ate their food and drank their water. He enabled his followers to develop a sense of self-worth alongside the grace of God. Snobbery, favouritism and discrimination had no place in his ministry. He was a very plain man who communicated the Gospel of Jesus Christ in simple language."

"He lived in touch with heaven a life of faith, prayer and meditation. His sympathies, hopes and joy – his all, were centred there. He was a chosen servant among God's many sons. He bore his sayings on his lips, and on his errands. No human frown he feared, no earthly praise he sought. But in the dignity of Heaven his burning message spoke."

Christine Leonard, his biographer added her own tribute: "A 'simple' farmer turned tram driver, James went to the mission field with no training. God had called him to do a new thing in the Gold Coast. He did not mix with other missionaries, nor did he benefit from the advice of academic institutions; he just listened to God and set things in motion accordingly. He knew his Bible and believed it, expecting God to work, expecting lives to change. James' clear mind had no preconceived ideas, so he was open to learn from the Holy Spirit. Prayer, in the sense of a two way conversation with God, must be one of the main keys to the man. Hearing God became so natural to him that he did not always realise where his wisdom came from. To James, many of the principles he applied were simply things that he had seen." (Leonard, 1989)

The Apostolic Church in Ghana remains strong in the 21st. Century and currently has a membership of over 300,000 people, spread across fifty-three administrative areas. It is involved in mission to a number of European countries, as well as to Canada and the United States. In recent decades many Ghanaian Apostolics have come to live and work in Britain, inspiring the UK Apostolic Church with their faith, their powerful praying and their love and service for the Lord.

Taking into account also that the Church of Pentecost has over 2.1 million members in approximately 15,800 congregations worldwide, we begin to appreciate the scale of the legacy that James McKeown has left behind. Of course numbers only tell a very small part of the story and there are doubtless thousands of individuals and families who could testify to the life-changing impact he had upon their lives.

One of James McKeown's favourite verses was: *"I will build my church, and the gates of hell shall not prevail against it."* Matthew 16:18 (AV) He would have been the first to acknowledge that it was not James McKeown who built the Apostolic Church Gold Coast or the Church of Pentecost but it was God, by the Holy Spirit, who accomplished the work through him, leaving an extensive and enduring legacy, not only among the people of Ghana but far beyond.

CHAPTER SEVEN
WILLIAM CATHCART

"To me, the very least of all the saints, this grace was given, to preach to the Gentiles the unfathomable riches of Christ, and to bring to light what is the administration of the mystery..."
Ephesians 3:8 -9

One evening in the Skewen Apostolic Assembly, just as the midweek prayer meeting had closed, a man in the congregation called Emlyn Hughes suddenly burst out with this prophetic word: "My servant, I have given you Australia". It was the mid to late 1920s and D.P. Williams was the pastor in Skewen at the time. Hearing the prophecy, Pastor Dan leapt over the table, behind which he had been convening the meeting, and told the departing congregation that he had been in prayer all that day for Australia. That prophetic word came to pass in an amazing way and William Cathcart was the man that God used to pioneer the Apostolic work in Australia and also in New Zealand.

HIS EARLY LIFE

William Cathcart wrote his own account of his life and ministry which was published under the title, *From Gloom to Glory*, and we shall draw excerpts from it to relate his story here.

Of his early years he says, "On May 12th, 1893, I was born in my native Scotland to my Scottish parents, but tragedy began for me at the early age of three years when my mother died. With three sisters and one brother, we were sent by our father to be reared by our grandmother and aunt in North Ireland. It was there that I heard for the first time about God's love and salvation for sinners, but I was too young to understand it. The message came to me in the words of old revival hymns sung by my aunt, who had a beautiful soprano voice. As I grew to manhood, I heard that those hymns were the favourites in the 'Great Revival of 1859' in North Ireland. I also heard talk about the wonderful experiences of conversion under God's power and that my uncle John was one of the local leaders."

He continues, "Although my mental grasp of all this was of a childlike nature, yet the spirit of it all seemed to include me. At the age of seven years, this was made so real to me that somehow it remained with me from that time on. This, no doubt, led to my own conversion at the age of sixteen; shortly after that, I left North Ireland and returned to my native Scotland. I soon found myself in the army and deeply involved in World War 1. I was severely wounded in battle in France in March 1915; and, after hospitalisation, I returned to battle until eventually, in 1918, I was among the 'incurables', who were practically expendable since we were of no further use for king and country." (Cathcart, 1976)

William's brother, John, who was serving alongside him in the trenches, died of mustard gas poisoning. William survived, but the Great War had a devastating effect on his health, bringing him eventually to a state of collapse. He was hospitalised in France and then transferred to England, where he spent much time in British Army hospitals. Suffering from tuberculosis and the debilitating effects of life in the trenches, he was physically very weak and scarcely able to walk. Mentally, like so many other survivors, shell shock had transformed him into a nervous wreck.

He was backslidden spiritually at this time, but, while William was convalescing in a hospital in England, God spoke to him and told him, "You are coming back to Me. I am going to heal you. I will give you a shepherd's heart and you will go to the uttermost parts of the earth for Me." This word from the Lord had a profound effect upon him and he writes, "I had a compulsion to weep and blend my tears with longings for forgiveness and mercy, when all at once I had the assurance that I was fully restored to God in spirit and truth."

William Cathcart was eventually discharged from hospital and was put into army rehabilitation work. Although he was physically, in his own words, "still a pitiable sight", the time in hospital and the subsequent period of rehabilitation "were days of spiritual rehabilitation more than anything else. The story of my life at that time was prayer, and faith in God, and I prayed when walking, when working, and prayer was my name for it, although it was more like 'talking to God.'"

He went to live in Glasgow, where he found himself completely alone in the world - no wife or home of his own, nor even relatives. He took board and lodgings and began to attend a Plymouth Brethren assembly close by. It was with this Christian group, at the first open-air meeting he had ever attended, that, out of the blue, the words of John 6:29 came into his mind and he got up on the small platform and William Cathcart preached the Gospel publicly for the first time. "At first I began weakly," he recalls, "but then I got an anointing and all the weakness was gone from my body, my mind was highly inspired, and the ministry of the Word just streamed out of me to the crowd! The 'approved brethren' just stood gaping at me and could not understand how this happened."

He continued to prove God both physically and spiritually. He learned much about spiritual warfare and saw God test his faith. He moved to another boarding house and it was there that he heard about the "Burning Bush" assembly on Renfrew Street. A friend of his new landlady visited the house and William was invited to join in their conversation about this church, whose minister was the "terrible Andrew Turnbull." William Cathcart writes, "I somehow knew immediately that was why I had to meet that woman with my landlady and to have tea with her, because God was using her as a finger post to point the way in which I should go..." (Cathcart, 1976)

THE BURNING BUSH, GLASGOW

William Cathcart first visited the Burning Bush assembly, on Renfrew Street, Glasgow in 1919 and he mentions the fact that they were at that time changing the name of the church, as recorded in Gordon Week's account of that year: "Pastors D.P. Williams and W.J. Williams again visited the Burning Bush Assembly... Their preaching was fully accepted and Pastor Turnbull and his elders decided to join the Apostolic Church. A prophecy through Pastor W.J. Williams changed the name of the Assembly to the Apostolic Church and recognised Pastor Turnbull as the leader. The word continued, 'I have in this land those in whose veins is the blood of the Covenanters and their cry is still before Me.'" (Weeks, 2003)

William Cathcart was, by his own confession, a direct descendant of a Covenanter: "Like Timothy, whom Paul claimed to be his 'son in the faith', the roots of my faith go back to the faith of my Scottish Covenanter ancestors, who witnessed their testimony of faith in Christ from the sixteeneth century." (Cathcart, 1976)

Pastor Joshua McCabe, who also became an Apostolic pioneer in Australia, was present on the occasion of William's first visit to the Burning Bush and this is his description of what happened:

"When he came into the AC before 1921, I never saw a more miserable looking devil than he was. He was a shell shocked case from the First World War... One day, he was walking past the AC in Glasgow. He heard the people singing. It was upstairs in a hall two storeys up. He was in such a state of nerves he just couldn't stand singing the choruses over and over again. There was a chap by the name of MacPherson[6], one of the elders. He followed him and said, 'Brother, don't you like the singing?' 'Oh,' William replied, 'I like the singing but you know they sang that song 23 times! I can't stand it.' The elder talked further with him and discovered that he was shell-shocked. He was told, 'God can heal you... Come next Sunday.' William's response was 'I'll never come back here again.'"

In fact, William did come back the following Sunday but discovered that Pastor Andrew Turnbull was away in Portobello, near Edinburgh, on holiday. He made his way to Portobello on the Monday for Andrew Turnbull to pray with him. Joshua McCabe continues, "He came to the meeting on the Thursday and you never saw such a change in anyone. From that time on he never had any trouble." (McCabe, 1990) According to His promise, the Lord had completely healed him.

While William was at the Glasgow Apostolic Assembly, the Lord called him, through a prophetic word, to be the organist. Tom[7], the young son of Pastor Andrew Turnbull, who had prophesied the family move to Glasgow in 1915 when he was twelve years of age, prophesied these words to William: "As David played the harp before the Lord, so you will play the organ before the Lord."

After the prophecy was given, Pastor Turnbull turned to

---

6   John MacPherson: elder and later an apostle in the AC
7   See Preface

William, who was shocked to realise that the pastor knew he was the one to whom the Lord had spoken, and said, "William, the Lord's called you to play now. Just sit down and give us the note." William writes, "I did not know one note of music, which fact I stammered to this man of God. I was still more surprised when he did not seem to pay any attention to this, but commanded me to sit down and play... Just then I had another experience where the mantle of power came over me and, to my surprise, as well as that of all the others sitting there, I began to play the tune in front of me, even though I knew not how to read music, and I continued to play it till the end of the verse." (Cathcart, 1976)

William had this amazing experience of being able to play purely by the power of the Holy Spirit only this once. However, he went on to learn to read music and play the organ and testified, "I was always conscious of being greatly helped by the Spirit of God as I played before the congregation."

As a Pentecostal movement the Apostolic Church believes in spiritual impartation. The clear Old Testament example of this is in 2 Kings 2:13-14, as Elisha takes up Elijah's mantle. The prime New Testament example is the anointing of Jesus falling on the one hundred and twenty disciples on the Day of Pentecost in Acts 2:1-4. The Apostle Paul also speaks, in 2 Timothy 1:6, of having imparted a spiritual gift to Timothy, "his son in the Gospel" through the laying on of hands. According to the same principle, William Cathcart came under the spiritual influence of this giant of a man called, Andrew Turnbull and received something spiritual from him which prepared and equipped him for his future pioneering work in Australia and beyond. Cathcart recognised this himself: "The Rev. Andrew Turnbull was a man of faith and of God, and his mantle began to fall on me, as he had indicated to me that God had shown him I would receive his mantle in this way of ministry." (Cathcart, 1976) What an amazing God we serve!

MINISTRY IN SCOTLAND

William Cathcart came into full-time ministry in Scotland in 1923. The report of an Apostolic Church Convention in Edinburgh includes this information: "Brother Cathcart was also called and set to be the pastor in the Church in Airdrie, called out from his work to work in the Church. Pastor Cathcart is taking the place of Pastor Richard Turnbull, who is, by the word of the Lord, moved from Airdrie to Stromness in the Orkneys." (Apostolic Church Missionary Herald, 1923)

Cathcart later wrote this about the call to Airdrie, which is a town about twelve miles east of Glasgow: "It was to be my first pastorate, and I was by no means desiring to go to this particular town for more reasons than one. I had been enjoying some success as a salesman, and I knew this call meant that I would have to say goodbye to any thought of prosperity in this world and to the accumulation of earthly goods. God had so wonderfully prepared me for this venture that I actually had no trouble whatsoever in surrendering to the will of God." (Cathcart, 1976)

During his time in Scotland, the Lord at times spoke to William Cathcart in visions, unfolding something of God's plan for his life. Alistair Gardiner[8], a past President and a historian of the Apostolic Church in Australia, writes: "It was about this time that God gave him his first vision of the divine predestinations for him. He was seated on a Glasgow tram on a typical Scottish winter's day. God showed him a sparkling blue sea and surf, bounded by golden sands and bathed in brilliant sunshine. It was certainly no place he could recognise or associate with. Some years later when Pastor Cathcart was in Sydney, he recognised the vision as an exact replica of Manly beach." (Gardiner, 1988) Until then he had not understood the significance of the vision.

---

8 Son of Pastor Alex Gardiner from the Burning Bush, Glasgow

In 1926, William received another vision and this time a clear interpretation. Alistair Gardiner explains: "...when pioneering the Apostolic vision in Dumfries, in the south of Scotland, God expanded his understanding. He dreamed he looked down a chasm in Wales and glimpsed that same scene as previously. However, this time two men beckoned him to come to them. He woke and as he began to pray, God revealed that the scene of the vision was in Australia, and that he would pioneer there and New Zealand." (Gardiner, 1988)

During his years of ministry in Scotland he came to be recognised as a church leader and apostle within the church. Under the influence and mentoring of Andrew Turnbull, a ministry in "signs and wonders" developed. William Cathcart writes, "One day at a convention in Airdrie he called me up to deliver the possessed and then the ministry began with some outstanding results. It was like New Testament days; we even heard demons come out with loud crying, in Jesus' name, for demons have to obey the command of Jesus. From then on, I was more and more enabled to deliver, and heal, and bless, so long as I kept in the Spirit." (Cathcart, 1976)

It was in Scotland that the seeds of, what Gardiner calls "a profound expository ministry, particularly in the realm of eschatology and divine government" were planted. It was this ministry that proved effective in his pioneering work in Australia and New Zealand.

On 28th August 1926 he married Sylvia Balfour at St Paul's United Free Church in Glasgow, with Pastor Andrew Turnbull officiating at the wedding. The Balfour family were part of the Burning Bush in Glasgow. Pastor Cathcart, who was based in Dumfries in 1926, wrote, "Soon thereafter we had to return to Dumfries to take up my pastoral duties once again, this time assisted by my wife. This is a great help to a pastor of a flock who needs to contact their shepherd by other means than just a platform sermon." (Cathcart, 1976)

At the same time, unbeknown to William Cathcart, God was also at work in a remarkable way behind the scenes in Australia, preparing the way for his future ministry there and in 1929, a group of Pentecostal Christians in Perth, Australia, wrote to the Apostolic Church in Great Britain, asking for affiliation and appealing for Pastor Andrew Turnbull to be their leader. They had saved about $60 and sent it with the appeal. The appeal from Australia was presented to the Apostolic Church Council in the UK in 1929. After some time spent in prayer and waiting on the Lord, the council came to the conviction that William Cathcart was God's choice. This was confirmed when Pastor Jones Williams prophesied that God had a man in the north whom he had prepared to go to that country. The man who prophesied knew absolutely nothing about the vision the Lord had given William some three years previously. The Lord was bringing His purpose to pass.

Actually, just prior to the Council meetings, William Cathcart had been seeking God about Australia and New Zealand in his personal devotions. Again, he received a vision in which there were cattle – some feeding on lush grass and getting bigger and fatter and there were lean-looking cattle. He could see they were hungry and not much more than skin and bone. Pastor Cathcart continues, "I began to cry to God so he could interpret it... I received the answer without delay, and I knew that the lush, overlong grass represented the glorious services that God's people and I were right then enjoying in Scotland... the lean and hungry cattle represented the people to whom I was being sent in Australia and New Zealand, and that these people were starving to share this type of food we were having in Scotland."

He immediately wrote to Pastor Andrew Turnbull about his conviction, but Andrew had already gone to Wales for the Church Council. Pastor Cathcart wrote, "Little did he (the prophet who prophesied) or any of those present at that conference know that my letter was in the mail up in the North country, telling my district leader (Pastor Andrew Turnbull) about the two visions the Lord had given me, and that they were about Australia and New Zealand." (Cathcart, 1976)

Although, because of ministerial commitments in the UK, Andrew Turnbull did not go himself in response to the appeal, by January 1933 there were three men from his church, the Burning Bush, pioneering in Australia – Cathcart, McCabe and Dickson. A fourth man, Pastor Alex Gardiner, joined this group in November 1934 and later took over from William Cathcart as the President of the Apostolic Church in Australia.

Pastor and Mrs. Cathcart and their son David, aged two, left Liverpool on 1st February 1930 on board the "Baranald" and arrived in Freemantle, Australia, a city 14 miles from Perth, on 1st March 1930. They were the first Apostolic pioneers "Down Under". They went by faith, not knowing if they would ever return and with no promise of support. However, they held on to this prophetic promise: "As the pebble that was thrown into the lake sent out ripples to every shore, so would His servant send out the message of the Apostolic Vision to every city and town in Australia."

They were missionaries of "the one way ticket." William Cathcart writes, "I had burned all my bridges behind me and there was no way back." The truth is – they emigrated to Australia and New Zealand. He went, as he said in his own words, "with an experimental knowledge of God Himself. I had been learning Christ in a hard school of experience, and the deep experiences through which I had gone, were now beginning to pay dividends." (Cathcart, 1976)

MINISTRY IN AUSTRALIA AND NEW ZEALAND
1930-1937

Alistair Gardiner describes how "they were welcomed by a

small group of about twenty people, who were Apostolic in name only. They had no knowledge of Apostolic doctrine, yet they were open and prepared for the truth from God's Word."

How had the Apostolic Church in Perth begun? Gardiner continues, "The Apostolic Church in Australia commenced in a wonderfully effective and scriptural manner. Miss Flett M.A., who had been a member of the Apostolic Church in the Orkney Islands, Scotland, had migrated to Perth and commenced teaching in various schools. And, like the early church, she went everywhere witnessing to the divine pattern of the New Testament Church." (Gardiner, 1988)

James Worsfold takes up the story: "...she taught religious studies, an approved syllabus subject. However, she spoke about the second coming of Christ, and the office and ministry of the apostle and the prophet, and gave out copies of *Riches of Grace* to her pupils, and as a result was dismissed from a number of schools. Miss Flett, who was in no way deterred by these dismissals, accepted them as part of her pioneering ministry in preparing the way for Apostolic Church ministers to campaign in the centres where she taught." (Worsfold, 1991)

The Pentecostal scene in Perth was one of splits and divisions. There were six separate Pentecostal assemblies in the city. Barry Chant, Australian pastor and church historian points out that this was "not caused by any reason of growth, but as a result of division." (Chant, 2011) Gardiner reports, "It was with one of these groups that Miss Flett and some other Apostolics from Scotland and Wales began to have fellowship; to share with them the truths that God had revealed in the United Kingdom, and to circulate copies of the *Riches of Grace* ...In 1929 this group, tired of the continual divisions in Pentecost, called themselves the Apostolic Church and wrote to be affiliated with the church in Great Britain."

It was this group of Pentecostal Christians that William Cathcart had come to lead. Australia was in the grip of a depression and William recalls, "We arrived with the grand sum of THIRTY POUNDS British currency, and with this we had to pay rent, set up our living quarters, keep alive and clothed, and pioneer a church assembly." (Cathcart, 1976)

Apparently fifty attended the first breaking of bread service in the Perth Assembly, which was conducted by Pastor Cathcart. The regular attendance soon rose to forty-five as he evangelised and preached the Gospel. This increase in numbers was partly due to one of those Pentecostal splinter groups joining the Apostolic assembly. This group was led by a Pastor George Taylor. He was to become the first Australian Apostolic Pastor.

Times were hard in Perth in 1930. Living expenses were high and money was scarce. After three months in the city, the Cathcarts came to the end of their resources. Alistair Gardiner gives this account: "Undaunted however, he began with two partners to sell tea from door to door under the name of the Triune Tea Company. Another Pentecostal leader started in opposition, calling his company 'The Try-Me Tea Company', with little success!" (Gardiner, 1988) One of the partners in the Triune Tea Company was Hector Gardiner. He was converted at revival services that William Cathcart had held above a large store in Williams Street, Perth in 1930. Hector must have been one of the early converts in Perth, under the ministry of William Cathcart. In May 1935 Hector Gardiner went to join Miss Dagny Pedersen in North China, as the first Australian Apostolic missionary to that nation.

In an article entitled "A Brother Beloved: An Appreciation of Pastor Cathcart", Pastor Joshua McCabe highlighted three particular qualities of the man – **He was a man of Faith; he was a man of Action** and **he was a man of Prayer** (Apostolic Herald, 1937). I will use these headings to further describe the seven years that William Cathcart spent pioneering churches in Australia and New Zealand, before he then moved to South Africa.

A MAN OF FAITH

Undoubtedly William Cathcart's faith had grown during his time in Scotland and he records this in his autobiography: "I had gone out in faith and this move to the uttermost parts required the uttermost faith; and well I knew that it was not organisation that we needed here; it was faith, and 'without faith it is impossible to please God.' God has to answer faith; it is His own principle; He cannot deny it! Faith in the God of the uttermost won the victory in the 'UTTERMOST PARTS.'" (Cathcart, 1976)

The challenges were great. There was a group of Apostolic people in Perth but no church as such, and Australia was in the grip of economic depression. But Pastor Cathcart ploughed ahead and God blessed: "We soon began to get converts – mostly men and of a real tough type of sinner... We took to the streets for services with police permission, and a good work began as converts were won out there in the open streets... Every day we expected to have to close the door; it was either lack of money, complaints from some people... but miraculously, we always managed to keep the door open." (Cathcart, 1976)

The group eventually moved from a hall above a grocer's shop, when God provided in a miraculous way. William was passing a church building in Perth one day, when he saw two men putting up a sign saying, "Revival Services" on the outside. Apparently one of the men turned to his helper saying, "That is Cathcart from Scotland and the Lord just spoke to me that we are fixing this sign for him, for he will take over this building in a few days." Cathcart only learned this later, but take over the building he did.

The story of how the assembly in Perth grew and developed

in God is a remarkable one. As well as preaching the Gospel, the people began to reach out in practical ways to the community. One particular incident provoked this, as Cathcart recalled, "One Saturday night in one of our street services I was challenged by a Communist as to why we preached, but did not feed the hungry. I took him up on it; although at the moment, we had not much left to feed ourselves." However, he took up the challenge and God provided. After a crowd had listened to the Gospel being preached on a street corner, they were then invited back to the church building for food. He continues, "...the outcome was that, apart from good publicity, the numbers increased and there was work for everyone to keep them busy, one way or another, so that they did not feel the frustrations of unemployment so bad at all." (Cathcart, 1976)

The Apostolic Church in Perth was also blessed with signs and wonders. In the *Riches of Grace*, September 1932 there was this headline: "ANOTHER CASE OF HEALING IN WESTERN AUSTRALIA – HEALED OF GASTRITIS AND PNEUMONIA - a story from R. Carson, 67, Brewer Street, Perth, W.A.

'I would like to tell briefly the way in which the Lord Jesus Christ, on two occasions, healed me. For six months I suffered from gastritis, which was caused by my work. Though I had heard many testify to the fact that Jesus healed, and I had seen the same, yet I never could lay hold of the truth for myself until every resource had failed.

'I dreaded the night-time coming on. One night I sat and listened to Pastor Cathcart preaching healing in the Apostolic Church, 24, Brisbane Street, Perth, W.A., and, as I had to go on duty three hours afterwards (being on night work), I felt I must do something; so, when the invitation was given to those desiring healing, I decided to put this doctrine to the test.

As the elders laid hands upon me, anointing with oil according to James 5:14, there and then the Lord healed me. Hallelujah! Again, on December 4th 1931, I was taken very ill with influenza and pneumonia. A well-known doctor in Perth, W.A., was called in and gave very little hope of recovery. The following morning Pastor Cathcart prayed over me laying on hands and anointing with oil. Two hours later the doctor was surprised to see the change, and, on examining me, said all trace of pneumonia had absolutely gone. Praise the Lord! Our God is a Great Physician.'" (Riches of Grace, 1932)

This was not the only testimony of healing from Perth in that edition of the magazine. The second read: "A CASE OF DIVINE HEALING IN PERTH, W. AUSTRALIA – HEALED AFTER 17 YEARS OF SUFFERING." This was the story of a Mrs. Reid who had suffered from bad eyesight from an early age. Her eyes were very weak and the left eye was crossed. Mrs. Reid wrote, "Time went on, but my eyes never improved, and I had to depend upon my glasses sorely. To go without them was painful... In August 1930, I became a member of the Apostolic Church, 24, Brisbane Street, and heard the Foursquare Gospel of JESUS CHRIST being preached... During the following November, when Pastor Cathcart was holding a Special Mission in Victoria Park, I went out for prayer, obeying the Scripture (James 5:14), and the GREAT EYE SPECIALIST, who caused the blind to see, honoured His Own Word and healed me. I took my glasses off, never again to wear them. PRAISE GOD, my eyes are perfectly straight." There was this footnote: "I have the glasses and also photographs of myself before being prayed for, and four opticians in Perth, W.A., have testified to me that my healing was marvellous." (Riches of Grace, 1932)

Speaking of Cathcart, Joshua McCabe writes, "It was typical of his further steps in faith to go to Adelaide (which is almost a foreign land to residents in Perth), to Melbourne, to Sydney, to New Zealand and to Brisbane. But God was teaching Pastor the 'life of faith'. The small assembly at Perth was only to pay expenses, but could make no provision for their Pastor, but again faith triumphed, for our pioneer, in real pioneer fashion, worked with his hands to pay expenses and ministered faithfully to the flock. However, the work grew and after the first twelve months the valuable time of the Pastor was not wasted on mundane things." (Apostolic Herald, 1937)

Looking at William Cathcart's life and that of other pioneers, we can wonder, "What is the secret of such faith?" Pastor McCabe gives this simple guidance, "Faith is gained in the daily life and surrender to the will of God."

A MAN OF ACTION

William Cathcart had a strategy when it came to church planting in Australia. Remember, he was a military man and his strategy bore all the marks of a military campaign: "An advance was made and ground taken; reinforcements brought in and the ground secured; then another advance and so on." (Burgess & Mass, 2002) However this strategy was not from any First World War manual. It was a plan that had been prophetically revealed to both Pastors Cathcart and McCabe while they were in Perth together. According to Alex Gardiner, it was "Divine in concept, prophetic in revelation, manifestly blessed and honoured by God and... scripturally sound in precedent and pattern" (Riches of Grace, 1937).

Let me give you just a taste of the strategy in the first seven years:

William Cathcart arrived in Perth March 1930

Through preaching, teaching the "Apostolic vision", praying for the sick, street work and helping the poor, a church was established in Perth. By the end of 1931 the membership had increased to over eighty and the work was continuing to grow steadily.

Joshua McCabe arrived in Perth 8th January 1932

An appeal was made to the UK for another family to come to Australia and on the 8th January 1932, Joshua McCabe and family, also from the Glasgow Apostolic Church, arrived in Perth. In an interview with Barry Chant, McCabe explains, "Cathcart came in 1930 to Perth. After he had been there he felt he should get another man to come – especially a man with prophetical ministry. As I had been a recognised prophet in the church in Scotland, I was the man who was chosen. That was in 1931, at the August Convention in Penygroes. I came away in November and arrived 8th January 1932. So that gave Cathcart the opportunity to move over to Adelaide where this little group had invited him to come. He had already been there and ministered. He came back to be with me to get me initiated with the folks in Perth." (McCabe, 1990)

Under McCabe's ministry the work in Perth progressed. Chant writes, "Cathcart welcomed the new arrival in Perth in January 1932 and they preached together for several weeks. Soon 200 people were attending regularly and McCabe hired the Perth Town Hall for a special series of meetings. There were more converts and new members. Shortly after, yet another of the original Pentecostal groups joined the Apostolics. Before long new assemblies were opened in Victoria Park, Claremont and Freemantle." (Chant, 2011)

William Cathcart moved to Adelaide January 1932

Adelaide was 1700 miles from Perth. Cathcart had already started to pioneer in this city before his family, including a newborn son, moved to be with him at the end of January 1932. Explaining his reasons for the move, he writes, "...one day I received a letter from two men who lived in Adelaide, South Australia, whom I had never met prior to this... The gist of the letter was that these men were affiliated with Pentecostal work in South Australia and when they had heard about me, they were so sure that the Lord had shown them to ask me to visit them, that they enclosed a third-class ticket by steamship from Perth to Adelaide... I had to leave Mother and sons and set out for fields unknown with no promise of support of any kind."

The journey took two days and two nights and Pastor Cathcart says, "I had done a lot of praying during those two days and nights." He arrived in the city with one pound, Australian sterling. "This is all I had in my possession to keep alive and open up a work for the Lord!" Eventually, after arriving in Adelaide early in the morning and after many bus fares, he got to where he needed to be. It was by then late evening.

It had been arranged that he stay with a German family in the city. He continues, "I was given a good supper and I was really hungry and enjoyed it, together with the fellowship. When the meal was over, we all got down to pray and the heavens opened and the Spirit fell with great power and joy, and spiritual laughter fell on us; I never doubted the results from then on."

At this time South Australia was also suffering from the depression – unemployment, mortgages overdue, no money for offerings, and no money for bus fares to come to church.

However a hall was rented and Pastor Cathcart describes those early beginnings, "Our services began with ten people present, then fifteen, then thirty and later sixty as we came to the sixth week. We rented the city hall for Sunday afternoon and evening services and hundreds began to come to hear the message! It was a repetition of the same scenes we had experienced in West Australia with souls saved, some people miraculously healed and many filled with the Holy Spirit." (Cathcart, 1976)

On 30th October 1932, Zion Temple was opened and by November this report appeared in the *Apostolic Herald*: "A big work is springing up in Adelaide, South Australia, to which Pastor Cathcart has transferred his operations and where he is having the joy and blessing of ministering on Sunday nights to over 800 listeners." (Apostolic Herald, 1932)

This move proved temporary because, by 1936 larger premises were required and the Draper Memorial Methodist Church was purchased and renovated by the Apostolic Church and opened on 1st November 1936. A further article comments, "Who could have thought when Pastor Cathcart, unknown and unheralded, arrived in Adelaide, that so great a work would be accomplished. The pioneer spirit of Pastor Cathcart shown in the mighty step taken in faith, in leasing, renovating and occupying Zion Temple has been imbued into the Apostolic Church in Adelaide." (Apostolic Herald, 1936)

Allan Dickson arrived in Perth January 1933
Joshua McCabe transferred to Adelaide February 1933

Gordon Weeks writes, "Due to the expansion of the Church in Australia an appeal for help had been sent to the Missionary Council in August 1932 and Pastor and Mrs. A.S. Dickson were called through prophecy to meet the need. They sailed from Southampton on 21st December 1932 and arrived at Freemantle on Friday 20th January 1933 and were welcomed in Perth Assembly by one hundred and thirty people on 21st January. Pastor and Mrs. McCabe were transferred to Adelaide from Perth on 21st February." (Weeks, 2003) William Cathcart knew the Dicksons from his time at the Burning Bush, Glasgow.

William Cathcart moved to Melbourne and meetings began in February 1933

Regarding this move to Melbourne, Cathcart writes, "Once again I was short of cash because the income was barely keeping up with the growing expense as the work grew and with all its demands. I was left with four pounds Australian currency which meant I was really making a faith move once again for all that I visualised doing in Melbourne. Who can do much with $16.00 American currency unless he really knows how to move on faith?"

With "an urge to go forward", Pastor Cathcart walked the city in a systematic way looking for premises and saw a sign for a Protestant Hall. Although he did not have the money, the hall was rented for five weeks. A deposit was put down and a brief advertisement was put in a Saturday paper. Thirty people appeared on the first Sunday, but the offerings were meagre and remained so in the weeks to come. With no money to pay the rent, he recalls, "I began to think I had failed somehow when a man walked up, and without speaking, pushed some money into my hand and said, 'The Lord told me to come here tonight and to give you this money. God bless you!' and he walked away... When I opened my hand, there lay the rent... and I could only weep at the goodness of God." (Cathcart, 1976)

Gordon Weeks continues the story: "Soon ninety people were attending on week nights and three hundred on Sunday evenings. On Easter Sunday afternoon one hundred and sixty people attended the first Communion service. On 20th April, Pastor John Hewitt arrived in Melbourne to join Pastor Cathcart in a Revival and Healing Crusade. From 23rd April, when one thousand two hundred people attended the first service, the crusade continued for nine weeks, during which seven hundred people were saved and over two thousand people were prayed over for divine healing."

(Weeks, 2003) The most dramatic healing was that of a Salvation Army woman who was instantaneously healed after being confined to a wheel chair for nine years.

Pastor John Hewitt was originally from Maesteg in South Wales, where he had been a member of the Apostolic Church. In his early twenties he had emigrated to Australia, but returned to the UK after some years and was recognised as an evangelistic apostle by the Apostolic Church Council in 1929. He returned to Australia and Worsfold records that he had, until 1933, been running successful Gospel campaigns in Queensland, New Zealand and South Africa under the banner of the Apostolic Faith Mission (Worsfold, 1991).

Cathcart and Hewitt knew each other from the Apostolic Church in the UK, but were by now living in different parts of Australia. One day William Cathcart was on a tram in Adelaide, praying quietly about contacting Hewitt, but having no idea where he was, when God intervened in a miraculous way. As he looked out of the tram window, to his astonishment, he saw Hewitt walking along the street in Adelaide. He left the tram and the two men met.

It transpired that John Hewitt was stopping over in Adelaide, en route by ship from the United Kingdom to Brisbane, where he was to take over the pastorate of a Pentecostal Church. He had left his wife and baby daughter on board ship and had felt impressed to visit the city. At this God-appointed meeting they agreed that it was God's plan for them to work together in Australia and that the Lord would bring this to pass in His time. So it was from the time of the 1933 crusade in Melbourne that he joined forces with Cathcart and the Apostolic Church and God greatly prospered his ministry and their work together.

On Sunday 4th June 1933, one hundred and seven people took membership of the Apostolic Church in Melbourne. During the service one member of the congregation was called to be the pastor of the Melbourne church and thirty three others were called into local ministries. Pastor John Hewitt ordained all these people there and then.

D.P. Williams wrote this about Pastor Cathcart in 1933 (by this time, the Cathcarts had been in Australia some three years): "Australia, from city to city, has flung her doors wide open to our beloved Pastor Cathcart, who has played a very prominent part as an excellent pioneer. He went out knowing no one, and faced a huge problem. By the Lord's help, he has handled a big situation against tremendous odds. Since then, three men have followed his trail, and repeated appeals are made for more men. We admire and commend the manner in which they have faced their difficult tasks, and the sweeping progress in Australia (where now Pastors Cathcart, Hewitt, McCabe, Dickson and Taylor co-operate) is a feature worthy of note in the annals of the Apostolic Church. These dear men of God have been encouraged by seeing the literal fulfilment of the Word of the Lord." (D.P.Williams, Souvenir Exhibiting the Movements of God in The Apostolic Church, 1933)

Alf Greenaway sent to Wellington, New Zealand, April 1934
Allan Dickson transferred to Auckland, July 1934

At this time Pastors McCabe, Cathcart, John Hewitt and his brother, Evangelist Isaac Hewitt, were also pioneering into New Zealand. By the end of 1934, there were six Apostolic churches there and ministers were sent from both the UK and Australia to support the new assemblies. Pastor and Mrs. Alf Greenaway from the UK moved in 1934. Two local men, E. Weston and Alf Jackson, were also called as pastors and Len Jones was recognised as an apostle.

As far back as 1925 there had been a group of twelve people who had had a Pentecostal experience and identified themselves with the Apostolic Church UK In 1927 their leader, Alex Wright, contacted Evangelist John Hewitt and later wrote to D.P. Williams, president of the Apostolic Church in the United Kingdom enquiring about Apostolic ministry. These links were maintained and, in October 1933, William Cathcart paid his first visit to the group in Wellington.

Two hundred people were present at the first meeting and the numbers continued to increase. John Hewitt joined him the following month and a Gospel crusade commenced, moving between various locations in the city. It drew congregations of up to seven hundred people. James Worsfold reports: "The ministry of divine healing came to the fore with many being ministered to by prayer and the laying on of hands, some being healed... Faith continued to rise, and it was during these services that a request was expressed for an Apostolic Church to be formed and set in order by Apostolic ministers." (Worsfold J., 1974)

When William Cathcart returned in June 1934, this time visiting Auckland, the Apostolic witness in New Zealand had expanded out from Wellington to four other locations. Pastors McCabe, Greenaway and J.H. Hewitt, Evangelist I. Hewitt and local men like Edward Weston, Alf Jackson and Len Jones, were the leaders God used to continue the pioneering work in this country and, under their ministry, the Apostolic Church in New Zealand developed and expanded. Cathcart himself did not visit New Zealand again till Easter 1940.

William Cathcart began to pioneer in Sydney in June 1934

The pioneering work in Sydney commenced with a Bible teaching campaign led by Pastor Cathcart. This was then followed by a Revival and Divine Healing Campaign led by John Hewitt and his brother, Isaac. Over one hundred and forty people were converted and a church of seventy members was established. At this time an independent church with over forty members also joined the Apostolic Church.

John Hewitt moved to Brisbane in August 1934

For four weeks John Hewitt held a revival campaign in Brisbane in 1934, and as a result a church was established and local elders and deacons appointed.

Alex Gardiner sent to Melbourne in September 1934

In September 1934, Pastor and Mrs. Alex Gardiner, with their three children, were sent to Melbourne from the Burning Bush in Glasgow. Gardiner, who had been the leader of the Glasgow assembly, was appointed senior leader in the Melbourne church and National Leader of the Apostolic Church in Australia.

In October 1934, Pastors D.P. Williams and his brother, Jones Williams, together with a deacon from the Penygroes assembly, visited the Melbourne church. To demonstrate the progress that had been made since William Cathcart arrived in Australia in March 1930, let me quote from Pastor Weeks: "After arriving in Melbourne on 19th October a great 'welcome tea' for four hundred people was held in the South Melbourne Town Hall on 20th October. Very warm welcomes were given by the leaders from Perth, Adelaide, Melbourne, Sydney, Brisbane, Tasmania and New Zealand." (Weeks, 2003) On 4th November Pastors Williams, Cathcart and others were at Melbourne Harbour to welcome the Gardiner family to Australia.

There are many stories I could have included in this brief history of how the pioneer, Pastor William Cathcart, opened doors in Australia and New Zealand for the Apostolic Church. Reading his autobiography one is struck by his honesty. He says, "As I look back over that venture of faith, I still tremble, for every moment was fraught with easy defeat, and faith alone could win such a challenge." He relates how the same questions would fill his mind as he entered upon every fresh challenge: "What would I do? Where would I go? How would I begin? How much should I pay for and how long should I take a suitable hall if I could find one?" (Cathcart, 1976) Although his material resources may have been very meagre, it is evident that the one thing he did possess in abundance was faith in God.

In researching something of the early beginnings of the Apostolic Church in Australia and New Zealand, it is the extraordinary speed with which God worked through William Cathcart to establish so many churches in so short a time that stands out. It takes my breath away! William Cathcart had only arrived in Australia in March 1930! In the years 1932-1934 alone, forty-four Apostolic assemblies were opened and every Australian state was touched.

But, of course, these things don't just happen. William Cathcart was a man of faith, but he was also a worker. Pioneering required many practical things to be done such as organising leaflets (30,000 were printed and distributed for the Melbourne Revival Campaign); some halls required alterations, for example the building of platforms and campaign newsletters had to be written, printed and distributed. He worked tirelessly and for long hours. Joshua McCabe made this assessment, "we found our brother always a man of faith and action." (McCabe, 1990)

Joshua McCabe paid this tribute to William Cathcart: "To few men is it given to see fifty churches in one land and the beginnings of several others in another land commenced as a direct and indirect outcome of the ministry of seven brief years. Such is the aggregate result of Pastor William Cathcart's ministry in Australia and New Zealand..."(Apostolic Herald, 1937)

He gave this further tribute in a 1990 interview: "He was a man that appealed to men. Wherever Cathcart had an assembly you could say that 50% were men. Most of us would have 75% women. But he seemed to have that command. People looked up to him. He was a godly man. He was a man who preached the word with power and dignity. He would tell us it took 60 hours to get a sermon. And he would preach for an hour and a half. His own wife got his measure. She said, 'Willie, you stand up there and you expect us to take in an hour and a half what it has taken you 60 hours to get'. He was a pioneer." (McCabe, 1990)

As you read this account of Cathcart's life, I trust you are saying, "GOD HAS NOT CHANGED. WHAT COULD THE CHURCH I BELONG TO ACHIEVE IN THE NEXT FOUR YEARS?"

A MAN OF PRAYER

E.M. Bounds wrote, "What the Church needs today is not more machinery or better, not new organizations or more and novel methods, but men whom the Holy Ghost can use – men of prayer, men mighty in prayer. The Holy Ghost does not flow through methods, but through men. He does not come on machinery, but on men. He does not anoint plans, but men – men of prayer." (E.M.Bounds, 2004) Of course this quote applies equally to women.

Cathcart was unquestionably a man of faith and action, but he was also a man of prayer. He felt that he had a calling to prayer.

It was back in those early days of convalescing in hospital, when he came back to the Lord, that God began to instruct William in the school of prayer. He learned how prayer could change his personal circumstances and his health; he learned the power of prayer over the enemy of our souls; he learned how through prayer God gives and gives and also speaks into our hearts. Through prayer and God's Word he learned to place himself more and more into the hands of God.

During a personal time of prayer in his boarding house in

Glasgow, William had been baptised with the Holy Spirit. He recalls, "I was talking to the Lord about a scriptural quotation I had just read in the book from Revelation 3:20, 'Behold, I stand at the door and knock'. I began to pray very simply and very trustingly, and said to the Lord that I opened my heart and would He come in? I had no sooner spoken those words by the inspiration of the Spirit of God in my prayer, than a mighty power laid hold of me, surging through the whole of my body, and quicker than you can read these words, I was filled with the Holy Spirit." (Cathcart, 1976)

Faced with the challenges of his pioneering ministry, he would often pray all morning. The first few weeks of pioneering in Melbourne were particularly hard, but his response was this: "I spent about six to eight hours daily in prayer. The spirit of prayer was tremendous and time flew as I travailed for that revival in Melbourne." (Cathcart, 1976)

Joshua McCabe wrote this concerning his example in prayer: "I have heard it suggested that spiritual work in the colonies is so much easier than in Great Britain. Let me dispel that notion forever... The natural respect for ministers that is found at home is not found here. The serious way people take to the truth of the Gospel at home is absent here and one has greater difficulties to fight. How did Pastor Cathcart meet his problems? On his knees. I have heard him deal with an enquiry, and when the conversation drifted from the spiritual things to things that did not matter he would say, 'Well, excuse me, but I must not waste any time. I must pray.' This was no mere twaddle, but was sincerely meant. I have known him pray for days on end. I know in his campaigns when things were hard, it was praying through that brought results. Pastor taught his fellow ministers to pray, he urged his members to pray. He prayed Australia into the Apostolic Vision. He endeared himself to us all, ministers, officers and members by being a brother indeed." (Apostolic Herald, 1937)

Cathcart knew that his call was to an international pioneering ministry, so, leaving the growing work in Australia and New Zealand in the safe hands of local leaders and the UK missionaries, at the close of 1936 he prepared to relocate to South Africa.

Pastor Alex Gardiner wrote a report on the Cathcarts' departure in February 1937. It provides a brief glimpse into what they as a family had faced during those early days in Australia:

"It is now seven years since Pastor and Mrs. Cathcart, together with their son David, arrived on the shores of Australia. Commencing their work in Perth with a small company of fifteen to twenty souls, they laboured incessantly night and day. In those days, the income towards the Wages Fund was approximately fifteen shillings per week, which necessitated the Pastor returning to his natural labour. Resuming his former occupation as a tea traveller, difficulty was found even in this realm to make ends meet, so that in the evening (when free from services) he made wooden horses as toys for children and sold them. Such is the adaptability required by pioneers, not only in the natural realm, but even in the spiritual realm. However, under the faithful and very able ministry of Pastor Cathcart, the work soon grew to larger dimensions, able enough to support him, together with wife and family." (Riches of Grace Jan 1937)

MINISTRY IN SOUTH AFRICA 1937 – 1939

The Cathcarts, now with three young sons – David, John and Peter, arrived in Durban on 2nd March, accompanied also by Isaac Hewitt. The journey from Perth had taken two weeks. They were coming to "another land to pioneer for Christ and the Apostolic vision", as Pastor Cathcart expressed it in the Apostolic Herald, August 1937.

They were met at the dockside by an Australian, Brother Elijah

Martin, and Pastor Cathcart's father-in-law, Mr. Balfour. Some preliminary meetings were held in a borrowed hall but, as he explained, "We felt little could be done until we had our own place. Finally a tent, seating 300, was obtained and pitched." He goes on to mention that they felt "very much strangers in a strange land."

John Hewitt and his family arrived from the UK to join them on 4th April and the first service that night was attended by one hundred and eighty people, with four making decisions for salvation. Pastor Cathcart writes, "Great things were in store for us, for that week we saw every night nine or ten to twenty five and even thirty five come out to the altar and decide for Christ. What a wonderful sight to see about thirty people kneeling for salvation while we called for Christian workers, whoever they were, to come and point these souls to Christ. Converted Zulus would come out to point their race to Christ. Converted Indians to point their race... We saw at least four nationalities kneel side by side night after night weeping before God."

In the first five weeks of pioneering in Durban six hundred people were converted and signs followed the preaching of the word. Pastor Cathcart continues, "One woman, literally dying on her feet with cancer, was instantaneously healed and a person with pernicious epileptic fits was completely delivered. People came forward testifying to healing from many terrible complaints and scores were helped. Pastor John Hewitt has never preached as he is preaching now." (Cathcart, 1976)

However, William Cathcart left Durban for Johannesburg at the end of the second week of the campaign. On arriving in the capital city of South Africa, he did what he had done in Australia – he started to search for a hall to hold meetings. This proved difficult, and after searching for two and a half weeks, still there was no hall. "There are many obstacles and many enemies but God is greater than all", he later wrote.

John Hewitt came to join Cathcart in Johannesburg. Hewitt was known in the capital from a previous visit in 1929. Pastor Isaac Hewitt remained in Durban to continue the work there. By this time Durban had an Apostolic Church with a regular attendance of one hundred.

Meetings were eventually started and a nucleus of a church was also established in Johannesburg. In 1938, Pastor Cathcart branched out to Cape Town and established an assembly in that city with the help of a Brother Bruyn from Durban. Cathcart relates how the wife of the South African Prime Minister attended the services in Cape Town.

The difficulties this pioneering team encountered in South Africa were great. Pastor Weeks lists some of them: "...the different languages, the intense inter-racial hatred (one church had over the entrance the words 'Hottentots and Asiatics not admitted') and the financial prosperity which made rents for halls exorbitant... But the chief difficulty was the attack on the teachings of the Church by opposing tracts and defamatory stories coupled with the 'conduct of people in this country who claim to have apostles and prophets, but who live abominable lives." (Weeks, 2003)

The opposition continued to prove very strong – the name "Apostolic" being a particular source for hostility. When application was made to register the ministers under the name "Apostolic Church", the approach was rebuffed because of two other groups with the name "Apostolic" in South Africa. There was serious hostility to any name resembling those movements which bore a similar name and had in the past brought reproach and shame upon their adherents.

As a result of decisions made by the UK Apostolic Church Missionary Board, John Hewitt returned to the United Kingdom in 1938 and became pastor of the Treorchy Apostolic Church, in South Wales. Isaac Hewitt went back to evangelistic work in

Australia. William Cathcart was also to return to Australia, but not before a UK pastor, Harry Copp, was sent out to take charge of the church in Durban. This was a fully functioning church with elders and Pastor Cathcart inducted him on 13th November. In the following January Pastor Copp held the first Apostolic Church water baptismal service in South Africa, when six believers were baptised.

William Cathcart left for Australia on 18th February 1939. In the April, he was present at the opening of the new Headquarters Church and Executive Offices of the Apostolic Church in Melbourne. The foundation stone had been laid by Alex Gardiner on 17th December 1938. Pastor Gardiner had succeeded Pastor Cathcart as President of the work in Australia. The prophetic vision had always been for the Apostolic Church to have its headquarters in Melbourne and again they were seeing prophecy fulfilled. The building had cost over £6,000 and William Cathcart was given the honour of opening it. To commemorate the occasion, he was presented with a golden key by the builder.

A report on the opening in 1939 commented, "Today, in the Commonwealth of Australia and New Zealand there are 30 servants of the Lord on the paid ministry of the Church, 65 assemblies have been opened, 20 missionaries are labouring on behalf of the Apostolic Church Missionary Movement in China, India and Japan, the majority of these having been sent out and are being supported by the sacrifices of the saints in Australasia."

All this had been achieved in God in just over nine years and Pastor William Cathcart had been the original spark for this great, pioneering work.

WILLIAM CATHCART RESIGNS FROM THE APOSTOLIC CHURCH

Early in 1939 and following the opening of the new headquarters in Melbourne, the Apostolic Church in New Zealand appealed to Australia for Alex Gardiner to become their National Leader. This was agreed and by the end of September 1939, the Gardiners were in New Zealand. William Cathcart once again became the National Leader in Australia, a position he had previously fulfilled prior to going to South Africa.

At the 26th January 1940 Apostolic Church Missionary Board meeting in Bradford, a letter from Pastor Cathcart, dated 4th January 1940, was included in the agenda. It was a letter of resignation. As he was no longer under the jurisdiction of the UK Board, the matter was referred to the Australian Apostolic Church, whose leaders urged him to reconsider. The UK board offered to help financially to bring him to Britain for further discussions.

It does appear there was a doctrinal issue regarding "British Israelism", although William Cathcart did deny this as a reason for leaving. The other issues were around the administrative structures of the Mission Board, which he felt restricted missionaries when they were serving on foreign fields. The background to this, no doubt, was his own experience in South Africa. Both the UK and Australian Apostolic Church had input into decisions and policies for the field. Cathcart had wanted to go to Rhodesia after South Africa but, as he wrote, "...being part of an organisation, I was told that delay was advisable and so we as a family left... for the return trip to Australia... I had arrived in Australia the first time with no ties obligating the organisation and hamstringing my efforts. Now, returning from South Africa to Australia... to fulfil what I was asked to do, I began to really be subject to the form of organisational government, and I began to learn that I had not been made for the organisation." (Cathcart, 1976)

This man who had pioneered from 1930 to 1937 in Australia with such amazing results, did not plant one church in Australia during his second presidency. This possibly demonstrates the struggles that he was experiencing.

By September 1940, the UK Board was aware of other difficulties in Australia and suggested that two national leaders, Pastors Dawson and Rowe, go out to Australia to see what could be done to help resolve them. They, no doubt, hoped that they could also bring about a reconciliation with William Cathcart. This was war time, so travel permits were difficult to obtain and the journey itself was dangerous, but they arrived safely, with the boat docking in Wellington en route. Whatever transpired, it seems that the threat of resignation was not followed through until late 1945. Until that time Cathcart remained as President of the Apostolic Church in Australia.

We thank God for this man, who gave over twenty years of his life in sacrificial service to the Apostolic Church Movement. Thank God also that William Cathcart has left us a ministry model to which we can aspire for our own lives – a model of Christ centred, Spirit empowered ministry.

William Cathcart was a giant for God. Charles Jennings, in *20th Century Testimonies* summed up his life in this way: "The life of William Cathcart can surely be described as proof of God's sovereignty, divine protection, supernatural interposition, faith, revelation and total surrender to His Saviour and Lord." (Jennings)

TWO CHALLENGES

A personal challenge

The story of William Cathcart is not a story from centuries ago. It is not a story from some great, world-wide revival, but it is the story of a man who simply believed God. It is a story in the spirit of those we read in the Acts of the Apostles.

Can you say, "Lord, here I am: write an Acts of the Apostles story across my life"?

A *church* challenge

In the preface to this book I mentioned that God spoke to a well-known minister one time and said, 'I've seen your ministry, now do you want to see Mine?"

How are we doing church? How are we doing ministry? I trust that the story of William Cathcart will help us to understand how God does ministry.

CHAPTER EIGHT
JACOB PURNELL

*"...Put your trust in the LORD your God, and you will be
established. Put your trust in His prophets and you will succeed."*
2 Chronicles 20:20

This verse became Jacob Purnell's guiding principal for life and ministry. To it he attributed the fruitfulness and prosperity he enjoyed in his service for the Lord. He expressed it in these words:

**"Faith in the Unchangeable God.
Faith in the prophets and their message."**

In writing this chapter I will be drawing on some autobiographical accounts, which members of Jacob Purnell's family have kindly made available, and also on testimonies he wrote in past Apostolic publications.

EARLY LIFE AND CONVERSION

Jacob Purnell was born of humble parentage on 8th January 1892 in Brynmawr, a small industrial town in South Wales. His parents, George and Mary Purnell, had eight children, of whom Jacob was the fourth. At the time of Jacob's birth they did not know the Lord, but, he writes, "...the God of all grace visited our home during the 1904 Revival and saved some of the family. I was then thirteen years of age. My conversion at this time was remarkable: I was saved in the vestry of Zion Baptist Church, Brynmawr. I was between the seats, rejoicing in the assurance of salvation; some wonderful wave of power swept over my soul. The Bible became my meat and drink... and I rejoiced in that blessing for many years. Sorry to state, a lukewarmness came over God's people and also over my soul, so that I became a religious, but lukewarm, young man, and lost the sense of victory. Then I did what most young men do, I married, which caused me to move to a place called Beaufort." The wife that Jacob chose was Lily Thomas, a young woman from Beaufort, and they went on to have four children of their own.

Jacob's story continues, "While attending Zoar Baptist Church, seated in the gallery between the hours of eight and nine in the evening, the voice of God came to my soul, calling for complete consecration. I yielded when the invitation was given, raised my hand as a sign, and then something wonderful happened in my life. My soul expanded. Holy desires were born within me. I became a sincere, active worker in the church. In the midst of my activities, the call developed, and the voice within spoke louder and louder, 'Leave this place!' I was in a struggle because of friendships forged and fellowship enjoyed."

It took some time for him to yield: "Eventually, I obeyed the voice and left the church I loved, to do His will. Definite leadings of the Good Shepherd were my experience. John 13:4 was the scripture given by the Spirit; He leadeth them out; He putteth them forth; He goeth before them; they follow Him; they know His voice. As I followed the Light, darkness increased, and eventually I found Matthew 10:34-39, to be perfectly true in my own experience. It was at this point of testing that the good hand of God imparted to me the definite experience of sanctification, and also the baptism of the Holy Spirit. Three months later, I spoke in an unknown tongue." (Purnell, 1933)

THE NEXT STEP

For a time after leaving Zion Baptist Church, Jacob Purnell found himself alone with no fellowship and no church to attend. He waited until the Lord gave him clear direction: "While praying in secret, I was overwhelmed with the Spirit, speaking in other tongues, followed by interpretation – the audible voice of God. The burden of the message was 'Stand thou alone. I will not fail thee. I will work.' I assuredly gathered that the Lord desired me to stand in the open-air alone, and that He would work. The scene, the time, the witness given at that first time I stood, I can never forget. I knew that as I stood alone from time to time, a glorious work was before me."

Jacob writes, "In a while, I met two angels. Yes, such they were to me, in the persons of brothers Thomas and James Seaborne. True as steel, they joined me in open-air work and, shortly after, another came along, Ephraim Morris, making four in all. The ranks were swelling. We decided to rent a meeting place, the name of which was 'Sardis'... here we had great times in prevailing prayer. The Lord gave us encouragement in saving a notable sinner. Two other sisters were also saved, making the number to seven... Sardis was the birthplace of the Apostolic Vision in the Monmouthsire valleys. Here God revealed Himself to us in the prophetic ministry in a wonderful way, implanting faith in our hearts to believe it was

His voice. We saw the vision of the plan of His Church." (Purnell, 1933)

Before long, news reached this small group in Beaufort that the Lord was also speaking prophetically to His people in a village called Penygroes, some fifty-five miles away. In 1921 Jacob and four others determined to attend the August Apostolic Convention which was held annually in Penygroes. Money was short, so they travelled by bicycle. The story is told of how, as they were going down the steep hill between Merthyr Tydfil and Hirwaun, the brakes on Jacob's bicycle failed. He called on those with him to try and stop him, but they mistook his shouts for shouts of "Hallelujah" and they replied with hallelujahs of their own! Miraculously the Lord intervened and Jacob came to a stop without injury.

He had already attended an Apostolic Easter Convention in a village called Dowlais. Eager to know more about the teachings of the Apostolic Church, he took the opportunity at the Penygroes Convention to speak to D.P. Williams, the President. D.P. promised that he would stop off at Beaufort en route to a proposed visit to Abergavenny later that month.

Gordon Weeks gives one account of what happened: "On Saturday August 27th Pastors D.P. Williams, T. Jones, W.J. Williams and O. Jones travelled by train towards Abergavenny. At Beaufort Mr. J. Purnell met the train and showed them the posters he had prepared advertising an 'Apostolic Church Convention 27th-29th August 1921'! After prophetic direction (on the station platform!), Pastors D.P. and W.J. Williams remained in Beaufort, while their companions went on to Abergavenny. To me this was a remarkable example of the humility of these men, for some men would have told the presumptuous young man to run his own convention! It is no wonder that this was the start of a mighty work in the Monmouthshire (now Gwent) Valleys." (Weeks, 2003)

Jacob had been at work planning great things for his group of seven people, not yet even linked to the Apostolic Church! This is how he headed the posters and bills:

> RED LETTER DAY, AUGUST 1921
> APOSTOLIC CHURCH CONVENTION
> AT
> SARDIS CHURCH (kindly lent)
> AUGUST 27th over AUGUST 29th.

Omri Jones, one of the leaders that accompanied D.P. Williams, gives his own account of the incident: "A very memorable moment came one Saturday evening, when the voice of God was heard on the station platform at Beaufort, giving directions to His servants, and telling them that He was starting a work there. Great were the results and many of the prophetic promises were fulfilled before our eyes." (Purnell, 1933)

APOSTOLIC BEGINNINGS IN THE MONMOUTHSHIRE VALLEYS

Purnell writes about what happened at that Beaufort Convention: "When I recall what a convention is, I smile! Yet I say, although at the time we were not Apostolic, the Lord was in it... We had a blessed time, I may state. The ministry of the servants was owned of God. It was on the Sunday afternoon that we decided to submit to God's order and sweet will. Seven of us were received into fellowship. Afterwards, the Lord spoke through the prophet and I was called and anointed to be pastor and overseer of a flock of six on August 29th." (Purnell, 1933)

Beside the two pastors, there were eleven others in the service. Pastor D.P. Williams spoke on the tenets and beliefs of the Apostolic Church and an invite was given to those present to become members of the Apostolic Church. Jacob Purnell, Ephraim Morris and others accepted the invitation. Pastor Jones Williams prophesied that Jacob Purnell was called to pastor the flock and Ephraim Morris was called to be the prophetic channel in the assembly.

They were later joined by the two pastors who had travelled on to Abergavenny on the Saturday. The Lord spoke through one of these men, the prophet Omri Jones saying, "I will use thee; I will bless thee; I will cause My Word to flow from here and every valley shall hear of my doings." Before long this promise was fulfilled. Jacob Purnell explained: "We were told of the Lord to apply for the school. This we did for Sundays. (This word was spoken in August 1921.) We obtained the use of the smallest room, on Sundays, for three meetings. The room seated about 30. It was more like a sideshow than anything else. Sanballat's followers came; they ridiculed, rushing in and out, but we were unaffected. We prayed on and praised God! The room being overcrowded, we looked for the best and largest room seating 200 to 300, which was packed each evening."

This new church caused a stir in the Beaufort area and the rumour was that strange things were happening there. As a result people came either out of curiosity or intent on mocking. Some of them, however, became convinced by what they saw and heard. They committed their lives to Christ and began to attend regularly. Ephraim Morris was used prophetically and people heard the voice of God through him.

Purnell writes, "Surely, the Church here was born in Apostolic fashion! Every night we held cottage meetings. Our homes were the Lord's. Every room was occupied by the crowds coming. We took the spoiling of our goods joyfully. God was working, saving. 'Tipit'[9] players, skittlers, boxers, card-sharpers were swept into the

---

9   A traditional Welsh pub game

Kingdom. Drunkards, swearers, amongst them a trophy of grace was saved (Phillip Williams, known to all by now). We saw, we have still on record, miraculous cases of healing from dumbness, consumption, cripples and incurables cured, God baptising many in His Spirit, speaking in tongues, prophesying. Without the touch of human hand, prophetic channels were born in revival power. Much persecution followed. Our membership reached in a short time 80. We recognised the fulfilment of the prophetic word." (Purnell, 1933)

Jackie Harris, retired pastor and apostle, who knew the above-mentioned Phillip Williams in his later years, told me this: "Before his conversion Phil had been a hard drinker and a feared, light heavyweight, bare-fisted, mountain fighter who represented his local coal mine, the Marine, as their champion. When he was drunk he boasted that he feared no man or devil."

Phillip William recalls, in his own testimony, "I gave my heart to Jesus Christ in Beaufort, Monmouthshire, in November 1921... under the ministry of Pastor Jacob Purnell and Isaac Roberts. God bless the memory of these men. My dear wife, for whom I do thank God with all my heart, was saved two weeks prior to me. She had been in a very bad state: physically she was anaemic, and also her mind was affected. The Lord wonderfully healed her, both in body and in mind, and it was this great change which I saw in her, in such a short time, that made such an impression on me... Many times did God have mercy on me when I was in the habit of drinking, robbing my wife and children and living a fast life. Oh! The mercy of God to one like me! ...I must confess, my sin brought me down very low. I lived in a house that was condemned, with my wife and five children, my dear wife very weak and anaemic." (Williams P.)

In fact the family lived in a "two up and two down" cottage in Ebbw Vale, but Apostolic cottage meetings began in a home nearby, under the leadership of Jacob Purnell and his co-workers, the Seaborne brothers and Ephraim Morris. Phillip Williams continues, "My wife, in her weakness, went to these meetings, gave her heart to the Lord, was anointed with oil and prayed for. The Lord did touch her, but gradually, and she was restored to full health. Praise Him!"

As a result of his wife's experience, Phillip started to read his Bible and came under conviction when sitting on a mountain. He said, "Spare me, Oh God, until the meeting tonight, and then I will surrender." That evening he went to the "Bethel" Apostolic Church in Beaufort, where Jacob Purnell was the preacher. Someone who attended that Sunday night service said, "...that night Jacob preached a clear and challenging Gospel message, then made an appeal to those who felt they should accept the Lord Jesus Christ as Saviour to do so, and to everyone's utter amazement Phillip Williams stood up and loudly cried, 'I'll take Him, Jacob.'" (Williams P.)

The Williams family were in serious debt and Phillip Williams made a vow that night, "that they would buy only what was essential until every debt was paid, and he kept that vow." This proved to be a struggle. He continues, "I remember one day, in my poverty and distress, seeing the mountains so high – in debt, no work, no clothes, a creditor coming to ask for money and I had none to give him. When he left my home, I fell on my knees in the condemned house, crying on God, and, as I considered the mountain too high, a thought from the Lord came into my mind: 'A little faith can remove a mountain.' God did help me. The day dawned after much struggle, and the mountain was laid low. All my debts were paid, and I was free to look in the face of all men. Praise Him for His grace and power!"

Phillip Williams' witness was powerful in the Beaufort and Ebbw Vale area following his conversion. He later became a pastor and an apostle in the Apostolic Church. He paid this tribute to

Jacob Purnell: "I must confess, it was a great day in my life, when God, through the prophet, Pastor J.O. Jones, called Brother Tom Seaborne and myself to hold up the hands of Pastor Jacob Purnell. At that time, many churches were opened in the Monmouthshire district and many souls were saved. Pastor Purnell was used more than any of us in soul-winning. He was a good shepherd who worked hard to establish the work and to train us in many ways." (Williams P.)

Some years later Tom Seaborne recounts: "As time went on, the work settled to a more definite pattern. On Sundays, meetings were held at Beaufort Hill Primary School; on Mondays and Saturdays at Sardis chapel and on Thursdays at the home of Mrs. Lloyd. This was an ex-army hut that had been erected after the First World War to help solve the housing problem. To all these places, people were coming and being saved." (Seaborne)

The growing church in Beaufort was soon in need of a building of its own. Once again God's people there proved the power and reality of His direction through prophecy. Jacob Purnell recounts: "During a visit of Prophet W. Jones Williams, in September 1921, the Lord spoke, saying that He would grant us a stone building, which would be a Bethel, indeed. Now, this is wonderful, as the cost of material was very high at this time, and seemingly impossible, but He who promised was well able." (Purnell, 1933)

With the assistance of the Apostolic Church Building Committee, a stone building in Beaufort, which had previously been used as a stable and a store, was purchased and renovated. This new church was opened in April 1923 and Jacob describes the event: "This was a witness to all that this work was to be a lasting one. Fifty were baptised in water at the opening of the new hall. Progress was remarkable. In August 1921, we were 7 in number. April 1923 finds us with 80 in membership and a lovely church in which to worship. Now, a remarkable prophecy came forth at this time (April 1923), through Prophet J.O. Jones. 'Jacob and Bethel are Mine... This is the place of My choice; rivers shall flow from here; every village and town will I touch; even to Newport. I will also send some of you to cities.' (Purnell, 1933)

Many years later, in 1973, Ephraim Morris recorded his own story of the beginnings of the Apostolic church in Beaufort and the surrounding areas of Monmouthshire: "Bethel, as a building could never claim merit for its beauty or artistry, nor will it ever take its place among the great buildings of our land, yet, created from an almost derelict barn of a warehouse – disused and vacant – here, in this converted slum shambles, God by His Holy Spirit dwelt, and it became the gateway to Heaven for many precious souls. In this place, nobodies became notables – men and women of half a century ago, who were oppressed by poverty, living in conditions undreamed of today, having no hope in this life, and hitherto knowing nothing of the salvation that grace had provided. Fifty years ago we shared our bread. We shared our clothes. No man had two suits or pairs of shoes, and more often than not no overcoat, and fortunate to have a second shirt! Money was scarce; many were in debt because of low wages, strikes and lockouts. This may sound exaggerated in this day and age, but the writer is one who lived through this era and experienced these difficulties." (Morris, 1973)

Morris paints a clear picture of the grace of the Gospel and the unselfish love expressed through the Beaufort church at that time. These were in stark contrast to the harsh social conditions that prevailed for many of the people of that town and surrounding area. In what he says we can surely hear echoes of the early church in Jerusalem: *"And the congregation of those who believed were of one heart and soul; and not one of them claimed that anything belonging to him was his own, but all things were common property to them."* (Acts 4:32)

Ephraim Morris comments, "In this atmosphere, men were raised as firebrands, full of zeal, with practical experience of God and their Saviour. With no social standing, no umbrella of financial security, no pretensions to superiority, nothing in this world to claim and own, yet these men had the treasures of revelation and things divine, and their preaching and power with God has not been surpassed."

Morris describes their single-hearted focus on evangelism: "The voice of God was heard in Bethel. There was a real reverence... The evidence of the presence of the Lord was shown by the number of souls saved, in the expansion of the Fellowship through the Monmouthshire valleys, in the growth of the church, but above all in the many, many trophies of grace, who lived anew among their neighbours and companions as glowing testimonies. In the pits where we worked we sang and testified; day and night on street corners we preached the Lord Jesus Christ. We had no mechanical means of transport, but we walked mile after mile over hill and dale, carrying the vision that had become our purpose for living." (Morris, 1973)

It was Jacob Purnell who spearheaded this pioneering, Apostolic work of God in Monmouthshire. God brought some tremendous people around him, as he freely acknowledged, but he was the man with the passion and the vision. He sought to foster that pioneering spirit in others. It is evident from the testimonies of Phillip Williams, Tom Seaborne and Ephraim Morris, that he imparted Christian truths and disciplines to those with whom he worked and also to those who were part of the churches that were birthed.

Reflecting on those pioneering years, Purnell explains, "This was a great demand on our faith. We believed, we cried to Him, we set to work. The work spread like fire in the valleys. Doors were opening. Each step we took was on the prophetic word.

Oh! How we proved its value – guiding, choosing, preserving; establishing - no tongue can tell. I make my confession. I am, and have been blessed of God, used of God, and won favour due to the power of the spoken word toward me. Its value is untold. 'HE SPAKE, IT WAS DONE; HE COMMANDED AND IT STOOD FAST'... We have proved beyond all doubt, through set prophets and local channels, that our God is a God to be inquired of. There are opposing forces of unbelief against the spoken word. But we have irrefutable proof of its reality and power in the lives and assemblies in Monmouthshire... Pray for prophets. They are men, but God speaks through them. I believe the prophets! The officers here are as one man, united, always willing to obey the apostleship and prophetic word. Worthy of note is the fact that during these twelve years, the presbytery has never been called upon to settle any variances or disputes. Faith in the spoken word has been the secret of success and unity in our midst." (Purnell, 1933)

Jacob Purnell inspired in others a confidence in the power of the prophetic word: "Anyone who remembers those early days cannot forget the wonderful utterances, the heart-searching and personal words from the Lord. Jesus was in the midst, and we believed the prophets and accepted them as any other calling in the church." (Morris, 1973)

However, it was not just prophecy that was important to Purnell. He inspired a desire in the people for all the gifts of the Holy Spirit. Ephraim Morris comments on this: "Paul knew the value of spiritual gifts, for he advised the early church to covet them... and this was our aim at Bethel. We found it rewarding. They gave us something different from the normal way of worship, for a church without them has little appeal or no appeal. What an asset and a testimony to have a spiritually gifted congregation, moved by the Holy Spirit."

Purnell was also recognised as a very able preacher of God's Word. Ephraim Morris wrote, "May I be permitted to speak of the ministry of the preached word at Bethel. It was profound, rich in conception and presentation, born of sincerity, clothed with inspiration and preached with tongues of fire." (Morris, 1973) When Jacob Purnell preached, miracles of healing and deliverance often followed the ministry of the Word.

Two examples of this are given in the *Riches of Grace*, January 1930: Evangelist W.M. Owens writes, "I have proved in a wonderful way that Jesus not only heals sickness, but casts out dumb spirits. My son was dumb from birth, and the doctor certified he could not speak. For four years he was dumb. Pastor Purnell anointed him, and cast out the dumb spirit, and the child spake, and has been speaking ever since, quite plainly, and was seen and heard at the last Christmas Convention at Beaufort. This case is of two years standing; the child is perfectly delivered. I praise God for His wonderful power." (Owen, 1930)

Mrs. M.A. Ellis testifies, "My son John was an invalid from birth, and until five years of age he could neither walk not talk. I carried him to many doctors, but none gave me hope... Pastor Purnell came and prayed with him, as we were watching him die. He revived. I carried him to the Apostolic Church at Beaufort and had him anointed by the pastor and the Lord healed him. He is now thirteen years of age, and a strong healthy boy. He has had no illness since. I praise God for His power revealed through this miraculous healing of my boy." (Ellis, 1930)

There was also a clear pioneering drive to Jacob Purnell's ministry and this was evidenced by the rapid expansion of the work. By 1933 the work in the Monmouthshire valleys had spread to such an extent that twenty churches had been established and other smaller groups had formed. There was a full-time apostle and also one pastor. Throughout the churches one hundred officers had been called. Twenty people had attended that first convention in Beaufort in 1921, but by 1933 the attendance had grown to nine hundred.

THE NEWPORT CHURCHES

Newport is now a city, but in 1932 it was an important town in south-east Monmouthshire, located about twelve miles north-east of Cardiff. In the spring of 1932, Jacob and family moved to Newport to pioneer and superintend the Apostolic work in that area. He writes: "The Newport churches are a fulfilment of prophecy uttered in Bethel in April 1923 *('Rivers will flow from here; every village and town will I touch, even to Newport.' J.O. Jones).*"

Over eight years went by following the 1923 prophecy and the Lord spoke again concerning Newport. Purnell continues: "...In September 1931, a prophecy came forth in Bethel, Beaufort saying, 'It is time for you to possess the land, and I have promised many of my servants shall minister in Newport in the near future.' I found myself in Newport in April 1932. We have made great progress here in twelve months. We have three assemblies established and still advancing. 'THIS IS THE LORD'S DOING AND IT IS MARVELLOUS IN OUR EYES.'" (Purnell, 1933)

Phillip Williams had been ordained in 1931 and took over from Purnell as pastor of the Beaufort District. The *Apostolic Herald,* June 1932, records that there were nearly one thousand people at Jacob Purnell's farewell service in Beaufort.

The Newport assembly, originally known as the Rockfield Full Gospel Mission, had formed a link with the Apostolic Church in the Hereford District and came under the cover of Frank Hodges, the apostle from Hereford. However, from the time of Jacob Purnell's induction the Newport church was transferred to the cover of the Welsh District. (Apostolic Herald, 1932)

After Jacob's first month in Newport the following report appeared in the *Apostolic Herald:* "At the end of April we praise

God to be able to report that the work at 'Rockfield' is making rapid progress. Many have received the right hand of fellowship with the formation of a very live Sunday School which has grown from one to six classes since Pastor Purnell's induction. Already we are feeling that a very wise and powerful servant of the Lord is in our midst, a man full of Apostolic faith, with the gifts of wisdom, knowledge and the Holy Ghost." The following month this update appeared: "The saints at Ystradmynach are now extending the work to a place called Llanbradach, where cottage meetings are being held. Nine have professed salvation, and others are prepared to cast in their lot here. Four have also received their baptism." (Apostolic Herald, 1932)

A CALL TO ESTONIA

1934 was a significant year for the Apostolic Church UK Prophecy had been received in January 1934 at the Apostles' and Prophets' Council that it was the Lord's will that the organisation of the Apostolic Church should be centralised. As a result several national appointments were made in the August of that year, including National Sunday School Leader and National Women's Leader. Jacob Purnell was appointed as the first General Superintendent of the Young People's Movement. He was still living in Newport at the time, but was later moved to Tunstall in the Potteries. (Riches of Grace, 1935)

Purnell had the privilege of leading the first International Witness[10] Rally during the 1936 Penygroes Apostolic Convention. The following report was given: "The power of the Holy Spirit fell while the whole congregation sang, during the rally, 'Yes, I know, I fully know, Jesus' blood can make the vilest clean'. Many on the platform and in the audience were moved to dance and otherwise express their joy and gratitude for so full a salvation." The meeting was three hours long! "There was not a dry face in the Temple as we heard some of the witnesses testifying of the way the hand of

---

10   The Apostolic youth were known as "Witnesses"

mercy had grasped them from the brink of the Abyss." (Riches of Grace, 1936)

In 1937, Jacob Purnell was appointed to the Apostolic National Executive, a role which he held for several years. Around this time his ministry began to take on more of an international dimension.

In 1939, church leaders in Estonia had sent an appeal to the Apostolic Church UK to send an apostle for at least nine months to help with the work there. The link with Estonia had been made in 1935 by Pastors D.P. and Jones Williams, along with colleagues from Denmark. Further visits by UK and Danish Apostolic pastors had followed in the succeeding years. In August 1939, Purnell was the apostle chosen to go and in the August Convention he was publicly separated to the task with the laying on of hands of the apostles. He and his family had by this time relocated from the Potteries to Brynmawr in South Wales. His farewell there was organised for 31st August, but it does not seem to have taken place. With the onset of war in September and tensions in the Baltics, the visit to Estonia was unavoidably delayed.

On the 1st September, Estonia declared its neutrality but this did not prevent the Russians from violating Estonian airspace and placing 600 tanks, 600 aircraft and 160,000 men along the Estonian border. On the 28th September, Estonia signed a ten year Mutual Assistance Pact with the Soviet Union, which allowed the Soviets to have 30,000 men stationed in military bases in Estonia. In return Stalin promised to respect Estonian independence.

In March 1940, Purnell flew to Copenhagen, having been advised that he could obtain an Estonian visa there within eight days. As things transpired no visa was obtained and he never reached Estonia. Instead he spent five weeks in Denmark before returning to Britain. (Riches of Grace, 1940)

When he came back from Denmark some debate appears to

have taken place behind the scenes between the Missionary Board, the National Executive and Jacob Purnell. The Missionary Board clearly felt that Purnell could have left for Estonia immediately following the Penygroes Convention. In the *Apostolic Herald*, June 1940, a "Report on Estonia" appears, written by Pastor Rowe. Purnell had been called and set apart publicly, according to what the leaders had believed was the revealed will of God, and therefore they apparently considered that some public explanation was required as to why this had not been followed through.

The report concludes, "But finally we have had to admit a present defeat in that this (visa) could not possibly be obtained, and consequently Pastor Purnell had to return home despite every effort on his part to fulfil the purpose of his going forth. Whilst this development is absolutely beyond our control, it does constitute a challenge to us as a Church in face of the revealed will of God... If there has been any failure on our part, it must be faced as a Church and valuable lessons learned." (Apostolic Herald, 1940) It was later acknowledged by the National Executive that Pastor Purnell was not to blame and that there had been misunderstanding between the different parties involved.

This experience did put Jacob Purnell under a great deal of pressure. It perhaps indicated that "personalities" were gaining prominence in the Apostolic Church UK. However, the whole incident demonstrates that the leaders involved were prepared to examine their own hearts and ask, "Have we failed God?"

A CALL TO CANADA AND THE UNITED STATES

A further call to minister overseas came in 1943. Gordon Weeks records: "During the Penygroes Convention a prophecy was given by Pastor J.D. Eynon calling Pastors D.P. Williams, W. McLeod, J. Purnell, W.J. Williams and himself to travel to Canada (and the USA) and minister through the churches there." (Weeks, 2003)

The trip was delayed until 1945 because the war was still in progress and travel was difficult. D.P. Williams and his wife, Mabel, set off first on 6th April and the others followed later. Jones Williams was unable to travel because he was very ill and actually died on 15th April, at the age of 53 years, while his brother and sister-in-law were still at sea. They arrived in Nova Scotia on 18th April then went by train to Montreal, where they received news of Jones' death.

Shortly afterwards D.P. himself was taken seriously ill with pleurisy and pneumonia. Mabel writes: "We almost gave up hope of his recovery. The following seven weeks we felt as though we were passing through the Valley of Achor, but praise God for the door of hope!" (Davies & Yeoman, 2008) God did intervene and D.P. Williams had a divine touch from the Lord and continued the itinerary. However, a further blow fell when, eleven months into the trip, news came from the UK that D.P. Williams' daughter, Mair, who was intending to join her parents in Canada, had contracted tuberculosis.

The delegation spoke at conventions and undertook evangelistic and pioneering ministry in various parts of Canada, including Nova Scotia, Ontario and Quebec. In 1946 D.P. Williams and James Eynon travelled to the United States.

During the tour Jacob Purnell also took ill with facial paralysis. He wrote to the UK Missionary Board asking for help with medical expenses and also requesting to be allowed to return to the UK after the Canadian Apostolic Church had received autonomy in October 1946. He was concerned that another extreme Canadian winter would have a detrimental effect on his medical condition. Unfortunately the UK Missionary Board turned down both these requests.

The delegation moved on to the States but, while they were

there, D.P. Williams and his wife received news that their daughter, Mair, was very ill in a sanatorium near Birmingham. They returned to Wales, arriving in Penygroes in November 1946. Just three months later Pastor D.P. Williams and his daughter both died within a few days of each other.

Jacob Purnell and James Eynon, friends and colleagues of Pastor D.P. Williams, were unable to attend his funeral because they were still in North America. They were the UK representatives responsible for giving autonomy to the Apostolic Church in the States over the Thanksgiving weekend 28th November to 1st December 1946. The meetings were held in East Lansdowne, near Williamsport, Pennsylvania, the first place in the States where an Apostolic church was established.

Worsfold writes that the prophecy in regard to the Canadian and States delegation through Pastor Eynon in 1943 was a "major discussion point in AC circles around the world... The whole matter, however, was to remain a mystery for many ministers and congregations. The various answers proffered still leave for many the matter unexplained. Some individuals close to the event have said that the motivation to send ministry to Canada was right but the selection of these certain individuals may not have been God's perfect will." (Worsfold J. E., 1991)

The Missionary Board had hoped that this delegation would plant churches and bring expansion to the work in North America, but this did not prove to be the case to any great extent. Sadly, the trip certainly seems to have brought stress to those involved. They found themselves involved in various internal administrative matters and many business meetings were held during their time there. There is no doubt that the UK Missionary Board was wary of administrative changes that were being discussed for North America and it was against one change of location for a UK Pastor in North America, and this seems to indicate some underlying tension.

Interestingly, when D.P. Williams enquired of the Lord regarding the need to return to the UK, the first words of the prophecy he received were these: "...I have seen desires in you to abide in this land..." We know that by this time some of his closest friends and colleagues had died, including his brother Jones and good friend Andrew Turnbull. He was missing them and commented in the Toronto Convention, "I can say, as one of old, only I am left." He was also concerned about the need for spiritual reform within the UK church. Worsfold comments that D.P. was "deeply troubled by the effect which the Constitution was having on the spiritual life and aspirations of many of the ministers and members of the church." (Worsfold J. E., 1991)

Did Pastor D.P. Williams, and those with him, see North America as a new start away from the constitutional ways of the UK? Remember, Jacob Purnell had already had an experience of the "committee structure" in the UK a few years earlier in regard to Estonia. It had not been a good experience.

After over eighteen months away from home and family, Purnell returned from North America in mid 1947.

HIS DEATH – JANUARY 1953

Jacob Purnell's long and fruitful ministerial career with the Apostolic Church also included pastorates in Skewen and Birmingham, although latterly his health was deteriorating. He died, at the age of sixty-one on 24th January 1953 in Birmingham.

He had lived for the voice of God but he also had faith to believe and obey what the Lord said through his prophets. Until the end his guiding principal remained:

Faith in the Unchangeable God.
Faith in the prophets and their message.

For Pastor Jacob Purnell faith was a gift from God that grew and developed as he read God's Word, heard God's voice and followed through with obedience. It was faith, not for himself, but to see men and women like Phillip Williams transformed, to see families (like the Owens and Ellis families) experience the miraculous and to see men like Ephraim Morris find their calling under God.

Pastor J. Omri Jones, who had ministered with Pastor Jacob many times following that first meeting on the platform of Beaufort Station in August 1921, wrote this tribute, "His faith in the spoken word of God was proverbial, and he attributed much of his ability to minister, to the fact of his assimilation of the revelation given by the spoken word, which he contended was the true medium of unveiling the written Word to the edification and guidance of the Church. Whilst he was very firm in the truth that every man should possess strong personal convictions concerning the will of God as to his life, he strongly believed in the directive word through the prophets to be the way of guidance for the church collectively. He would appear sometimes to be austere in his dealings as he stood unflinching for what he believed to be the will of God; but to those who knew him, this austerity was only apparent, for beneath was a heart full of compassion and love toward the flock of God, for he recognised the ownership of the sheep, and that he served the Lord Christ." (Jones O. , 1953)

Even on his deathbed Jacob Purnell's zeal to win others for Christ was not diminished. Omri Jones relates: "A touching incident took place during the service, when Mrs. Purnell stood up to say that the last service for the Master that her late husband performed on his deathbed was to lead their only son, John, into the light of salvation." (Jones O. , 1953)

The day after the funeral a local man was heard to comment in Beaufort, "Beaufort has produced four great men (naming three who had gained a name in the political world) but Pastor Purnell surpassed them all." Another added, "The only complaint I have to make against Mr. Purnell is that what he preached he practised!"

This poem was written as a tribute to Pastor Jacob Purnell by Mildred Rees, Smethwick, Birmingham:

The Master called our loved one home
From this sad, dismal earthly plane;
He saw how spent and tired he was,
He knew, and understood his pain.

He took him from this scene of strife,
He took him to His loving Breast;
He took him into endless life,
He took him, for He knew 'twas best.

On earth our brother served his Lord,
And preached His name for many years;
The sword of truth was in his hand,
But in his eyes, compassion's tears.

Right to the very end he hoped,
And prayed that God would lend him breath
To once again go through the land,
Defeating pain and fear and death.

But God in His omniscient might,
In His all-seeing wisdom came,
And gave not that which we had hoped,
But peace and freedom from all pain.

He did not send him health and strength,
But said, "My glory you shall see,"
He gently took him by the hand,
And said, "I want you here with Me!"

And we can leave him safely there
With Jesus and the heavenly host;
While here on earth we serve the Lord,
The Father, Son, and Holy Ghost.

CHAPTER NINE
JOSEPH OMRI JONES

"Now you are Christ's body, and individually members of it. And God has appointed in the church, first apostles, second prophets, third teachers..."
1 Corinthians 12:27-28

We have so far looked at six of our church fathers; men who had a God focus in their hearts; men who had God's character and God's works written across their lives; men who witnessed and experienced the power of God. Let me now introduce you to Pastor Joseph Omri Jones, known as Omri Jones.

Omri Jones was an appointed prophet in the Body of Christ. The Apostle Paul writes of the importance of the office of the prophet in 1 Corinthians 12:28: *God has appointed in the Church: first apostles, second prophets...* and in Ephesians 2:19-20: *So then you are no longer strangers and aliens, but you are fellow citizens with the saints and are of God's household, having been built on the foundation of the apostles and prophets, Jesus Christ Himself being the corner stone...*

The rich blessing and rapid expansion in Britain and overseas which the early Apostolic Church experienced was in a great part attributable to the supernatural direction of God's voice through the appointed prophets. D.P. Williams expressed it in this way: "If we are called as an Apostolic Church to witness for something above another, we witness to the unassailable truth that we are a standing body that is an evidence of the existence and value of the prophetic ministry." (Williams, 1931)

Our forefathers greatly valued the ministry of the prophets. Sad to say, in recent decades there appears to have been a moving away from that dynamic dependence on the prophetic voice to bring strategic revelation and direction. James Worsfold, writing in 1991, gives his perspective on this subject: "It is the observation of this writer that since the 1950s the function of the prophet in the Apostolic Church around the world has, in many instances, settled for the manifestation of the gift of prophecy. It would have needed in this movement a minister (who was also recognised as a prophet) to receive a charism of exceptional spiritual boldness to rise to the level of prophetic ministry that was given in the first twenty years of the movement's life." (Worsfold J. E., 1991)

PENTECOST COMES TO LLWYNHENDY

Omri Jones was born in 1892 to Sarah and Thomas Jones, a draper, in the village of Llywnhendy, near Llanelli in Carmarthenshire, South Wales. It is situated about six miles from Penygroes. Looking back many years later, Omri wrote about the beginnings of a powerful move of God in this village:

"The Apostolic[11] work in the above district (Llwynhendy and

---

11   Pre 1916 this group came under the Apostolic Faith Church

District) began in 1911. Previous to this date, meetings had been held at Clifton House, Llwynhendy (which is the home of Pastor Thomas Jones), for the space of three years. Having received a definite call from God to sever his connections with the Baptist denomination, Pastor T. Jones reluctantly obeyed and commenced meetings at his house. He and Mrs. Jones were joined by a brother named William Thomas, of Byrn, who is now in glory. They gathered faithfully together not knowing what the Lord had in store for them. On Sunday afternoons they went together to a place called Bank, Cwmfelin, where there were many poor people, to hold Sunday school in the open and to preach the Gospel to the elderly people. Many were the trophies won for Christ there. They were joined in this work by another sister, who is now a faithful worker among the brethren. As time went on, they felt a definite leading to wait upon God for an outpouring of the Spirit."

He continues, "On Sunday evenings throughout the three previous years to 1911, the house had been filled after chapel services by 'Revival brethren'[12]. In January and February 1911, the prayers and the waiting were rewarded, for the Spirit was poured out upon many and great was the rejoicing, and the praising and magnifying of God became very fervent indeed. Immediately after the great baptism of the Spirit that was then experienced, many souls were saved, and the saints felt they could no longer continue in their chapels on account of the coldness and indifference which prevailed among so-called Christians. So the house was filled – two rooms, passage, and staircase, while the power of God was working in a wonderful manner, saving, baptizing and healing many people." (Jones J. , 1933)

It was following this visitation that the gifts of the Holy Spirit were revealed in the services and Omri, who was nineteen years of age at that time, was used for the first time prophetically. The members of the group grew in their experience of the gifts and saw many people saved, healed and filled with the Holy Spirit as

---

[12] People saved during the Welsh Revival, also known as "Children of the Revival"

the power of God was manifested in the Jones' home. Omri Jones explains that through prophetic gifts, "God began to establish order in the assembly, electing an overseer and elders and deacons to care for the flock. As time went on (the house being far too small) the council schools were obtained to hold services on Sunday. By this time, we had come in touch with our Apostolic[13] brethren from Penygroes. The great boon in these gatherings was the incomparable manner in which the voice of God was heard through the channels of prophecy. Pastor W. Jones Williams was mightily used in the midst." (Jones J., 1933)

THE JONES FAMILY

Thomas Jones and his son, Omri, had both been ordained in the Apostolic Faith Church prior to the breakaway and formation of the Apostolic Church in Wales in January 1916. Omri was saved on 21st March 1911, just after the outpouring of the Holy Spirit on the group in Llwynhendy. He was baptised in the Spirit in December of that year and ordained as a prophet by William Hutchinson, the leader of the AFC, in March 1912, at the age of twenty. Thomas Jones was recognised as an apostle in 1915. (Weeks, 2003)

D.P. Williams, in his book, *Cradle of Mystery*, gives the background to this prophetic call: "Special meetings were held in the council school at Llwynhendy at which the word of the Lord came through my brother Jones, and I was to anoint and lay hands upon Pastor[14] Joseph Omri Jones and to impart to him the gift of prophecy. Immediately we laid hands on him. A prophetic ministry flowed through him and, in due time, he became one of the most valuable prophets in the Body of Christ." (Williams, D., 2006)

Worsfold highlights the importance of the ministry that this father and son brought to the Apostolic Church in Wales when

---

13 This refers to the Apostolic Faith Church pre 1916
14 This incident took place in 1911, but Omri Jones was not ordained as a pastor until 1919

it broke away from the AFC in January 1916: "D.P. Williams and Thomas Jones remained for a time the only apostles. They had both been called and ordained to that office while they were members of the Apostolic Faith Church. In 1920 Andrew Turnbull (the leader of the Apostolic Church in Scotland) was called through a public prophetic word given by Jones Williams at the Penygroes Convention. The prophets too were a small group; Jones Williams, Omri Jones and Ernest Boulton had all been called and ordained as prophets while ministers in the Apostolic Faith Church. They remained the only major prophetic voices in the Apostolic Church in Wales until 1922." (Worsfold J. E., 1991)

Following the formation of the Apostolic Church in Wales in January 1916, Omri Jones assisted his father in administering the finance of the new group. They did this from a room in the family home at Clifton House, Llwynhendy. The breakaway assemblies sent their tithes to Pastor Thomas Jones and he and his son were responsible for paying the salaried pastors. Omri was ordained as a pastor in 1919 and was appointed as pastor of the Apostolic Church in Llanelli.

Thomas Jones had another son who also served in the Apostolic Church, Pastor David "Kongo" Jones. This son had been a Baptist missionary in Africa for seven years and was inducted into the Apostolic pastorate in Penygroes on 24th May 1918. (Davies & Yeoman, 2008) He later served as a pastor in Pontypridd and then Swansea for a time. (Williams, D., 2006) (Riches of Grace, 1922) He was given the honour of speaking at the opening of the Apostolic Church Bible School in October 1933, which met in the Babell[15] in Penygroes, and he subsequently lectured there. (Riches of Grace, 1989) It is a measure of the respect in which Pastor Thomas Jones was held that he was accorded the honour of opening both the Apostolic Temple in August 1933 and the new Apostolic Church Bible School building on 23rd April 1936.

---

15 The original Apostolic Church in Penygroes until the "Temple" was opened in 1933

CONSCRIPTION AND CONSCIENTIOUS OBJECTION

In March 1916, just two months after the break with the Apostolic Faith Church, compulsory military service was introduced in the UK Gordon Weeks writes, "This presented no problem to men like Rev. Boddy[16] or Pastor Hutchinson but for many believers it brought a real crisis of conscience. Many were arrested because they refused to serve in the military forces and were treated harshly by the authorities." (Weeks, 2003)

Conscription was not popular and in April 1916 over 200,000 people demonstrated against it in Trafalgar Square. For a Welshman conscription presented two particular issues. Firstly, Wales was overwhelmingly Liberal in political consciousness at that time. For a Liberal Coalition Government led by Prime Minister David Lloyd-George, who was himself Welsh, to pass such a law was problematic. Secondly, as Professor Densil Morgan[17] comments: "The non-conformity tradition in Wales was pacifist in tone. 'We had been brought up in a tradition that was wholly unmilitaristic, peaceful if not pacifist...' wrote the son and grandson of a Calvinistic Methodist minister." (Morgan, 2011)

Omri Jones was Welsh speaking and from the Baptist nonconformist tradition. Welsh language newspapers and prominent Welsh ministers, including Baptists, were openly against conscription. However, there was a contradiction. As Morgan explains, "Despite being deeply pacifistic, Welsh nonconformity found itself almost wholly in favour of British intervention in the war." (Morgan, 2011)

The *Wales at War* website explains, "When conscription was passed in 1916 authorities in Wales made a big effort to make sure no one got away with avoiding the call-up." There were some 1,000 conscientious objectors in Wales - a small number when you compare it with the 280,000 who left Wales to serve in the War.

---

16   Leader of the revival in Sunderland
17   Head of Theology at the University of Wales Trinity St. David

The Military Service Act passed by Parliament in March 1916 did have an exemption for clergymen, but Omri Jones was not called as a full-time, salaried pastor until 1919. (National Library of Wales, 2015)

Morgan states that those who refused service on religious grounds were to be employed in alternative occupations. Whatever his personal reasons, in 1916 Omri Jones was imprisoned for two years as a conscientious objector. This would seem to indicate that he declined to be part of any alternative work associated with the war. Nearly six thousand men were imprisoned for resisting military authority at this time.

There had been prophetic words about imprisonment at the AFC conventions in Swansea in 1911 and in London in 1914. D.P. Williams recalled these prophecies at a later date: "Many of you, dear saints, will remember the meeting in Belle Vue, Swansea, when the Lord said that some of those who were in the congregation would be within prison walls, and we had not the least idea what the Lord meant. But as you know, the young men who decided not to take up arms, in obedience to the prompting of the Spirit, fulfilled the word. The word of God was actually carried out before our eyes." (Weeks, 2003)

Commenting on the same prophecies in Porth Apostolic Convention in November 1921, D.P. Williams said, "We thought we were going to be put in jail because of the Holy Ghost and we made a terrible mess trying to sum up what the Holy Ghost meant. But we have since found out that the young men went through prison doors because as conscientious objectors they thought God had called them to stand for peace."

Government policy was that conscientious objectors were imprisoned at least one hundred miles away from their homes. Whilst spending twelve months of his sentence in Wakefield Prison, Yorkshire, Omri Jones befriended two other conscientious objectors, David Rennie and Herbert Ogilvie. They were members of an Open Brethren Assembly in Aberdeen.

In time he spoke to them about the baptism of the Holy Spirit, as he recalled many years later at the 1965 Penygroes Convention: "We were very friendly then although I was trying to get them to believe in tongues. Mr. Rennie gave me some hard hits before giving in, but we won him over. One day Mr. Ogilvie was thrown on his back in the cell and we thought he had died – but he was speaking in tongues." (Weeks, 2003)

Speaking at the Penygroes Convention in 1919, D.P. Williams reminded the congregation, "A few years ago the Lord told us to pray for Aberdeen and today we have our two brothers from Aberdeen among us, Bros. D.T. Rennie and H.W. Ogilvie." Clearly Omri's friendship with these men was in the plan of God. In later years both of them became pastors in the Apostolic Church. David Rennie became the UK Apostolic President and Herbert Ogilvie pioneered in the United States and South Africa.

As Christmas 1918 approached a prophecy was received in Omri Jones' home church saying that he would be home for Christmas. Hopes were dashed when the Government announced that all trains were needed by the troops during the Christmas holidays and that it would be unwise to let conscientious objectors travel. Hearing this, Thomas Jones asked his wife, "What of the prophecy through our maid-servant, Maggie, of which you told me that our son Omri would be home for Christmas?" She replied, "It was God's word and He knows His business." That was Friday 22nd December 1918.

The following day there was a knock on the door and there was Omri. God's word had come to pass. The Governor of Wakefield Prison told him, "Jones, if you desire to go home, I shall not stop you; there's the door open, but don't forget you shoulder the responsibility." "And here I am!" said Omri. (Davies & Yeoman, 2008)

At that time William Phillips, pastor of an Apostolic Church in Aberaeron, about fifty miles away, was staying with the Jones family. A prophetic word had been received in Penygroes that the local council was intending to arrest Pastor Phillips and place him in the army, so D.P. Williams had written to him. After some enquiries he was able to verify this and he fled for refuge to the home of Pastor Thomas and Sarah Jones in Llwynhendy.

When Omri arrived that morning the whole household, including William Phillips, gathered together for a time of praise and worship. Omri prophesied, "I have a word to declare to My servant William. Hearken! The hounds are at your heels. Go from this place and journey to the town where My servant Isaac lives (i.e. Dowlais). Be happy and minister the Word to My people and I will meet you there. I will then give you a further word of wisdom." (Davies & Yeoman, 2008)

After two years in prison, Omri Jones was clearly still walking in the Spirit. He had grown and matured spiritually through powerful encounters with the Lord during his young life and he had developed in character as he learned to trust God through the hardships of prison life.

FAMILY LIFE

In his family life Omri also experienced serious trials and sorrows. His first wife was Annie Rowlands from Llanon, near Aberystwyth. Sad to say, she died from pneumonia within months of the marriage. His second wife, who was from Pontypridd, died in 1923, giving birth to their son, Kenneth. Omri then married Gwladys Hughes, a converted opera singer. They went on to have three children; Moelwyn in 1929, Mair in 1930 and Howell in

1932. Gwladys was better known as "Mrs. Omri Jones" and she was a powerful preacher, serving alongside her husband.

Many will remember their daughter, Mair Omri Jones, who was a Gospel singer. She sang a number of times at Christian events at the Royal Albert Hall. Mair, whose married name is Perkins, is still alive and her family are serving the Lord in the UK.

Mair told me a remarkable story: At one time her father was pastor of the Apostolic Church in Cardiff. The house where the family were living was infested with cockroaches. One day Pastor Phillip Williams was visiting and, on hearing about the problem, he put Omri through some strict questioning: "Are you paying your tithes? ...Are all things well in the family?" Omri answered "yes" to all the questions, so Phillip Williams started to pray in the name of Jesus and cursed every cockroach that was in the house. From that day the house was free of these insects, but the houses on either side were still infested!

In the *Riches of Grace*, November 1929, there is a fitting tribute to Omri's parents, Pastor Thomas and Sarah Jones, on the occasion of their golden wedding anniversary: "Of the spiritual fathers of the present Apostolic Church, no one is more revered than Apostle Thomas Jones; while Mrs. Jones has proved herself a loving 'mother in Israel' to the converts in the various assemblies of Llwynhendy and district." (*Riches of Grace*, 1929)

Over the years Omri often ministered with his father, who, until his retirement in 1934 at the age of seventy-six, still had the care and oversight of five assemblies.

PROPHETIC MINISTRY

The Apostle Paul, in Ephesians 3:4-5, states that ...*the mystery of Christ... has now been revealed to His holy apostles and prophets.*

Thomas Vaughan Lewis, one of the fathers of the Apostolic Church said, "As you know, the prophet is the second office in the Church. We read in Eph 4:7-11, that Christ, after He ascended, gave gifts of men to the Church. They are five in all, and the prophet is one of them. Take note, they are the gifts of the Ascended Christ, so the New Testament prophets are prophets for the Church. A prophet is not a 'preacher'. He does not get his message by the study of Scriptures, but by direct revelation. He speaks under the control of the Holy Spirit." (Lewis, Riches of Grace, 1933)

In the *Souvenir Exhibiting the Movements of God in the Apostolic Church,* we get an early insight into the role of the prophet in the Apostolic Church. The Apostolic system of church government was theocratic rather than democratic or congregational. This meant that, through prophecy, individuals could be called by God to fulfil different offices within the local church.

How did the Apostolic Church grow from just nineteen assemblies in January 1916 to become a world-wide movement within a very short space of time? It was achieved through prophetic ministries that were Jesus given and Spirit anointed. The recognised prophets spoke words, not from a sanctified intellect or a holy imagination, but as the Spirit gave them revelation and insight from the Head, the Lord Jesus Christ.

Omri Jones was one of these early prophets. He had been recognised and ordained as a prophet in the Body of Christ at the age of twenty. How did the Lord Jesus Christ, the Head of the Church, *"in whom are hidden all the treasures of wisdom and knowledge"* (Colossians 2:3) use Omri Jones to both reveal and further the purposes of God in the Apostolic Church?

In January 1920, Omri Jones was part of an Apostolic delegation to Belfast, which went in response to an invitation from Benjamin Fisher, the pastor of a small Pentecostal church in the city. At the end of the two week mission thirty-five people were saved, eighty seven accepted the right hand of fellowship and the assembly became part of the Apostolic Church. A further visit was requested for July, but this was rescheduled on the grounds of a prophetic word saying, "Write and tell him not to hold the convention in July but in the second week of June." The delegation was to be led by Pastor William Phillips. Plans were made and a circular was sent around the churches on the mainland inviting people to come to Belfast in June 1920.

D.P. Williams writes: "Alas, however, on June 1st, the Sinn Feiners fired upon the Orangemen at Seaforth Street, Belfast, and the riots commenced. Murder, and the shedding of blood, took place on a large scale all over the city. As the press published these things, letters came to Pastor Phillips saying that they (the writers of the letters) did not feel like going to the convention in Belfast."

The riots continued into the second week and some of the guest speakers sent word to Pastor Phillips saying that they were no longer going. "When Pastor Phillips read the last letter in the presence of Pastor Thomas Jones of Llwynhendy, the prophet J. Omri Jones being also present, Thomas Jones remarked, 'That's the end of the Belfast Convention.' Then the word of the Lord proceeded out of the mouth of prophet, Omri Jones, 'Go thou, for I am God of land and sea. I would add that the bullet is not yet made to slay you; therefore, go thou and I will cause thee to return to the Mount (i.e. Penygroes, the Convention being in August) with the first fruit of that land with thee." (Williams, D., 2006)

Gordon Weeks concludes the story: "The visit was richly blessed and, when Pastor W. Phillips returned to Wales for the August Convention, twenty-five members of the Church travelled with him – first fruits indeed." (Weeks, 2003) In that convention, Pastor W. Phillips and Evangelist Evan Jones were called through prophecy to go to Ireland. They arrived in Belfast in October 1920.

In 1921, Omri Jones prophesied at the first convention in Beaufort, which was described in Chapter 8: "I will use thee; I will bless thee; I will cause my word to flow from here and every valley shall hear of my doings." And so it all came to pass as the word of the Lord had said! Following this first visit in August 1921 he became a regular visitor to Monmouthshire, bringing prophetic ministry as the work spread through the valleys. In the June 1932 *Apostolic Herald,* he receives this acknowledgement: "Pastor J. Omri Jones has travelled Monmouthshire to meet the demands, not of schisms and quarrellings (for there were none), but of the quick movements and goings of God. The year 1932 sees twenty Apostolic Assemblies in the Monmouthshire Valleys." (*Apostolic Herald*, 1932)

At the August Penygroes Convention 1925, Omri Jones gave this interpretation of tongues: "I AM THAT I AM. And behold, if Man will fail Me in these days, have ye not heard, even in convocations on this Mount, that this work which I have begun shall not fall to the ground. It shall rise, My people, for My Word have I sent forth; and I have gathered from among the nations; into an insignificant village have I gathered, saith the Lord, but remember that I would send forth My Word even at this hour again, and I will declare, in spite of the unreasonableness of your imaginations, that this mount is an ordained Mount, and I will manifest My glory yet again, yet again, saith the Lord, and not many years hence shall there be forty nations represented in this convocation." (Convention Report, 1925)

Did that word come to pass? Certainly, there have been forty nations represented over the years when the convention was held in Penygroes, but not necessarily all at one time. Undoubtedly doors have opened up to preach the Gospel in other nations through the overseas visitors that came to the annual Penygroes Convention and many young people in that place heard and responded to the call of God to go to the mission field.

In 1925, Omri Jones was also used prophetically to reveal that Pastors William Lewis and T.V. Lewis (who were not related) were to be recognised as apostles in the Body of Christ. T.V. Lewis tells the story: "At Blaenclydach were Pastors T. Rees, W.H. Lewis, Omri Jones and Hugh Evans. I joined them, and spoke on the text, *'And the Lord was with Joseph, and he was a prosperous man.'* Pastor W.H. Lewis preached on, *'Did not our hearts burn within us while He talked with us on the way?'* After he spoke, the Lord used Pastor Omri Jones and said: 'You that have been saying, 'The Lord was with Joseph'; many a time you have said 'Here am I!' – are you willing to say, 'Here am I, now?' The oil shall fall on your head. And thou who hast been making the hearts of this congregation warm with your message, the oil shall fall on your head, too. Pastor W.H. Lewis fell on his face, and hid under the table, prostrate, and crying, 'I am unfit!' In fact they had to pull him out from under the table in order to ordain him to the apostleship. I was also ordained an apostle at the same time; although I never expected it; but the Lord had revealed the fact that both the Lewis's would be called at that convention, to Pastor Dan and others some time previous." (Lewis, 1973)

This brought the number of apostles in the Apostolic Church to eight, covering Wales, England and Scotland. There were five ordained prophets at this time and a further apostle in Denmark. God was expanding the foundation so that the building could grow. Four years later, in October 1929, a Conference of Apostles and Prophets was held in Bradford; there were eighteen apostles and six prophets present in the meetings. By 1935 there were thirty-five apostles. The number of recognised prophets had also increased, but three were now overseas pioneering with apostles. (Weeks, 2003)

Omri Jones was bold and courageous in his prophetic ministry. On one occasion he challenged the spirit of Welsh nationalism that was at times evident in the church. On another occasion his courage was seen when in a meeting in Skewen, in 1926, he gave a directive word of prophecy to a man called Cyril Rosser, who was unknown to him at the time. In the obituary he wrote for Rosser many years later, Jones explains himself what happened that night: "It is with sorrow and a strange sense of loss that I write this appreciation of Pastor Cyril Rosser, my old friend. I have been very closely associated with him since the night he was called, through me, during a memorial service in Skewen, South Wales, to be a shepherd without a flock at Neath. He was unknown to us before that night but the prophetic word made it quite clear to whom the call was given, and never from then until his dying day did he look back." (Jones, J.,1965)

As a result, the Neath assembly opened with five people in March 1928 and continued to grow. This directive prophecy was a key step for Cyril Rosser and his wife, Ida, in finding the will of God for their lives. In time they went on to touch thousands of lives in West Africa with the Gospel.

The clarity of the revelation which Omri Jones received was remarkable, and his courage to speak forth what God was telling was indisputable. The following story is evidence of this: From 1922 Apostolic missionaries had been sent to Argentina, but in 1930 D.P. Williams received a letter informing him that "the work had gone to nothing" there. As D.P. was weeping over this situation in a prayer meeting in Skewen, Omri Jones began to prophesy: "Wipe your tears, My servant. In three days you will receive another letter that will open the fields beyond your comprehension." (Weeks, 2003) In three days a letter had arrived from Pastor D.O. Odubanjo of the Faith Tabernacle Congregation, Lagos, Nigeria. As missionaries were sent to that country the doors swung wide open and a mighty work of God was established. (The beginnings of the Apostolic Church in Nigeria are described in Chapter 11.)

In February 1933, Omri Jones went to Denmark with D.P. Williams, who wrote about what occurred when they met with the Danish leaders: "The prophetical ministry that came through

Pastor Omri Jones was profound, searching and enlightening, until our souls were ablaze with light. We were overwhelmed by its foretelling and revealing power. Often were we brought face to face with Him who knows every heart, who weighs every thought and scrutinizes every action. We listened with rapt amazement on those words of wisdom and life. At last – melting moment this! - the cloud burst, hearts were rent, groans and sighs of contrition filled the air, until every man lay helpless and broken at the feet of Him Who spake." (Apostolic Herald, 1933)

This experience undoubtedly had a positive impact on the work in Denmark. One of the Danish Apostolic leaders commented that 1933 was a year of beginnings. Later that year the church opened a Bible School and there was also further expansion in the Church's evangelistic campaigns. Two extra tents were purchased for Gospel missions. Finally, by the end of 1933, two new churches had been opened in Copenhagen.

Omri Jones visited various nations during his ministry, such as France, Italy, Denmark and North America. In 1935, during a ministry trip to Italy and France with Pastor Hugh Dawson, he prophesied that there would be a chain of assemblies from Le Harve to Marseilles. That word has come to pass. Today, we have assemblies from the north, including Le Havre, down to the south, including Marseilles.

In the 1936 Penygroes Convention he prophesied: "Behold, by My Word I am saying unto you, I am opening doors, and I desire to send many from among you, many from among you. There are more than have been revealed as yet. There are other doors in other lands that are opening; and I declare again, the business of the Lord requireth haste." (Riches of Grace, 1936)

By August 1936, the Apostolic Church had pioneered and sent missionaries to Ireland, Argentina, New Zealand, Denmark, France, Nigeria, Italy, India, Australia, the States, Canada, China and France. Further links had been made in the Gold Coast (Ghana), Estonia, Latvia, Japan, Egypt, Algeria, Sweden, Norway, Germany and South Africa. There were twenty-six missionaries and their families on the field, including some from Australia and Denmark. There were also two missionaries waiting to go to Canada and Ghana and some replacements were ready to go to Nigeria.

In the years following this prophecy the number of missionaries on some existing fields increased. Between 1936 and 1955 further works were established, either by the UK or other Apostolic countries, in Ghana, Japan, Hungary, Vanuatu, Israel, Papua New Guinea, Togo, Cameroon, Jamaica, South Africa, Rhodesia, Norway, Germany, Switzerland and the New Hebrides.

EVANGELISTIC MINISTRY

Omri Jones' ministry was not just prophetic. It was also evangelistic.

In the 1928 Penygroes Convention a Gospel van (known as "the chariot of the Lord") was dedicated for use in evangelistic missions in South Wales. Omri Jones was often involved with the evangelistic team, driving the vehicle for them at times. Among those he led to the Lord was Tom Saunders, a future President of the Apostolic Church. As the Gospel van travelled, members of local Apostolic assemblies would come and support the team each day where possible. The team would sleep in the van and hold meetings in the open-air or in the tent that they carried with them.

In the August 1932 *Apostolic Herald*, there is a report of the Gospel Van visiting Tai'r Gwaith, near Garnant. Omri Jones is in the picture and the report states: "Sixty-nine souls have surrendered to the Lord up to the time of writing, and two have been baptised in the Holy Ghost. Hallelujah!"

This evangelistic spirit never left Omri Jones. Mel Seaborne, former President of the Apostolic Church, mentions in his tribute to Omri Jones that, in his later years, he met a man in his eighties who had never read the Bible, so he bought one for him and sought to help him read and understand it. (Riches of Grace, 1979)

APOSTOLIC MINISTRY

In the August 1939 Convention an announcement was made that Omri Jones and Jones Williams, both of whom had been prophets for many years, were being called into the apostleship. They were to function in the dual office of apostle and prophet.

The emphasis on the dual office was perhaps the best way to present this revelation to the Convention congregation. The danger was that people would get the wrong impression that the headship ministries of Jesus were a ladder of promotion; that these two pastors had reached the rung of prophet and were now being promoted to the top rung, apostle. Hence the clear message that they would operate in the dual ministry. Following this calling he took on more responsibility at a national level within the Apostolic Church. In 1941, he was appointed Secretary to the Ministry Committee and, a few years later, National Women's Leader. At the time of this calling Omri Jones was in America, on a mission trip with D.P. Williams. Word was sent to America informing him and he was anointed on his return.

He was one of the main speakers at the 1941 New Year's Convention in Glasgow. He was there to preach but he was also used prophetically. This was wartime and he prophesied: "I would remind you that the nations are in the balance at this time. The nations are coming within reach of those judgements that I have foretold. I am dealing with the nations. You may endeavour to exalt one nation above another, but all the nations are in My Hand."

As God had previously used Omri Jones to speak against a

nationalistic spirit in the church, God was now using him to speak against any nationalist triumphalism in his people. (Herald of Grace , 1941) What is evident from this prophecy is that he still maintained a global perspective on God's purposes. This is one of the marks that differentiates a prophet from someone who simply exercises the gift of prophecy, bringing "edification, exhortation and consolation" to the local church (1 Corinthians 14:3). The words of the prophet often have a much deeper and a much wider scope and application.

He does not appear to have prophesied again at the Penygroes Convention until 1946, when it is clear that his courage and boldness had not diminished. We know from Worsfold that some tensions existed within the leadership of the Apostolic Church at that time. There was concern about the stifling nature of the constitution and the centralised structure of church government that was in place. A review was also taking place regarding the role of the prophet in the church. (Worsfold J. E., 1991)

I believe Omri Jones endeavoured, as an apostle and a prophet, to speak into the situation at the 1946 Convention. He chose as his text 1 Corinthians 3:9: *For we are God's fellow workers; you are God's field, God's building.* Among the many things he said was this: "Humbly do I say that I have been the witness of great things since 1911 in the Apostolic Church. Wondrous things has He done for us, but I am afraid that even as it was in the case of the Corinthian Church, we have allowed factions and strife to creep in oft-times... There should be no strife among us, brethren. God has been too good to us... Whose Church is it? It is the Church of God... God owns this field. This field does not belong to any of us, it belongs to God..." (Apostolic Convention Report, 1946). It was a message challenging leaders to work together.

THE PLACE OF PROPHETS IN THE CHURCH

The Apostle Paul, writing to the Ephesians, says that the Church is *built on the foundation of the apostles and prophets.* Ephesians 2:20. Prophets are part of the foundation.

In the examples I have given of the prophetic ministry of Omri Jones, I trust you have seen something of the strength and depth and dynamic revelation that prophets bring to a church. The content of their prophecy is foundational. It includes direction, expansion, identification, teaching and sending. Our early fathers considered it vitally important to the purposes of God. They did not, however, consider the prophets infallible. Mistakes were made and the leaders were fully aware of the dangers. Although aware of its weakness, our fathers saw prophecy as something very valuable and precious.

Our forefathers paid a high price in regard to prophecy. Pastor D.P. Williams at the 1925 Convention said, "We have been the off-scouring, and we have been buffeted, and have been thought that we were off our heads." When Pastor D.P. Williams and a group went to the States for the first time in 1922, certain Pentecostal leaders in the UK sent a letter to a Pentecostal paper in the States warning churches about this Apostolic delegation. The letter was "inserted in thousands of Pentecostal publications in America", but did not succeed in hindering the work. (Weeks, 2003)

In 1936, a pamphlet entitled, *The Apostolic Church's Error* was published by a Pentecostal pastor from Manchester, called Nelson Parr, attacking the concept of the "set prophet" and his function in the Church. Our fathers, personally and as a movement, paid a price for believing in the ministry of the prophet in the New Testament Church. Warren Jones, previous National Leader of the Apostolic Church UK, in the preface to *Cradle of Mystery*, reminds us that the truth of revelatory prophecy, while now accepted by many, was at the time of our forefathers, revolutionary. (Williams, D., 2006) But, as the Old Testament verse says: *...put your trust in the LORD your God and you will be established. Put your trust in His prophets and succeed.* 2 Chronicles 20:20

The evidence is this: from 1916 the Apostolic Church did prosper and succeeded in establishing a worldwide work that was directed and expanded through the prophetical gifting of men. That fact is without doubt. Some of our greatest missionary endeavours in the early days were built on apostles and prophets pioneering together. The question could be asked, did the quality of apostleship that Jesus gifted to the Church make the prophet, or, did the quality of the prophet that Jesus gifted make the apostle? One of our forefathers said, "A strong apostle will make a strong prophet." When I asked a seasoned apostle about this, his answer was, "A strong prophet will inspire an apostle."

I also spoke to Danny Thomas, now retired after long service as a pastor and missionary. He said, "In those early days, they taught that the relationship between the apostle and the prophet was like the human relationship of marriage." This unique and God given 'marriage' has given much to the Body of Christ over the years, and to the Apostolic Church in particular. As a movement, there is at the present time a dearth of prophets. Perhaps our cry should be not, "Lord, give us more prophets", but "Lord, strengthen the 'marriages' we already have between apostles and prophets."

Let me finish this section with quotes from D.P. Williams, which will help us to understand the great motivation that our fathers had for the prophetic.

"The Holy Ghost is a prophetic Spirit; He is working everywhere to a prophetic end. He has a goal in view; not an 'evolution' but an 'involution'. God is working towards that goal; everything is prophetic, and we are carried on the prophetic ministry of the Holy Ghost, in tears, prayers and laughter." (Davies & Yeoman, 2008)

"The secret of our unity in the Apostolic Church is that God speaks in the Church. It is His voice that has united us. It is His voice that keeps us together. He has called us in this sense to gather His own people together, that people may know that His temple is

going up, and that in His house the voice of the Father is heard."
(Davies & Yeoman, 2008)

THE PASSING OF A PIONEER

Omri Jones retired in the Neath district. He died in 1979 and was buried in Skewen. During his many years of ministry he served the Lord as the district pastor in Llanelli, Pontypridd, Skewen, Ammanford, Penygroes, Llandybie, Cardiff, Aberdare, Bradford and Neath.

I personally remember Pastor Omri and the affection people had for this man, even in old age. He married my mother and father and the way they would say, "Pastor Omri" whenever they saw him, spoke volumes to me of the love and regard they had for him.

My father recounts this funny, but amazing story about him. On one occasion Pastor Omri was travelling by train to a church appointment. The shoes he was wearing had no soles. In fact, before he left his home he had put cardboard inside them. He was travelling on the train when suddenly, through the open window of the carriage, a pair of shoes landed at his feet. He picked them up and they were exactly his size!

Pastor Mel Seaborne, the then president of the Apostolic Church, paid this tribute to Omri Jones: "In the passing of 'Pastor Omri', as he was affectionately known, the Apostolic Church has lost one of its earliest pioneers, a man of God who served the Lord with distinction... He has left a memory which we cherish, but more – he has brought to the Church a ministry that will live on in the lives of others with eternal implications. He was a pioneer of Apostolic truth, but he was also a pioneer of the purpose of God for his day and generation." (Riches of Grace, 1979)

CHAPTER TEN
WILLIAM R. THOMAS

"I am under obligation both to Greeks and to barbarians,
both to the wise and to the foolish. So, for my part,
I am eager to preach the gospel to you who are in Rome."
Romans 1:14-15

William Roger Thomas was born on 26th July 1909 to Thomas and Rachel Thomas, in Plasmarl, Swansea, one of nine children. The family was prosperous and even had its own horse-drawn carriage, which would be the equivalent of a luxury car today.

In his young days, he was known to his friends as "the hooded terror". He would put a paper bag over his head, with two holes for his eyes, and get up to mischief in the neighbourhood. He was a good rugby player and represented Swansea District on the rugby field. (Thomas A., 2015)

However, everything changed sometime after his sixteenth birthday in 1925. William's mother, who had become a Christian in 1919, attended the Apostolic Church in Swansea and persuaded him to come with her to some evangelistic meetings there. He only agreed to attend because a deal had been struck between mother and son: if William came to the evangelistic meetings, he would be given money for the new suit he wanted. (Apostolic Herald, 1936)

William's daughter, Violetta, writes, "Dad spoke of the occasion as follows: he entered the hall quietly and sat at the back. During the sermon, he thought his mum must have told the preacher all about himself because the message fitted him perfectly. At the end of the meeting he tried to leave quickly but a deacon stopped and asked him, 'Why do you not give your heart to Jesus?' This made him cry and pray and there in the doorway he gave his life to the Lord." (Thomas V., 2015)

William himself wrote this about his conversion experience, "My heart was seeking a greater satisfaction... then Jesus met me... and His love and beauty changed and transformed my soul... Oh, what a change! I was then taught concerning the baptism of the Holy Spirit and, after six months of humbling and mortifying experiences, the Lord graciously bestowed upon me the divine Gift. This divine indwelling gave me new impetus and inspiration to follow the Master." (Apostolic Herald, 1931)

An indication of the powerful impact his conversion experience had upon him, is the fact that he burned the rugby caps that he had won and also his collection of 78 rpm records of well-known singers of the day. William Thomas would say that he came out of that hall with two new suits: one that eventually wore away; the other, spiritual and eternal, that was renewed day by day.

HIS MINISTRY IN THE UK

By 1931, at the age of twenty-two, he was called to be part of an International Evangelistic Band, otherwise known as "The Revival Trio", made up of William Thomas and Pastors John Hamilton and J. Bonar Thompson. Gordon Weeks writes, "The Church in the UK was engaged in ceaseless evangelistic efforts, including the use of deaconesses and other sisters in preaching and campaign work. The magazines were full of reports of this activity. In addition, during this year, two International Evangelistic Bands were formed for aggressive activity throughout the country. (Weeks, 2003)

The *Apostolic Herald,* September 1931, provides this information: "The function of these bands will be to move up and down the whole country, as the Lord directs, conducting big revival and healing campaigns. At the time of going to press the first band is labouring at Tonypandy in Wales, and from there will go to have three weeks' campaign in Penygroes. The second band is engaged in a big tent campaign at Shrewsbury till 17th September, and will then be holding meetings in London from 19th September till 22nd October." (Apostolic Herald, 1931)

The report of the Shrewsbury Tent Campaign includes a remarkable incident. The first two weeks of meetings were held in a tent, approximately two miles from the centre of Shrewsbury. This location was inconvenient because of the distance people had to travel, but nine adults were saved and also a number of children.

After the first fortnight, the campaign was moved into a hall in the centre of Shrewsbury, which proved more convenient. From this point, the emphasis of the ministry was the baptism of the Holy Spirit. One evening, towards the close of an address on "The Anointing with Fresh Oil", a young man, who had been saved in the tent, rushed forward to the front with his face buried in his hands, pouring forth in unknown tongues as the Spirit gave him utterance. He knew absolutely nothing about the baptism of the Holy Spirit or new tongues, but the Lord gave him both.

In November of that year the team moved on to hold meetings in Barking, where two people were converted and ten became members of the local church.

The Revival Trio were also used in church planting. They would move into a town for approximately a month and rent a hall or use a tent, holding meetings every night. The team was multi-talented. Each could play the organ, sing and preach, so they would all take turns. At the end of the month, any people who wanted to be part of the Apostolic Church were taken into membership and the new plant was handed over to the local apostleship.

An example of their pioneering work was in Neath, South Wales. They held services for a month and, at the end of the campaign seventy new members were added to the existing assembly.

In 1932, William was ordained into the pastorate and was sent to Plymouth. A review of his ministry in the June 1936 *Apostolic Herald* explained: "In 1932 he was ordained pastor of the assembly at Plymouth. It was stipulated, however, through the prophetic ministry at his ordination, that his incumbency at Plymouth was to be preparatory to his assumption of an office in a wider sphere. This intimation was confirmed when shortly thereafter he was nominated missionary to Italy." (Apostolic Herald, 1936)

CALLED AS A MISSIONARY TO ITALY

William's daughter, Violetta, writes, "At 23 years of age he was called prophetically to go to Grosseto, Italy. He went to Italy in January 1933 as a single man but he was, in fact, engaged to be married to Lillian Jones. Lillian was one of the first two women to attend the Apostolic Church Bible School in Penygroes." (Thomas V. , 2015)

When Pastor Thomas, or "Pastor Willie" as he was affectionately known, left on his first stint of service to Italy, D.P. Williams gave him three pieces of advice: "Willie, you are going into a Catholic country: grow a moustache because no Catholic priest has a moustache, so you'll stand out. Willie, when we have money for a salary, we will send it. If not, God will provide. Willie, it is too early for you to get married. Wait until you return after your first missionary service in Italy." (Thomas A. , 2015)

As a result, William went to Italy alone, arriving in February 1933. He was met by the first resident Apostolic missionaries to the country, Pastor and Mrs. George Evans. This couple had previously been pioneers in Argentina and had moved to Italy in 1929. He stayed at the Evans' home in Grosseto, a city in the central Italian region of Tuscany. In the pictures taken at this time there was no moustache!

The first few months were spent learning Italian, but after only two months he was able to preach his first message in his adopted language. In the first report home, Pastor Thomas wrote, "The time had arrived for my introduction to the Italian Churches, and with prayer and desire we commenced our journey. In the company and under the guidance of one of the Lord's servants (Pastor Evans), I was introduced to Rome, Naples and Civitavecchia... From Naples we returned to Civitavecchia, via Rome. Arriving at our destination about seven o'clock, we were just in time for the meeting. And what a meeting; one would have thought that one was in Penygroes Convention, if it were not for the fact that one was in Italy. The joy was intense, the praise was spiritual, the preaching was powerful, the glory was supernal, and the Christ was supreme." (Apostolic Herald, 1933)

After spending a few days in Civitavecchia, William returned to Grosseto "blessed, encouraged, and grateful to God our Saviour, Who doeth all things well." The original intention was that, when he had fully settled and adjusted to his new life in Italy, he would relocate and link up with the Apostolic Church in Naples. However, this did not happen.

During the 1934 Penygroes Convention, George Evans and his wife were called to go and pioneer in Montreal, Canada, and they moved shortly after. As a result, Willie Thomas made Grosseto his base. The superintendent of the work was an Italian, called Pastor Alberto del Rosso, who was based in Civitavecchia, a town in the province of Rome.

THE PROPHETIC MOTIVATION

It is important to understand how Italy, and in particular, the Holy See at Rome, were viewed by Evangelical and Pentecostal Christians in the early twentieth century.

During the 1926 Penygroes International Convention, Italy and Rome were referred to in a prophetic word through Pastor Jones Williams: "In my movements in the Church I am not only moving you to the uncivilised world in regard to the missionary cause, I am making a direct move in the body of the Apostolic Church towards and against the 'great Babylon'. I am revealing to you that My battle is against the 'great whore' at the end of the age."

Pastor Worsfold comments on the above prophecy: "It is reasonably clear that the major motivation which led the Apostolic Church Missionary Council to provide ministry in Italy is rooted in the revelation which came to them through prophetical ministry, and that this was typical of most missionary activity which the Council embarked upon. In company with most evangelicals and Pentecostals, the Apostolic Church believed that the centre of the vast movement of anti-Christ activity was in Italy and that the Roman Catholic Church was the major expression of that power." (Worsfold J. E., 1991)

Prophetic names from the book of Revelation, such as "Babylon", "Anti-Christ" and the "Great Whore", are not generally taught about or even mentioned in church today. It appears that for many Christians the focus has moved away from the return of Christ and end-time events. However, if we understand something of the prophetic agenda that God has for this world, as detailed in Revelation, we know that there are some confrontations coming between the LORD GOD omnipotent and the "prince of the power of the air", Satan. Believing that Jesus is coming back to this earth as King of Kings and Lord of Lords will not only encourage us to be fully prepared for His return, but will also motivate us, as it did our early Apostolic fathers, to work for His return and long to see His Kingdom "stretch from shore to shore".

In November last year, I was sitting next to an Italian lady at our daughter's wedding. We started to talk about various happenings that were taking place across the world and she said these words to me, "It is as if we need some superman to come and sort everything out." I nearly fell off my chair, but I was able to explain to her how the Bible speaks of two people who are coming: Anti-Christ and the Lord's Christ.

It was evident that there was a prophetic call for the Apostolic Church, and William Thomas in particular, to work in Italy. At Pastor Thomas' farewell in Swansea on 18th January 1933, D.P. Williams mentioned an incident from his own life: on one occasion when he was in the south of France, he stepped over the border into Italy and touched Italian soil. Standing on a mountain, he looked towards Rome and claimed it for Jesus Christ.

APOSTOLIC BEGINNINGS IN ITALY

The story of how the Apostolic Church began in Italy is a remarkable one. What follows is an excerpt from D.P. William's book, *Cradle of Mystery*:

"In the year 1909, a Christian gentleman went to Florence, Italy where he held meetings in a dwelling house, and preached the baptism of the Holy Ghost for believers. Two members of a Baptist church were obedient to this vision and were filled with the Holy Spirit.

In 1914, a young Baptist pastor, who had just finished his training, returned to Florence to commence a work there, heard about the baptism in the Holy Spirit, held tarry meetings according to the scriptures, and there a young man, named Alfredo del Rosso, was baptised. This young man later became the first Apostolic pastor ordained in Italy, eventually taking charge of the A.C. work.

By invitation, on 21st February 1927, Pastor D.P. Williams, his brother Jones Williams, Ps. Sigurd Bjorner (A.C. Copenhagen), and Dr. Carl Naesser visited the Italian assembly, or rather, the saints whom Ps. del Rosso had gathered in several homes. There at Civitavecchia a hall was hired, del Rosso was ordained a pastor and two others appointed deacons.

At Grosseto a group of believers intimated their desire to be considered to join the Apostolic Church and two brothers were separated as elders.

After a visit to the August Penygroes Convention of 1929, Pastor del Rosso returned to Italy as the chosen of the Lord to superintend the Italian field, accompanied by Pastor and Mrs. B. George Evans. Their aptitude for languages helped them and soon the Italian language was mastered sufficiently to enable them to speak to the flock. In the will of God, they were stationed at Grosseto where, in due time, a splendid hall was built.

At the inauguration Pastors A. Turnbull, F. Hodges, W. Jones Williams and Dr. Carl Naeser officiated. Many souls were saved and bodies healed.

Though the Italian converts were poor, circumstantially, their fervency of spirit was blessed of the Lord and many were the enquirers. Other centres were also visited and the Lord worked with signs and wonders in each place.

In 1933, Ps. W.R. Thomas (a redoubtable footballer in his youth) consecrated his powers of mind and body to the Lord's work in Italy and, at this time, he, and his family are doing a grand work with substantial numbers of citizens joining the various assemblies." (Williams, D. , 2006)

MINISTRY IN ITALY: 1933-1940

In May 1933, a ministry team from the UK, including Pastors D.P. Williams, H.Croudson and Jones Williams, visited Italy some three months after Pastor Thomas had arrived. They started their ministry in Grosseto on Saturday, 13th May 1933 with a service in which Willie Thomas sang in Italian. (Apostolic Herald, 1933)

However, what would have captured people's hearts in the UK was this report from D.P. Williams: "At that time in Rome, under the nose of the Pope, a small company of believers gathered and it was felt the time had come to set the assembly in order." (Williams, D. , 2006) Pastor del Rosso writes, "After an illuminating address by the President, an invitation was given to those desiring the right hand of fellowship to come forward. Twelve responded to the call. It seemed good unto the Lord to choose an elder and a deaconess from these. Thus, after much labour and prayer, the Apostolic Church in Rome has been established." (Williams, D., 1933)

Right in the heart of Rome, where the Pope lived and ruled, an Apostolic Church on the pattern that Paul had set down in the New Testament, was now in place, bringing to mind the prophetic word concerning Rome at the 1926 Penygroes Convention.

The pioneering continued and in January 1934, an assembly was opened by Pastors del Rosso and George Evans in Catania, Sicily. The government authorities had also granted permission for the opening of an assembly in Cagliari, Sardinia. In the same year a Young People's Movement was commenced in the Grosseto church.

There were, however, some black clouds on the horizon. Shortly after a church conference in Grosseto in August 1934, the Italian Government ordered all regular evangelistic work and services to cease in the country. Five years previously, laws had been passed in Italy abolishing certain cults. Pentecostal groups were now identified as one such cult.

Willie Thomas' report of this conference, in the *Apostolic Herald*, November 1934, states: "Pastor del Rosso addressed the audience with characteristic fervour and enthusiasm, and the place was shaken... Unfortunately, since that time, the Church in this part of the world has been passing through a period of crisis. All evangelical work has had to be suspended. We trust, however, that in response to our co-operative prayer, the present difficult position may be rectified." (Apostolic Herald, 1934)

His report the following month reveals the determination of the Italian believers to continue to witness and preach the Gospel: "Denied the privilege of public meetings, the saints in Italy are engaging eagerly in private gospel work, and the truth which can no longer be proclaimed from the pulpit is now being broadcast by means of personal evangelism."

The news from Italy also included an account of two amazing miracles. Pastor Thomas had been asked to pray for a child who had swallowed a nail an inch and a half long: "The boy was suffering extreme pain, and his parents were distracted. The Pastor... laid his hands upon him and anointed him with oil, and on the following morning when he was taken to the hospital for examination, it was discovered that the nail had passed through the stomach without occasioning the slightest damage to it. The doctors were astounded."

The second miracle was that of a child who had been dumb from birth. Again, prayer was made and the child "was enabled in the name of Jesus to articulate sufficient language to allow it to converse with its astonished parents! The touch of Christ has still its ancient power!" (Apostolic Herald, 1934)

Although there were difficulties through these years, there were also great manifestations of God's power. The following account appeared in the *Apostolic Herald*, July 1935:

"Pastor Thomas received a telegram at 6.00pm one evening, to go to Pian-di-Rocca because a member of the Apostolic Church was ill. Pastor Willie knew that this woman had suffered in the past from a 'strange and depressing illness.' The village was about 20 miles from Grosseto. Pastor Thomas would have travelled there on bike (borrowed). At 7.00am, the following morning, Pastor Thomas was at the lady's house. On arriving he discovered that she had been unable to leave her bed for some time, and had to be bound to it, because the acute nature of the pain, which she was suffering, made it impossible for her to remain long in one position. Her whole body was shaken by terrific spasms of agony and her physical strength was quickly being exhausted."

The story continues, "Pastor Thomas started to talk to the lady about Jesus and noticed that her agitations became more and more. As he continued to talk about Jesus, the woman tried to break the bandages that were holding her and began to cry out in a loud voice, 'Kill me! Kill me!' The yell was terrible and she was repeating the words 'Kill me!' over and over again at the top of her voice. Pastor Thomas became aware of the demonic and he was asked whether he was Jesus. While the woman was still screaming, Pastor Willie took authority over the demon in the name of Jesus and commanded the evil spirit to leave the woman, just as they did in the days of first-century Christianity, and immediately the demon left the woman's body, tearing her violently as it did so, and emitting an unearthly howl. Ten minutes later the sister was out of bed and taking something solid to eat (she had lived on nothing but milk for ten days previously) and half an hour later she was sitting with the pastor in the evangelistic service in the town. There many, who had been daily expecting to hear of her death, were astonished to see her present and to hear of her marvellous deliverance. News of this remarkable experience is now being spread throughout the district and is causing no small stir." (Apostolic Herald, 1935)

From his base in Grosseto, Pastor Thomas continued to visit outlying villages in the area, undaunted by the opposition. He stated, "Many are the difficulties confronting us which cannot openly be declared, difficulties religious and political. But God is greater than the difficulties... During the past few months no less than eight new members have been added to the local church.

Saved under the pastor's ministry, they are continuing regularly to attend the services, and are exhibiting the joy resulting from a consciousness of sins forgiven. Particularly among the young people is the power of the Spirit at work." (Apostolic Herald, 1935)

However, sad to say, it appears that Pastor Thomas' colleague, Pastor del Rosso, either out of fear for his own life or to maintain his relationship with the authorities, was not fully supporting the British missionary in Grosseto. On 17th July 1935, he wrote to Pastor Thomas ordering him to comply with the Government orders to close all church services down.

Nonetheless, God is still on the throne. Stones had been thrown at the church during the services and some particularly wealthy individuals in Grosseto had raised a petition to have it closed down. The church in Grosseto had received this prophetic word saying, "Those who have done this have prepared their end with their own hands." Within six months, three of those who were agitating against the church were dead. This not only put fear into the hearts of the people but also faith. As a result, the meetings moved clandestinely into homes.

At this time a retired policeman, Guido Ulivagnoli, was converted. He became a key figure in the development of the Apostolic Church during the war years, when there was no resident UK missionary in Italy, and also in the years following the war. He was in a house meeting which was raided by the police. The police knew who he was, but he refused their request to attend the police station later. As a result, all those meeting in the home were arrested and Guido Ulivagnoli led the procession of captured Christians to the police station. As it transpired, they were all acquitted.

Alberto del Rosso did eventually resign from the Apostolic Church in December 1935. Gordon Weeks writes, "Pastor del

Rosso had withdrawn from the Church as he wished to travel widely without any accountability to the Church leadership." (Weeks, 2003)

Up until this time Willie Thomas had travelled everywhere on a borrowed bicycle. In January 1936 and due to "the liberality of an anonymous donor" in the UK, he acquired a bicycle of his own to travel around the Grosseto area!

Persecution against the Church and other Pentecostal groups continued. In February 1936 a report appeared in the *Apostolic Herald*, headed "Italian Incidents": "It is a remarkable fact that persecution has played an important part in the purification and purgation of the Church, and has thereby contributed in no small degree to its development in spiritual strength, even if it has at times depleted its numerical strength. There are some plants which, according to the botanists, are fertilised by the wind. The Church resembles these inasmuch as it is the wind of persecution, scattering the seed of the Word of God, which prevents the Christian community from becoming self-centred and effects the dissemination of the germs of spiritual life. This is what has been happening in the Assembly at Grosseto, Italy recently." (Apostolic Herald, 1936)

The Rome, Civitavecchia and Grosseto churches all continued to progress. News from Grosseto included the healing of a young man from an incurable disease, as Pastor Thomas relates: "He hobbled into our assembly... For fourteen years he had suffered untold inconvenience and physical pain... That night, however, the Lord healed him miraculously, and saved his soul as well." Around the same time, a Catholic priest was converted and two elders, who had left the Grosseto church six years previously, were restored. (Apostolic Herald, 1936)

These were the years of Mussolini and his fascist dictatorship in Italy and the threat of war in Europe. In January 1937, Willie Thomas sent a report home, headed, *In the Face of Fascism*: "In the midst of terrible difficulty and confusion the Apostolic Church in Italy continues to stand fearlessly for the whole counsel of God. Despite the concentrated opposition of the political powers and the spiritual warfare waged against the work of God by the principalities of Hell, the truth of Christ holds ground." (Apostolic Herald, 1937)

This report also contained news of the salvation of fourteen young men in Grosseto. Mussolini had been mobilising an army for an attack on Abyssinia and these men had volunteered to join this force. Pastor Thomas writes, "It was a glorious sight at one of our recent meetings, to see them all prostrate before God, repentant and seeking pardon for their sins from the Redeemer... But while things are going so well at Grosseto, we are sorry to report that great opposition is being encountered in Rome. The official persecution directed against the Pentecostals has led to the disbandment of all companies of baptised believers. All Pentecostal movements have been – as movements – destroyed." (Apostolic Herald, 1937)

It was at the end of this eventful year that Pastor Willie Thomas returned home to the UK on furlough to marry his fiancée, Lillian, whom he had not seen since January 1933. They were married in Swansea and spent their honeymoon at a church conference in Scotland. He then returned with his new bride to Italy that same year. Lillian served alongside him throughout the years in Italy and also in the UK In time they had seven children - five girls and two boys: Valeria, Violetta, Elizabeth, Joan, Beryl, William John and Andrew.

Persecution continued and freedom to meet was further restricted, as William describes in a 1939 missionary report: "For several months now our church in Grosseto, Italy, has been closed down by the Italian authorities and no public worship of any kind has since been permitted... In the meantime, private cottage services are being held, and, although the law prohibits the gathering of more than ten together, much blessing has been experienced in the households of the saints. In face of such a challenge from every realm, religious, social and political, one is surprised to learn of signs of growth... It would almost seem as though the early days of the Church were being repeated and history lived over again. We remember that when the disciples were scattered abroad the Church began to grow. And many conversions have taken place, many healings and many filled with the Spirit of God since the closing of the Church. Bless God that persecution does not destroy blessing. Not under any circumstances." (Jones W. , 1939)

Andrew Thomas, William's son, relates how, by the late 1930's, as the result of the alliance between Mussolini and Hitler, the Thomas family were seen as "British spies" and "enemies of the Axis of Iron". His mother often had to clean his father's jacket when he came home because it was covered in spit from those who called him "British spy" as he walked in the streets of Grosseto. (Thomas A. , 2015)

THE WAR YEARS

At the end of May 1940, Willie Thomas was in a cottage meeting when a Christian woman, called Corinna Ducci, gave this prophetic word: "And I say to you, my servant Thomas; go home, pack your bags and go back to your home. I'm bringing you here in the future, but not forever."

He went home to his wife and two young daughters, packed four suitcases and at nine o' clock the next morning, caught a train north. Pastor Andrew Thomas explains what happened a few days later: "The Blackshirts[18] arrived at the Thomas home in Grosseto to arrest the family as 'citizens of a hostile country', because Italy

---
18 Fascist followers of Mussolini

was declaring war on Britain. But the Lord had already spoken and the family was preserved." Had they been captured, Pastor and Mrs. Thomas would have been put into an internment camp and their two daughters would have been placed in a Roman Catholic orphanage.

Their first attempt to cross the Italian border was blocked, but when they tried again the next day the border guard was more sympathetic saying, "I should not let you go, but I have children too." They crossed the border into France and catching a train to Paris they found themselves sharing a compartment with the son of the British Consul in Paris. He took compassion on their predicament and invited them to stay at the Consul's house.

In Paris they could hear the guns of the approaching German invading army. The family made their way to Le Havre and caught the last ship that sailed for England. Pastor Andrew describes the journey: "The ship from Le Havre made a stopover in Guernsey in the Channel Islands, and the family took a room in a small hotel, promising to send money to the hotelier by post, because now they had spent all that they had. The following morning they left, and a few days later, the island was occupied by German airmen. They landed at Plymouth, along with the soldiers who were rescued from the beaches at the evacuation of Dunkirk. God led them safely." (Thomas A. , 2015)

In the early months of 1940, Pastor Thomas had sent two appeals to the Missionary Committee for permission to return to the UK, but both requests were turned down. However, this rider was included in the May minutes, "We have no desire to compel him to stay against his will." In May, the Missionary secretary was instructed to arrange tickets and money with the travel company for the family to come home without any further need to contact the Missionary Board. The minutes containing these directives never reached Pastor Willie Thomas in Italy, but the Lord stepped in, through Corinna Ducci, and told him to go home.

After his departure, the church in Grosseto was cared for by Guido Ulivagnoli, known as the "Marshal". It was this man who held the work together throughout the very difficult years of the war. In December 1941 this touching appeal for prayer was included in the *Herald of Grace*: "Without any means of conveying our greetings to the band of Italian saints gathered around the Marshal, we can only appeal to one and all to remember them during the coming season at the throne of grace. With Pastor W. Thomas back among us, we feel the separation less severely and we join him in spirit as we unite in commemoration of the Gospel news which first came to this country from Italy." (Herald of Grace, 1941)

Andrew Thomas recounts: "On one occasion, the so called 'Easter Blood' of 26th April 1943, a prophetic word had encouraged the church group 'to go to praise the Lord in the countryside' on the Easter Sunday, and it was while they were singing, away from the city, that Allied bombing struck the centre of Maremma (this is the geographical region of which Grosseto is the centre) leaving hundreds of civilians dead... But the church was preserved - even the organ, an old harmonium pedal, which had been wrapped up in a tarpaulin and buried in the garden of one of the members of Poggione (suburb of Grosseto). When Grosseto was liberated by the Allied forces in 1944, the hall at Via Oberdan was re-opened as a place of worship for military allies. When the organ was dug up they said it sounded even better than before!" (Thomas A., 2015)

Meanwhile, during the war years Pastor Willie Thomas was appointed pastor of Blackburn, Dover and then Ebbw Vale assemblies. When the family first moved to Blackburn they were given twenty pounds to set up home and the wage was £15.00 per month. It was while they were there that Willie and Lillian's twin daughters, Joan and Beryl, were born.

Violetta writes, "During the war Dad was pastor in Blackburn, where an Apostolic church with only seven faithful members, was about to close. After moving in, Dad held special meetings (for salvation, healing and Apostolic doctrine) for three months. After this period the Lord blessed so much that the membership had gone to seventy-seven, and all the church debts had been paid." (Thomas V. , 2015)

A copy of an unexpected letter from "The Marshal" to Pastor Thomas is printed in full in the August 1943 edition of *Herald of Grace*. It had arrived on a circuitous journey via America and provided a welcome update on the situation in Italy: "By the Grace of God you will find our faith and our promises intact. God bless you all! ...I send you warmest regards from all to all. I embrace you fraternally and sincerely." (Herald of Grace, 1943)

Pastor Willie Thomas volunteered to temporarily look after the Apostolic Church in Dover, Leaving his wife and family in Ebbw Vale. The town had suffered unrelenting German air attacks. He was there in June 1944 at the time of the Allied invasion of Normandy.

Andrew Thomas describes one of his father's enduring memories of his time in Dover: "My father, while on pastoral work, went to visit a particular deaconess. He found her sitting on top of a pile of rubble that had been her home. She was holding a pan, the only thing she had brought with her before leaving the home on the sound of an air-raid alarm. Pastor asked her how she was, and she replied, 'All saved, glory to God!'" (Thomas A. , 2015)

After the relief work in Dover, the family were together again in Ebbw Vale and in October 1944 Willie Thomas appealed to the Missionary Committee to be allowed to go back to Italy immediately. The Church had already agreed a policy regarding the reintroduction of missionaries to the countries affected by the War. It stated that before any missionary went back to reside in a country, all war hostilities should have stopped and then a delegation would visit to investigate the feasibility of the missionary returning.

A RETURN VISIT TO ITALY IN 1946

In May 1946, Pastor Hugh Mitchell, the National Missionary Secretary and Pastor Willie Thomas visited Italy. News had filtered through that the assembly in Grosseto was still in existence, but nothing else was known about the situation of the Italian churches. On their arrival, Pastors Mitchell and Thomas discovered that the church in Civitavecchia had been reopened but was now under the control of the U.S. Church of the Nazarene. In line with Guido Ulivagnoli's letter of 1943, the Apostolic assembly in Grosseto had survived.

As a result of the findings of this visit, it was agreed by the Missionary Committee that Willie Thomas and family could return to Italy "on the understanding that we are expecting to see an expansion in the work immediately. We wish to make clear that the length of his stay in Italy will depend entirely on the results of his ministry." (Apostolic Missionary Committee Minutes, 1946)

Pastor Thomas was interviewed by the Missionary Board and left in no doubt what was expected of him: "We pointed out to him the purpose of the Committee that aggressive steps should be taken for the expansion of the work to other large towns in Italy besides Grosseto (Rome being particularly mentioned) and the decision of the Council, in August last year, that Brother Guido Ulivagnoli should be called out into the ministry as soon as the position of the Italian finances permit." (Apostolic Missionary Committee Minutes, 1946)

CONTINUED MINISTRY IN ITALY

In February 1947 there was a prophecy identifying William Thomas as an apostle and also stating that his call to Italy was not a permanent one. (Apostolic Church Council Minutes, 1947) Visas were granted in July of that year for the family to return to

Italy. However, due to financial constraints on the Missionary Committee, these plans were postponed and William returned alone in April 1948. The cost of living was high in Italy, but the Missionary Committee decided to take a step of faith and the whole family finally returned later that year.

The region in which Grosseto is situated was very poor at that time, and, like other parts of Italy, was held fast by superstitions and witchcraft. People feared the "evil eye" and many consulted fortune tellers and magicians.

Andrew Thomas writes, "When the young family returned to Grosseto after the war, they were looking for a house and went to visit a vacant house that no one wanted to rent because it was called 'the house of the spirits'. Every family that had lived there had left in a hurry because of unexplained noises, footsteps and voices. Because of this 'reputation' the landlord was offering the house for a very low rent... My mother told me that, after agreeing to rent the house, they prayed in every room asking for peace and God's protection and 'deliverance from evil'. There were never any problems or complaints and the house was a means to get the family started again in Grosseto." (Thomas A. , 2015)

Violetta recalls, "I remember dad's fervour, when we went back to Grosseto as a family in 1948 and he started to work on gathering what was left of the congregation after the war. He was so busy, with four daughters to teach - we didn't know Italian- and there were meetings every day - Bible study for all on Saturday, three meetings on Sunday, Monday: discipleship- teaching - preaching - convening - outreach- strictly for the young men, to prepare them for the pastorate etc. The church was growing fast and he needed to delegate the work. It was spreading all over Italy -whole families were joining. We went to as many meetings as we could because the Lord was powerful in the meetings. We didn't want to miss anything. Tue: sisterhood, Wed: prayer, Thurs: all the young witnesses. Fri: free day, but Dad spent most of his free time writing on many Biblical books and subjects. The church was young, needed teaching and he couldn't be everywhere at all times, even though he travelled to oversee the work continuously. The books were written for a growing church but also and mainly out of his great love to know more and more about God and His will, and to pass it on to others. He never liked the administration side of the work. His whole work was on the spiritual side." (Thomas V. , 2015)

In the Missionary Committee minutes from 1948 through to 1955 there were repeated requests for Bibles in Italian, money to build and furnish church buildings and to support full-time evangelists. The Apostolic work in Italy was starting to fan out from its base in Grosseto to other parts of the country. There were further requests for a duplicator and an organ and also for the UK to recognise different callings in men. Resources were severely stretched for the Missionary Committee and for the Thomas family, due to the rising cost of living after the war years.

Sadly, in January 1949 William and Lillian lost a son, William John. Violetta writes, "Where we were living the winter was harsh and the baby did not survive. One of the sisters in the church said to Dad, 'Now you will never leave Italy completely. There will always be one of you here.'" The child was buried in Grosseto. (Thomas V. , 2015)

When Lillian became pregnant again, the family received a prophetic word that they would have a boy; they were to call him Andrew and he would serve the Lord in Italy. That has all come to pass. They did have another son, in May 1952, and they did name him Andrew. Today, Andrew Thomas, who is based in Rome, is a recognised pastor and apostle and has served the Lord for many years in the Apostolic Church in Italy.

The Apostolic Church in Italy continued to expand and experienced many miraculous interventions from God.

Casermone was a huge abandoned barracks, some miles from Grosseto, that was being used to house families from all over Italy who had lost their homes and belongings because of the war. An opportunity arose for Pastor Thomas and the saints in Grosseto to evangelise the people living in this disused military base. One of the families in the camp was called Ciampelli. The wife, Nerina, was suffering from advanced tuberculosis. Nerina was prayed for and was miraculously healed.

This brought such a spiritual awakening to the camp that the Catholic priest stopped going to perform the mass. While his congregation decreased, the Apostolic church in Casermone increased. But this miraculous healing had another providential outcome for the Apostolic Church in Italy. Violetta writes, "These people had moved to Casermone to live from all over Italy and now they were telling their relatives the Good News and making contacts for future places of worship." (Thomas V. , 2015) Andrew Thomas explains, "Those displaced people later became the seed for the later expansion of the Apostolic work in Italy. (Thomas A. , 2015)

Andrew writes that, after their return to Italy, his father felt the need of a prophet to work alongside him: "One evening, in the church in Grosseto, while the congregation were praying about this need... the Lord spoke to my dad and said, 'Are you my apostle? Come down from the pulpit and lay hands on my servant Theseus Benelli, and he will be a prophet in my church. Obeying promptly... he laid his hands on the head of beloved Theseus and suddenly, for the first time, his mouth opened with the powerful cry, 'Thus says the Lord'... God made use of this 'channel', gushing like clear water that night, and to this day, putting in the hands of the apostles, revelations accurate and true to be implemented." (Thomas A. , 2015)

There was another occasion when a man came into one of the

meetings in Grosseto with every intention of stabbing Pastor Willie Thomas at the end of the meeting, as the people were leaving. He had a concealed dagger, but, during worship, the presence of God convicted the man and he gave his heart to Jesus. Before he left, he handed the dagger over to Pastor Thomas. (Thomas V., 2015)

The local authorities were still opposed to the work of the Apostolic Church in Grosseto when Willie Thomas returned, but in time it became known as the place where communist sympathisers were converted and this helped it to gain some acceptance. The police were glad to see that these ex-communists were no longer attending the political rallies which were causing problems in the area.

In the *Apostolic Herald*, April 1951, we see something of the progress that had been made since Pastor Thomas and his family returned in 1948. The Marshal, Guido Ulivagnoli, and his wife had moved to live and pioneer in Siena, about fifty miles north of Grosseto. Pastor Pecorini, "inspite of fanatical persecution", was evangelising the villages and towns around Castellammare di Stabia, a town approximately twenty miles south of Naples. Theseus Benelli, who was now a recognised prophet, has been ministering in Castellammare and an elder, Vincenzo, from that church has been in Grosseto ministering. Casermone, Pastor Thomas reports, "has become the upper room of the Apostolic Church in Grosseto and surroundings. In this assembly we have witnessed dozens of persons coming through in the baptism of the Spirit; our elder there is a stalwart for the vision and for the Lord." He continues by mentioning "our evangelist, Guadagnoli, will be soon visiting Castellammare together with his wife. This too will be a blessing to the work in the south... The duplicator that the church now has is being used to send Bible studies, prophecies, hymns and sermons... to the north and the south." (Apostolic Herald, 1951)

In this report he also expresses his vision for the Italian

Apostolic Church: "I want to get the Italians themselves to take up the work and bear as much responsibility as possible. I believe that our duty, as foreign missionaries, is to get the local people themselves to take on the work of the Lord; themselves to bear the burden to the measure that they are able." (Apostolic Herald, 1951)

In an interview with the Missionary Board at the Penygroes Convention in August 1954, Pastor Thomas informed the Committee that there were now at least 1,500 members in the Italian Apostolic Church. There were forty-one assemblies with 1,100 members in the Grosseto Region; nine assemblies with 340 members in the Castellammare Region and one assembly at Syracuse in Sicily with 15 members. (Williams, D. , 2006)

Pastor Thomas Turnbull, the chairman of the Mission Board visited Italy in September 1955 and found that Pentecostal believers were still experiencing persecution. However, Pastor Thomas had received some advice from the British Embassy in Rome about a possible way of improving the situation. He was advised to write a short history of the Apostolic work in Italy, including details of administrative and financial procedures and submit it to the Embassy. The Embassy in turn would then take the matter up with the Italian authorities, to arrange for a letter to be sent to the police in the districts concerned, asking them not to interfere with the Apostolic churches there. (Apostolic Church Missionary Committee Minutes, 1955)

These minutes also indicate that a special committee was to be set up in Italy, including all apostles, prophets and the national evangelist, with a view to looking at the administrative arrangements and forwarding their findings to the UK Missionary Board. Three apostles were to be recognised in Italy and steps taken to register all the buildings under the name of the church. Pastor Thomas, who had already ministered to Pentecostals groups in Switzerland at the end of 1954 and at the beginning of 1955, was now to go to Lugano to minister to Pentecostal Christians there. On his previous visits to Switzerland, he had received financial gifts to further the work in Italy. (Apostolic Church Missionary Committee Minutes, 1955)

One of the final minutes from this Board meeting states: "We feel that the time has come to send another apostle to Italy from the British Isles, with the necessary qualifications to ensure the continued progress of the work, spiritually and administratively." In 1958, Pastor Iorwerth (Teddy) and Ruth Howells and family, were sent to Italy and their first base was Turin in the north.

Pastor Willie Thomas told a fascinating story of what happened prior to the Howells' coming to Turin: "I cannot forget, personally, being alone with the prophet in this great city, when searching for a rented house ready for the coming of Pastor Howells. We were together in a cheap hotel. Shortly after our arrival, and preparing to retire for the night, the Lord spoke powerfully through the prophet assuring me that He was about to fulfil His great purpose which He had already revealed to us in the past concerning the establishment of a vital Apostolic centre in the city. The next day we found a residence for the Pastor and were enabled miraculously to make all the necessary preparations for his coming with the family." (Apostolic Herald, 1961)

As far back as the Apostolic Church Council Meetings in February 1947, the prophecy which revealed the calling of Pastor William Thomas to the apostleship said, "Concerning My servant Thomas, he is not to be in Italy for a long time but I would advise you to send him there for a period of time, until another can be prepared and equipped for that responsibility, then he should return to minister in this land." (Apostolic Church Council Minutes , 1947)

Pastor Thomas and his family moved to Rome in 1956 and the evangelising and pioneering continued.

The Apostolic work in Sicily is of particular note. In 1962 Pastor Thomas writes, "It all began with a prophetic word uttered about ten years ago in our Grosseto Assembly, when the Lord graciously spoke to us of His plan to establish an Apostolic testimony in the island of Sicily." By January 1962, there are eight assemblies on the island and the plan is to launch out into Malta and North Africa. (Apostolic Herald, 1962)

The report mentions a man called Pastor Antonio Arrigucci. I know, from my many trips to minister in Italy in recent years, this man was a much-respected servant of God. His story started in Grosseto many years previously. Pastor Thomas writes, "We thank God for this dear brother, saved many years ago in Grosseto when greatly afflicted with a stuttering tongue, but gloriously delivered when sealed with the Holy Spirit of promise. He is now a faithful apostle of the Lord producing the signs of his apostleship in Sicily."

The report continues with this story of healing from September 1961: "A little girl smitten with tetanus, in great spasm and lockjaw, incapable of speaking, was immediately healed through prayer and laying on of hands. The news soon spread far and wide – to the glory of God." (Apostolic Herald, 1962)

In the early 1960s, Pastor Willie Thomas returned to be President of the Apostolic Church UK

CLOSING YEARS

Willie Thomas retired from ministry in 1974, but the years in Italy were deeply impressed upon his life.

The focus of this chapter has been his years of missionary service in that land. He and his family had proved God through much opposition and many trials. Throughout his ministry he had seen the Lord accomplish much, not only in the churches but also in the lives of many individuals. Many had been saved, many healed and many delivered.

William Thomas established in Italy the God-given ministries of apostle and prophet for the Body of Christ today and, under his ministry, many other Italians were brought into their Christ-given callings in the Church. As Paul birthed Timothy, so Pastor Thomas birthed men like Pastors Ulivagnoli, Arrigucci, Pecorini and many more. He birthed in them the evangelistic and pioneering spirit of Jesus. When he left Italy in 1964, his legacy was a church that possessed an aggressive evangelistic drive.

The Lord had spoken prophetically, many years previously, that Willie Thomas would not finish his ministry in Italy. This reminds me of what Paul says in 1Corinthians 3:6, *I planted, Apollos watered, but God was causing the growth.* Perhaps, one of the greatest things that Pastor Thomas left was a work with a solid foundation upon which someone else could further build and develop. And that is exactly what happened when Pastor Teddy Howells took charge of the work when Pastor Thomas returned to the UK.

Today in Italy there are 123 Apostolic churches with over 9,000 members, plus 57 associated churches with a further 9,500 members. The Italian church is missions orientated, reaching out with the Gospel into Albania, Benin, Togo, Equador, Peru, Bolivia and Romania. The Apostolic Church in Italy today is testament to what William Thomas, with many Italian men and women alongside him, planted in those early days. In his retirement he went back there to minister often. His daughter, Violetta, writes, "His heart was still in Italy."

William Thomas died on 6th February 1993, at the age of eighty-three. Violetta said this of her father, "He didn't want to be a social success. He just wanted to do his best for the Lord and to prepare others to work for God." Surely he fulfilled that ambition.

CHAPTER ELEVEN
CYRIL ROSSER

"I thank Christ Jesus our Lord, who has strengthened me, because He considered me faithful, putting me into service, even though I was formerly a blasphemer and a persecutor and a violent aggressor. Yet I was shown mercy..."
1Timothy 1:12-13

EARLY LIFE AND CONVERSION

Cyril Rosser was born in 1900, one of four children born to George and Louisa Rosser, who lived in Windsor Road, Neath, in South Wales. He attended the Alderman Davies School in the town and was described as a "mischievous little boy". His father, an alcoholic, died in the First World War in 1915. Cyril left school at fourteen years of age to become an errand boy for a local grocery store in the town. No doubt, his wages helped the family after his father's death. In time, Louisa married again. Her second husband was Alfred Taylor and she had a further two children.

At the age of seventeen Cyril joined the army, lying about his age, and was posted to the front. God's hand of protection was on him, because the story is told of how, on one occasion, he left his colleagues in the trenches to fetch more ammunition. When he returned, they were all dead. After the war he went to work at the local oil refinery and played rugby for the works' team. One of those who opposed him on the rugby field, a Mr. Dick Bufton, described him in this way: "Cyril was a very tough and rough customer." (The Neath Guardian, 1965)

Cyril Rosser married Ida Moses and, in May 1926, Ida persuaded him to attend a service at the Forward Movement Mission Hall, in Neath. This Mission was pioneered by the Joshua brothers, of Welsh Revival fame. According to Geraint Fielder, a Welsh missionary and broadcaster, in the early years of the twentieth century this Mission Hall was probably the most successful evangelistic church in Wales. (Fielder, 2000)

Cyril Rosser describes what happened when he visited this Mission: "I was persuaded by my wife one day to attend a place of worship. More out of a desire to please her than from any other motive, I accompanied her. But, after having entered the church, I became aware of a sense of an unseen presence... That night the preacher proposed to deal with faith, and in addresses to follow on the two succeeding Sundays, with hope and charity respectively... I celebrated my third attendance at the church by inducing my dear mother to come with my wife and me."

On his third visit to the Mission not only did Cyril experience conversion but so did his wife and mother. He writes, "Charity was, of course, the subject with which the minister dealt, and, such an able discourse did he give upon it and such was the power of the Spirit in the service, that I was deeply convicted. An intolerable consciousness of my guilt dawned upon me. I became aware that I was a sinner. 'Give God a chance', said the minister. The expression appealed to my sporting instincts. I resolved that I would give Him an opportunity to help me and so, when the invitation was given for anyone who desired to signify their acceptance of Christ by coming to the penitent form, I rose and went forward. To my amazement, my wife and mother followed me. They had evidently been waiting for me to take the lead." (Apostolic Herald, 1934)

Recalling this experience, he wrote, "I cannot say that on that occasion I was conscious of any change. Emotionally I experienced nothing, although I had faith to believe that I was converted. This did not satisfy me, however. I wanted the confirmation of my feelings. Consequently, I attended the prayer meeting on the evening following, with this in mind. I was not disappointed. The realisation came to me as I was on my knees. I shouted and sang for joy. And meditating on the experience of the night before, I reflected that I had not sworn since my conversion on the previous night. This, for me, was something of a triumph, accustomed, as I had been, to blaspheme so continually. That made the matter beyond all doubt. I was really and truly regenerated – born again by the Spirit of God." (Apostolic Herald, 1934)

Cyril Rosser's sister, Winifred, was converted in September of the same year. She married Fred Poole, who later became an apostle in the Apostolic Church and pioneered in North America.

Meanwhile, Cyril started to testify to his work colleagues. They were very sceptical, but something happened in the work place that did convince them of the change in Cyril's life. In the *Apostolic Herald,* November 1934, there is an article headed, *Blasphemer Becomes a Believer. How God Laid His Hand Upon Me For The Nigerian Mission Field*, by Pastor Cyril Rosser. In it he recounts, "One day, however, an opportunity arrived for the truth of my statements to be demonstrated. A piece of iron weighing a considerable amount fell on my foot. The men who were standing by expected to hear a profane ejaculation. They did not, and presently, one of their number walked up to me and, patting me on the back, exclaimed, 'Cyril, old boy, I'll believe now what you said to me a few days ago about you being converted.'" (Rosser, 1934)

In the article he describes the life he had been living: "Before I came to know the Lord I was an open sinner. I frequented public houses and gambling dens, and was notorious for my use of unclean language. Hardly six words could I utter without inserting one of those abominable expletives, and all my conversation was punctuated with oaths and blasphemies. Indeed, so far did I carry my impiety that, on one or two occasions, I publicly avowed my atheism, blasphemously calling upon God (if there was one) to demonstrate His existence by striking me down dead." (Rosser, 1934)

CHURCH LEADERSHIP IN RESOLVEN

Cyril Rosser explains how, just four months later in September 1926, he, Fred Poole and a Mr. Johnny Jones began to minister in a village about seven miles from Neath: "We went to take charge of a little church in Resolven. Only about five or six attended this place. The work was difficult. We commenced to visit homes. Oddly enough, the man who opened the door of the first house at which I called was an African. And, still more strange, the first convert that we had in that little assembly was a negro[19] boy. In the light of what has since transpired, these circumstances become remarkable. Truly it is wonderful how, when rightly understood, the smallest details of our lives appear prophetic." (Rosser, 1934)

Fred Poole tells an interesting story from those days in Resolven: "Many were the experiences we had at that place. With another brother I took a hand-bell to wake up the sleepers in Zion. As I rang the bell my friend shouted 'Fire!' You should have seen the people come out of their houses. 'Mr. Jones, where is the fire?'

---

19   This word was not considered offensive in the first half of the twentieth century

He replied 'In Hell, fire in Hell!' I'll never forget that Sunday."
(Apostolic Church Convention Report, 1940)

It was through an American preacher that Cyril heard about the necessity of water baptism and the gifts of the Holy Spirit. This preacher was visiting the Neath area and taught for three days from I Corinthians 12 and 14, on the gifts of the Holy Spirit. "Oh, I thought, if only there were such a church today as Paul describes in these chapters! I was soon to discover that there was." (Rosser, 1934)

THE ROSSERS AND THE APOSTOLIC CHURCH

Cyril Rosser was invited by a friend to the Apostolic Church in Skewen. He visited the assembly a number of times, but not as much as he would have liked because there was opposition from his family. Fred Poole, his brother-in-law, in his testimony at the 1940 Penygroes Convention, openly acknowledged that at that time he was opposed to the Apostolic Church and preached against its teachings.

When Ida agreed to go with him to the Skewen assembly for the first time, Cyril prayed that "there would be no manifestations or anything that would be likely to prejudice her against the service." His prayer was not answered and to his surprise, his wife was not put off by the moving of the Holy Spirit in the service. Pastors D.P. Williams and J. Omri Jones were based in the Skewen Assembly at that time.

Cyril recalls, "On the next evening, accordingly, we returned. This time the prophet was present, and during the course of the meeting the Lord commenced to speak. He intimated His intention to call an overseer for a local church. Naturally I was curious to know who the new shepherd was to be, and what a surprise when I heard my own name mentioned! On reaching home, I began to seek confirmation in the written Word. I was as yet not completely convinced of the authority of the prophetic utterance. The first passage to which I was directed was in Deuteronomy chapter 28. It read, *And all these blessings shall come upon thee and overtake thee, if thou shalt hearken unto the voice of the Lord thy God.* After such unquestionable reassurance it was impossible not to accept the call, and I was thereupon anointed as the overseer of the Neath Assembly." (Rosser, 1934)

The truth is, the Neath Assembly did not even exist at that point in time! In the meantime Cyril Rosser became a member of Skewen Apostolic Church in January 1928 and was filled with the Spirit in February of that year. (Apostolic Herald, 1936)

In the *Souvenir Exhibiting the Movements of God in the Apostolic Church*, published in 1933, Pastor Rosser wrote this: "It was at Salem, Skewen, that the Lord began to speak concerning Neath, and a people He had there. Although Salem was pregnant with the Eternal Word for three or four years, even to the calling of a shepherd without a flock, it was not until March 1928, that the Lord said, 'Go!' unto five members, and He gave birth to His Church in Neath, calling it 'Carmel,' a place where the fire would fall, as it has on numerous occasions." (Rosser, 1933)

Pastor D.P. Williams completes the picture for us with these comments at the Rossers' 1934 farewell service from Neath: "God had spoken years ago in Skewen, promising that an assembly should be opened in the town of Neath, and in a later word the Lord said He had His hand on a young man in the valley. Brother Rosser was at that time serving the Lord in a Mission Hall at Resolven, and had no knowledge of the Apostolic Church. Through the instrumentality of one of his workmates he was invited to the Apostolic meetings and in a very short time God spoke and said that the time had come, that this young man was His choice, called to be an overseer in the town of Neath – a shepherd without a flock. But the Lord had promised that He would gather a flock." (Apostolic Herald, 1934) And God did gather a flock in Neath!

THE NEATH ASSEMBLY

The Apostolic Church in Neath was called "Carmel", and was situated in Queen Street. It was opened in March 1928. Cyril Rosser wrote this about the early days in Neath: "At first the opposition was tremendous. My most intimate friends were the most bitter in their antagonism. Eventually, however, a prophecy was given in the church to the effect that, within three months, our most inimical opponent would come and affiliate himself with us. And, sure enough, three months later our most belligerent detractor came to our service one day and made a public apology for his uncharitable attitude towards us! He is now an energetic Apostolic." (Apostolic Herald, 1934)

A 1931 report gives this update on Neath: "The Assembly here, under the charge of Overseer C.H. Rosser, is growing and flourishing. Recently, three souls, one a Roman Catholic, accepted the Lord as their only Saviour, and a wanderer returned to His Father and home." (Apostolic Herald, 1931) The following year the headline read, *Revival Outbreak at Neath, South Wales*. The Second Evangelistic Band had held a five-week mission in Neath and eighty-one people had committed their lives to Christ and thirty had been baptised in the Holy Spirit. (Apostolic Herald, 1932)

It was during this campaign that Fred Poole, Rosser's brother-in-law, had a defining experience. After being twice rejected for the London City Mission (the famous Dr. Martyn Lloyd Jones had examined him prior to one of his interviews), Poole wrote, "Alone, in the secret, in my own bedroom, one Sunday morning in February 1932... I cried unto the Lord... God spoke to me and said, 'Go, to the Apostolic Church.' I said, 'Lord, I do not believe this prophecy business is from you; but if it is, will you speak to me by name this morning. I will go to the Apostolic Church." (Apostolic Church Convention Report, 1940)

And that is what happened. He went to the service and a local prophetic channel spoke and Fred Poole was called by name. "If I had typed out my prayer and given it to the prophet and said, 'Prophesy that!' it could not have been more accurate," Poole confirmed. Another report describes the incident: "A young man (Fred Poole), not an Apostolic, attended a Sunday morning service. The brother, up against the wall, so to speak, not knowing what step to take, prayed before going to the meeting and asked the Lord to call him by name in that meeting as proof that the Lord desired him to follow in this way. When he came to the meeting, the Lord did so... The brother responded and received the right-hand of fellowship. The reality of the incident impressed all, and the condescension of God brought the assembly into tears. Until now this brother has been a local preacher, and had charge of a Mission." (Apostolic Herald, 1932)

Cyril Rosser was recognised as a pastor in 1932 and called as an apostle at the Christmas Convention of the same year. However, at the Neath Easter Convention the following year, this prophetic word was received: "I have given you one apostle; I have another that I am preparing; and he shall go to another nation." That "another" was Fred Poole and in 1940, he and his family left for North America.

By 1933, the Neath church had planted an assembly in Glynneath, about eleven miles away and a house meeting had started in Resolven. (Rosser, 1933) In April of that year, Pastor Andrew Turnbull visited the Neath Assembly. During a week of services, "over twenty saints stood up to testify of the blessings received, for the Lord's saving and healing hand had extended in power during the week of the Pastor's stay." (Apostolic Herald, 1933)

CALLED TO NIGERIA

In March 1934, the Apostolic Church Council decided on a number of overseas moves. Pastor Noah Evans, based in France, was to be sent to Calabar, East Nigeria, and Pastor and Mrs. Rosser were also to go to Nigeria, but no town or region was specified. The Rossers had been particularly challenged about missionary service when Miss Pedersen and Mrs. Berg, Apostolic missionaries to China, had been on furlough in the UK in 1931.

Cyril wrote, "My wife and I were profoundly affected by their testimonies and felt that we had done so little for the Lord. We attended the great International Convention later that year and there, under the ministry of the spoken and the written Word, we surrendered our lives to God. One night we made a mutual agreement to dedicate ourselves to missionary work. China was the field of service that we had particularly in mind. The Lord, however, has decided otherwise, and we gladly submit to His direction." (Apostolic Herald, 1934)

Speaking of this call to Nigeria he said, "In my heart of hearts I had no call for Nigeria, but God's voice called me to go, and I gave Him implicit faith and obedience. But I found the call of God to me right in the heart of Nigeria, as a consequence of following." (Weeks, 2003)

THE APOSTOLIC CHURCH AND NIGERIA

One of the key events in the opening of the Apostolic work in Nigeria hinged on a prophetic word. It was a word concerning a letter that D.P. Williams was to receive (previously mentioned in Chapter 9). Gordon Weeks describes what happened: "A letter from South America saying that the 'work had gone to nothing' caused Pastor D.P. Williams many tears in a prayer meeting in Skewen, but through Pastor J.O. Jones a word of prophecy told him: 'Wipe your tears, My servant, for in three days you will receive another letter that will open the fields beyond your comprehension.'" (Weeks, 2003)

A letter did arrive in three days and it came from a Pastor D.O. Odubanjo of the Faith Tabernacle Congregation, Lagos, Nigeria. From Lagos to Skewen is a distance of over 4,500 miles. How long would a letter take in 1930 to travel that far? Certainly more than three days.

How did Pastor D.O. Odubanjo, in Nigeria, even know about the Apostolic Church in Wales? At this time, Nigeria had been experiencing a mighty revival which had stirred up opposition and persecution against the leaders. In these difficult circumstances, the Faith Tabernacle Congregation in Lagos asked for help from their partnership group in the USA. Help was refused.

Gordon Weeks continues the story: "So the leaders decided to seek missionaries from the UK.. just at this point a copy of the Apostolic magazine, *Riches of Grace,* was handed to Pastor D.O. Odubanjo. A Welshman, Mr. Silas Williams, who worked as a hairdresser in a Lagos hotel (his mother and sister attended the Apostolic Church, Swansea and had sent him the literature) passed the magazine on to a Nigerian friend and it eventually reached Pastor Odubanjo." (Weeks, 2003)

Pastors Dan and Jones Williams, with Pastor Andrew Turnbull, sailed for Nigeria on Wednesday 9th September 1931. A group of seventy Apostolics from various parts of Wales and England were on the quayside to wave the pastors off. Their ship, the RMS "Adda", arrived in Lagos two weeks later, to a very enthusiastic welcome.

The group toured different parts of Nigeria and, wherever they visited, congregations were large and the Lord manifested His presence with signs and wonders and the salvation of many people. Before the pastors returned to the UK in November, the Faith Tabernacle Church grouping in Nigeria, with fourteen thousand members, joined the Apostolic Church in Wales.

At the Apostles' and Prophets' Council in January 1932, one item on the agenda was the appeal from Nigeria for a resident missionary or missionaries. The Nigerian church had also detailed the kind of man they required: "We, as Africans, need a man from you, full of the Holy Ghost, a gentleman, cheerful, sympathetic, unassuming, level-headed, law abiding, non-fanatic, and lowly in nature like yourselves, a spiritually-devoted and elderly-mannered man with a thorough education, a graduate if possible, a good revivalist, a good speaker and preacher, and one that makes himself accessible to all people making no difference in his treatment on account of colour, absolute faith in divine healing without the use of medicine, modesty, not given to wine and filthy lucre, not a striker, not given to lustful immorality. Such are the qualifications of the man suitable for our need as Africans." (Adeboyega, 1978)

In response to this appeal, the first Apostolic missionaries sent to Nigeria were George Perfect, an apostle, and Idris Vaughan, a prophet. They arrived in Lagos on 2nd June 1932. They went with this prophetic promise ringing in their ears; "I will be more to them in that land than I have been to them in this."

George Perfect was fifty-three years of age and he left his wife and family behind in Scotland. He did two tours of duty in Nigeria: June 1932 - May 1935 and November 1936 - December 1938. The Nigerians said this about him, "He is a man like Jesus." What higher commendation can anyone receive?

Idris Vaughan was thirty one years of age. His wife had died at the end of 1931 and he left his two young sons in the care of relatives. He had been pioneering in Ireland since 1922 and went on to serve in Nigeria until 1945.

Pastor S.G. Adegboyega, in his book, *Short History of the Apostolic Church in Nigeria*, wrote this about the influence of these two men: "They taught us sound doctrinal truths from the written Word of God. They expounded to our understanding and acceptance the mysteries of the Word of God concerning the Body of Christ... Frankly speaking and without controversy, the present Pentecostal movements... in our country today (the book was written in 1978) could be safely attributed to the advent of the Apostolic Church missionaries from the United Kingdom who rendered sacrificial and selfless services for the promotion and growth of the Christian work in Nigeria." (Adeboyega, 1978)

Pastor Adeboyega had been one of the leaders of the Faith Tabernacle Church. He became an apostle in the Nigerian Apostolic Church and gave great support to Pastor and Mrs. Rosser during their years in the country.

The reports from Nigeria, prior to Pastors Perfect and Vaughan arriving, spoke of a church continuing to know revival. In fact, Nigeria had been experiencing revival "winds" since 1916. This is what Pastors Dan and Jones Williams and Andrew Turnbull experienced on their visit. By the time George Perfect and Idris Vaughan arrived, Apostolic Church membership had risen to fifteen thousand people. (Apostolic Herald, 1932)

The two pastors were based in Lagos and travelled around the churches. In a series of articles headed, *The Nigerian Revival*, George Perfect explains that the truth which they brought to Nigeria was "the good news of the promise of the Spirit." Having read these articles and the accounts of revival which they contain, I have no hesitation in saying that what they were experiencing was the Acts of the Apostles all over again, or, as Perfect said, "A better title would be 'the Acts of the Holy Spirit'. According to the promise of God's Word, *all* were being filled with the Holy Spirit.

ARRIVAL IN NIGERIA

Cyril and Ida Rosser were the first Apostolic missionaries to go as a couple to Africa. They arrived in Lagos on 29th November 1934. "They were met by Pastor Perfect and two black brethren. After that they were escorted to their new home in the town of Ebute Metta. There they were awaited by forty sisters who accosted them with shouts of 'Welcome, Sir!' and 'Welcome, Ma'am!'" (Apostolic Herald, 1935)

After a period of overlap, with George Perfect remaining until May 1935, Cyril Rosser became the superintendent minister of the work in Nigeria. His colleagues in the work were Pastor Noah Evans, who had arrived in June 1934, and Idris Vaughan, who returned from furlough in July 1935. The Rossers set about getting to know the country and the people of Nigeria. Nigeria is four times the size of Great Britain and at that time there was no missionary car available. It was necessary, therefore, to travel long distances by bicycle, lorry, train, boat or on foot.

In early 1935, this report was sent home: "At present we are at Creektown, having arrived at Calabar a week ago... Pastor Evans, Mrs. Rosser and I made the voyage in a small motor launch and arrived safely at Creektown. What a reception the people gave us! Five hundred of them marched to meet us, lining both sides of the road... The next item of interest was a trek to Ibonda. This is a place some four miles distant, and the journey there was our first experience of a tramp through a tropical forest... Mrs. Rosser had a new experience, that of riding in a rickshaw... After one and a half hours plodding through the bush we reached our destination." (Apostolic Herald, 1935)

The purpose of this trip into the forest was to further establish a church group that had come together despite the superstition, ju-

ju worship and witchcraft which were prevalent in the area. They did not leave Ibonda till very late: "We did not begin to make tracks home until night had fallen. It was pitch dark and our company was preceded by lanterns. We were about a hundred in number, and as we marched along we made the forest ring with our shouts and songs... At 9.30p.m. we arrived back in Creektown, tired but happy."

The report continues: "On Monday, January 28th, at 4 o'clock in the morning, we set out, accompanied by about 50 members of the Creektown church, on a tour of the outlying mission stations. Our party must have cut an amusing figure. Pastor Evans and I were mounted on bicycles and Mrs. Rosser was again in her rickshaw." (Apostolic Herald, 1935)

What a contrast to two months previously, when they had been surrounded by all the sights and sounds of London! (Apostolic Herald, 1935)

The following month, Cyril and Ida Rosser, accompanied by Noah Evans, journeyed to the north of the country. They spent a week with a group of one hundred and fifty believers in Ekot Ekpene. The outcome was that this group joined the Apostolic Church and prophetical ministry indicated that there were great things in store for them.

Pastor Rosser describes God's provision for their onward journey: "We advanced towards the town of Aba, but discovered, on investigation, that we did not have sufficient money to pay the cost of a motor lorry to transport us there. Accordingly, without mentioning the circumstances to anyone, we applied to God for the necessary amount, in prayer and, presently, to our joy, the leader of the new assembly, approached us and volunteered to provide a vehicle suitable for our conveyance." The report further informs us that on this mission trip they visited an area that was known for cannibalism; a local chief offered land to build a church; the weather was very hot and they experienced hot winds that made their throats dry; they encountered a terrifying insect and they ministered in an area that was predominately Muslim. (Apostolic Herald, 1935)

Gordon Weeks provides some indication of the progress that was being made: "In Nigeria two thousand seven hundred believers attended the Easter Convention in Ilesha and on 17th May (1935) a new church building, with seating for six hundred people, was opened in Ebute Metta, Lagos." (Weeks, 2003) The expansion of the work was rapid, and Cyril Rosser later commented, "One of the greatest difficulties of our work in Nigeria is for us... to keep pace with the work the Spirit is doing. He goes too fast for us." (Herald of Grace, 1940)

Rosser was also proving God in his personal experience. He had a hearing defect for many years and had prayed for healing, but nothing changed. In fact, the deafness seemed to get worse in the heat of Nigeria: "He was lying in his bed one morning, reading his mail from the homeland, when, suddenly, he heard what he imagined to be a loud report in his right ear... He thought something had fallen outside, but after investigating, found nothing there. To his astonishment that morning, however, he discovered that he was able to hear the very smallest sounds." (Apostolic Herald, 1935)

In July 1935, Pastors Rosser and Vaughan held a revival campaign in Lagos. This campaign was preceded by weeks of prayer. Rosser saw Lagos as a Gospel-hardened city, like many he knew in the UK He was also aware of the low level of spiritual life in the Lagos church. The church spent time in prayer and the results were evident: "Souls were saved every evening (at least 100); many were healed of diseases; and a large number were saturated with the divine power of the Holy Spirit." (Apostolic Herald, 1935)

Everything was moving forward and the Lord was directing them prophetically to evangelise in the principal towns. The twin ministries of apostle and prophet were working together to further the Gospel and the Apostolic vision in Nigeria.

Cyril Rosser was taking steps to draw the Nigerian Apostolic Church together. The first Nigerian apostles had been recognised in 1933. At the same time, Pastor I.G. Sakpo, was ordained as a prophet. With Rosser as superintendent, the calling and recognition of Nigerian leaders continued. None of the money collected in Nigeria was sent to the UK because it was determined that the tithes and offerings taken in the assemblies would be used to pay the full-time African ministers and workers.

Pastor Rosser was given a car, which helped greatly with the travelling. On one occasion he had to rush two hundred miles to the Ilesha area: "A violent persecution had broken out and several members of the church had been arraigned before the local magistrates... to give an explanation of their having started an open-air meeting." On arriving he found that one of the church members had been publicly flogged. When Pastor Rosser arrived, this man simply said, "I was glad to suffer for Jesus." (Apostolic Herald, 1935)

In 1936, a National Nigerian Council was held to review the administrative arrangements. The work in Nigeria was expanding rapidly and, through prophetic guidance from Pastor Noah Evans, it was decided to reorganise the work in Nigeria. Whereas everything had been centred in Lagos, there were now to be four areas: Lagos, Ilesha, Calabar and Zaria. Each area would have a European missionary as superintendent and these superintendents would be in direct contact with the Missionary Board in the UK The Missionary Board was asked to send men to fill these area roles.

During that year Pastor Rosser had suffered ill-health and, in November 1936, he and Ida came back to Britain on leave. Pastors George Perfect and Robert Kay went out to Nigeria in the same month. The Wellings family had left earlier in the year to replace the Rossers temporarily. Idris Vaughan was home on furlough the following year and reported that there were now one hundred and eighty five assemblies in the North and West of Nigeria and in Eastern Nigeria there were seventeen thousand members in one hundred and sixty-six assemblies. (Weeks, 2003)

SECOND JOURNEY TO NIGERIA

Pastor William Taylor, a missionary in northern Nigeria, died from dysentery on 1st July 1938 in Kaduna. He was the first Apostolic missionary to die in Africa. After spending some time in the UK, based in the Hereford district, the Rossers set off on their return to Nigeria in October of that year. They went back to this new administrative structure. Cyril Rosser was returning to replace George Perfect as the superintendent of the Lagos Area and the President of the Nigerian Council.

Prior to the Rossers' return, serious animosity and ill-feeling had arisen between Pastor D.O. Odubanjo and George Perfect. This was in respect to church monetary affairs. However, T.N. Turnbull identifies polygamy as the major issue. (T.N.Turnbull, 1959) Weeks, on the other hand, states that the issue that really came to a head was the "no medicine" policy. (Weeks, 2003) Many Nigerian believers considered it sinful to take medicines of any kind. (James McKeown encountered the same issue in the Gold Coast. See Chapter 6)

Rosser writes, "In 1932, when Pastors G. Perfect and I. Vaughan arrived in Nigeria they told Pastors Odubanjo and Adeboyega, in confidence, that they would not use medicine while living in West Africa, but they stated that they intended to take quinine with their food to protect them from malaria. The Nigerian pastors agreed to this and this was not disclosed to any other pastor or to the Church until the conflicts in this year." (Weeks, 2003)

Pastor Odubanjo, because of his personal difficulties with Pastor Perfect, disclosed to his Nigerian colleagues that the European missionaries were using medicine, and so it spread across the Nigerian Church. The "no medicine" policy had been a key belief in the Faith Tabernacle Movement and it had been carried over into the Apostolic Church in Nigeria.

There was correspondence between The Nigerian Council and the UK Missionary Board and various meetings took place, with some leaders taking the position that all European missionaries should leave the country. Despite the efforts of Rosser and others, the issue rumbled on without resolution. In April 1940, he wrote to the Lagos presbytery saying, "Dear Brethren, I have patiently borne the ungentlemanly and unchristian attitude of Pastor Odubanjo and the Lagos Assembly (excluding the elders), believing that matters might be adjusted, but the longer I wait, the more evident it becomes, that Pastor Odubanjo has no intention of mending matters... I feel the time has come when I should obey the Scripture's injunction according to Matt. 10:14, *Where people will not receive nor hear you, shake the dust from off thy feet.*" (Weeks, 2003)

In consequence, over one hundred churches broke away and the Apostolic Church was left with only five assemblies in the Lagos Area. Assemblies also broke away in other parts of the country, but the Lagos Area was the hardest hit. It was in no small measure due the labours of Pastors Rosser, Adeboyega and Sakpo that the Apostolic work on the western side of Nigeria was not only saved, but began to grow again to the glory of God.

After two years' service in Nigeria, the Rossers were due home on a six month furlough in 1940, but they asked for this to be postponed. Pastors Vaughan and Evans had been transferred to the Calabar Area, which meant that Cyril and Ida Rosser were the only missionaries remaining in the Lagos Area. They found themselves once again without a car, because of heavy financial demands on the Missionary Fund. In fact, they did not arrive back in the UK until June 1943, having then been away for four years and eight months. On their return, the Missionary Board drafted a minute to the effect that they were to be given time to rest and recuperate from the rigours of living so long in a tropical climate and they were not, for the time being, to undertake any ministerial activity.

With the strong support of the Nigerian pastors, a remarkable work had been achieved in the three and a half years since the split in 1940. By 1943 the Lagos Area was divided into four districts, comprising forty-five assemblies.

THIRD JOURNEY TO NIGERIA

It was still wartime and, from May 1944, the British Government had imposed overseas travel restrictions, making it difficult to find berths on ships. Writing in the May 1945 *Herald of Grace*, Pastor Rosser gave this background regarding his return to Nigeria: "A strong conviction possessed me that, if we were prepared to travel separately, we should get away much sooner. We both weighed the project and counted the cost. My wife's reply was, 'If it is the quickest way it is the best way.' So I passed on our suggestion to the Missionary Secretary. Within a short time I got a telegram offering me to sail alone." (Herald of Grace, 1945)

When Rosser arrived in Lagos, Pastor Adegboyega greeted him with these words: "Our joy is only half full; it will not really be full until Mrs. Rosser arrives." She was offered a passage from the UK the day after Cyril left. Once back in the Lagos Area, Pastor Rosser found the evangelistic fervour still alive and strong and the work had held together very well. He paid this tribute to the Nigerian leaders: "It is a compliment to the untiring efforts of the native brethren left in charge, who have acquitted themselves admirably. With deep gratitude and humility I say quite frankly, we could not have done better." (Herald of Grace, 1945)

There were several administrative tasks that Pastor Rosser was to undertake on this tour of service: the national structure of the Apostolic Church was to be reduced from four areas to two; some operating principals for church government were to be introduced; a schools policy was to be implemented in the Lagos Area; land was to be purchased for a house in Ebute Metta; and training was to be organised for Nigerian leaders. Behind these changes was the desire of the UK Missionary Board that the Nigerians should grow in their callings and experience the challenges of leading in their own country. These were the preparatory steps toward autonomy.

By 1945, there were sixty-two churches with 3000 members in the Lagos Area. Pastor Rosser wrote, "Our policy has always been to adhere to truth, especially the truth of the vision that has been given us as Apostolic brethren. Even when the threat of a breakaway was hanging over our heads, such as no other area has yet experienced, we, along with some of our loyal and faithful brethren here (Pastor S. Adegboyega being worthy of special mention in this connection) held fast to the principles of truth, and truth has, as it always will, prevailed. Having since then regained many of the lost assemblies, we are establishing new ones in four out of the five districts within the Lagos Area." (Apostolic Church Missionary Report, 1946)

When the split happened, the Apostolic Church lost their only church in the city of Lagos, while holding on to others in the wider Lagos Area. Although Ebute Metta is only three miles away from Lagos, the Apostolic Church did not have a witness in the capital city. Pastor Rosser wrote, "Ever since the Lagos Assembly broke away from us in 1940, through false ideas and control that we could not and would not tolerate, I have prayed that God would give us an entry into the capital again." He had been invited to meet a group of twenty people in Lagos and, afterwards, they decided to come under Apostolic cover. Within a week, an open-air campaign was held in Lagos, which saw thirty people converted. There was also news of two further churches opening in the Ebute Metta district.

A Bible school was set up in Ebute Metta to train leaders for the growing number of churches that were being established in the Lagos Area. Pastor Rosser was the main lecturer and people from the UK supplied books. In addition, a schools' policy was set up and a Nigerian National Executive had been formed. These were all important steps toward the attainment of the goals that had been set.

During this third tour of service in Nigeria, Ida suffered from time to time with health problems. By April 1947, they were back in the UK for a well-deserved furlough.

FURTHER SERVICE IN NIGERIA

The Rossers returned to their work in Nigeria in October 1947. However, this tour of service was brought to a conclusion when Cyril Rosser tendered his resignation from the Nigerian Field in August 1948, due to some disagreements that had arisen between him and the Missionary Board. Pastor and Mrs. Rosser returned to Britain and he became Apostolic pastor in the Aberdare District.

The one positive thing that came out of this tour of missionary service was that Pastor Adegboyega became the first African superintendent of the Apostolic Church in the Lagos Area. He was a very able man and had worked closely with Pastor Rosser, proving himself a faithful and loyal man of God.

Cyril Rosser was called to return yet again to Nigeria in May 1953 to handle the fall-out from the divisions resulting from the Latter Rain Movement in the Gold Coast and Nigeria, which were mentioned in Chapter 6. He was accompanied by Pastor Vivian Wellings, also a past missionary in Nigeria. Ida joined him a few months later but by the July the pastors had moved over to the Gold Coast, on the instructions of the UK Missionary Committee.

In the Gold Coast, the superintendent of the work, Pastor James McKeown, had resigned and set up a new denomination, taking many Apostolic churches and members with him. The only UK representative that was left was Pastor Albert Seaborne. Pastors Rosser, Seaborne and Wellings had the task of securing the properties and the bank accounts of the Apostolic Church in the Gold Coast. Some of the African leaders stood with them, including Pastor David Tenobi.

Pastor Rosser, Pastor David Tenobi and others, had meetings with James McKeown and the breakaway group, but nothing was resolved. Court cases ensued and Rosser was asked to remain in the Gold Coast for six months.

Meanwhile, in Nigeria, the Ilesha Area of the work had lost four UK staff members to the Latter Rain. One of these did return to the Apostolic Church in July 1954 and proved a great strength to Pastor Rosser as he sought to re-establish the western side of the work in Nigeria. Pastor and Mrs. Rosser came back to Lagos in March 1954, and then moved to Ilesha and lived on the church compound there.

The Ilesha area was an important part of the Apostolic work in Nigeria. There was a Bible school, an educational training college, some domestic training schools and a school system in place. Pastor Rosser was familiar with this area from 1947, when he went there for a time as a relief superintendent. A power struggle ensued for

Pastor Rosser to take back control of the Ilesha and Zaria areas of the work. There was at least one forced expulsion from a church house and letters had to be drafted to the Government, informing them of changes. UK missionaries, who were in Nigeria at the time, reported that Pastor Rosser was a very weary man and near to collapse. However, certain African pastors had taken a stand against the rebellion, and, by July 1954, the report was that the Ilesha and Zaria areas had returned to the cover of the Apostolic Church.

When the Rossers came home in March 1955, the schools work was still in place, as well as the training college and the Bible school. Pastor Rosser had been ill at times during this tour and he had faced severe challenges, but he had proved God's faithfulness in holding together the work in the Gold Coast and in western Nigeria. The Missionary Committee commended him: "We would place on record our appreciation and thanks to Pastor Rosser for his exemplary service on the field during a very critical period."

THE LAST MISSIONARY JOURNEY TOGETHER

The Rossers arrived back in Nigeria in February 1956. The plan was that they would live in Ilesha and then move to Lagos in the October but, by June, both of them were unwell.

On medical advice, they returned to the UK, arriving on 31st December 1956. Pastor Rosser took on the responsibility of the Pontypridd church and later the Neath District. Ida's health continued to deteriorate, but in September 1960 they were accorded a very special honour. They were invited by the Nigerian government to go back for the Nigerian Independence Celebrations and an aeroplane was sent to transport them. This was undoubtedly an indication of the high esteem in which they were both held.

THE DEATH OF IDA ROSSER

Ida Rosser, who was a qualified nurse, had served the Lord faithfully and tirelessly alongside her husband and loved the Nigerian people amongst whom they worked. She led weekly meetings of prayer, worship and Bible study, as well as teaching health and home skills. Over time, the tropical climate and conditions had taken their toll on her health.

She died in January 1962, in hospital in Bridgend, with what we know today as Alzheimer's disease. As Pastor Rosser knelt beside her bed and thanked God for her life and their time together, the nurses were in tears. Mrs. Heulwen Robling, a member of the Neath church wrote, "He held his pastorate with dignity while having to watch Aunty Ida suffer with what we know today as Alzheimer's disease... (When) Aunty Ida passed away... he was broken hearted and grieved deeply for her in private, with tears near the surface." (Robling, 2016)

At a memorial service in February 1962, at Ebute Metta, Pastor Adeboyega gave this tribute to Mrs. Rosser, "She loved our nation! She loved our people! She loved our Church! She loved!" In the eulogy, the congregation of over 500, was reminded of her spiritual counselling; her classes in midwifery; her encouragement in domestic science; her leadership of the deaconesses and, above all, her example, zeal, enthusiasm and her Christianity. In fact, every assembly in the Lagos Area held a memorial service for Ida Rosser on the same day. Over 100,000 would have been present in all these services!

FINAL JOURNEY TO AFRICA

In November 1962 Pastor Rosser set off for Ghana once more, this time to act as relief superintendent while other missionaries were home on furlough. He went also to mediate in some tensions that existed in the Ghanaian church and with some issues with the breakaway group from 1953, now called the Church of Pentecost. On this occasion he travelled with a small group of other Apostolic missionaries and their children.

When he arrived in Ghana he was met by Pastor and Mrs. Johnson and their daughter, Sheena. (The Johnson's also had two other children with them in Ghana.) He wrote, "After sorting and dispatching our baggage we set off for Somanya, the place where we first set foot in 1953 (Pastor Wellings, the late Pastor and Mrs. A Seaborne and I), in the recovery of the work in Ghana." (Apostolic Herald, 1963)

The same edition of the *Apostolic Herald* included this report of the Ghanaian Christmas Convention, December 1962: "Unconventional Convention! 100 Saved at Koforidua... We soon felt the wave of revival in the air... we felt the dew of heaven falling upon us, and felt certain we were going to experience the 'rain' God promised way back in August at Penygroes." (Apostolic Herald, 1963)

There were some encouraging moments for Pastor Rosser during this convention. Firstly, a Ghanaian apostle, who had left the Apostolic Church in 1953 and had recently rejoined was given a tremendous welcome. Secondly, the sight of over five hundred people from the Accra assemblies at the convention made him jump for joy. As he wrote, "I well remember the days, way back in 1953, when we had no members at all at Accra." There were now seven assemblies in the Accra District. Thirdly, by the end of the convention there were over 6,000 people in attendance. Finally, he rejoiced in the fact that "it was not the excellency of preaching, but the power of His presence bringing over one hundred souls to Christ throughout the five days we were gathered in this unconventional Convention." (Apostolic Herald, 1963)

Two thousand people attended the opening of a new church building in a suburb of Accra in January 1963 and a second church building opened elsewhere in the city in the February. The blessings continued and more assemblies and people returned to the Apostolic Church in Ghana.

In September 1963 the headlines read, "Revival Scenes at Asamankese". Pastors Rosser and Perfect had first visited a group of Christians interested in Apostolic teaching in this town in 1935. The group had broken away toward the end of the 1930s but had returned. On this visit in 1963, Pastor Rosser witnessed twenty-three people saved, six filled with the Holy Spirit and twenty-one people healed. He also reported that other towns where the Apostolic Church was first established were showing renewed interest. An evangelistic campaign was running in Ghana with this slogan, "Christ for Ghana, Ghana for Christ."

There was continuing fallout from the breakaway in 1953 and there had been an attempt not only to oust James McKeown from the leadership of the Ghana Apostolic Church but also to deport him from the country. There had been tentative moves towards the Ghana Apostolic Church rejoining the Apostolic Church Ghana. There had been long-running disputes over land and monies between the two groups, with cases being brought to law. It took the intervention of the President of Ghana to bring some semblance of order to the situation. The Ghana Apostolic Church, with James McKeown still its leader, was advised to change its name. It became the Church of Pentecost on 1st August 1962. A procedure was also put in place to resolve disputes over property.

In 1963, UK Apostolic leaders were still open to discussion about reconciliation, with the hope that autonomy for the reunited Ghanaian Church would then follow, but Church of Pentecost leaders were insisting that the Apostolic Church Ghana should join them and this proved a stumbling block. Pastor Rosser and the UK Missionary Board rejected this completely. As a result there were no further attempts at reconciliation and the focus was turned to establishing the Apostolic Church in Ghana on a firm administrative footing: the headquarters were to be in Accra; a Bible school was to be set up; six new Ghanaian apostles were recognised and a National Council of Apostles and Prophets was to be established. Authority was transferred from the UK to that newly inaugurated National Council and the Apostolic Church, Ghana was granted autonomy on 20th June 1964.

At this point Cyril Rosser came home, but he came home an ill man. The National Council of Ghana requested that he return as the principal of their new Bible school, but his failing health would not allow him to take on such a responsibility and he was due to retire in November 1964. By the December, he was in hospital.

THE DEATH OF PASTOR ROSSER

When he came home from Ghana in August 1964, Pastor Rosser went to live in Neath with a couple whom he had married in 1962, Ken and Heulwen Robling. They wrote, "When he made his home with us we got to know this great man even more. He had such love for everyone and filled our home with laughter and joy." In the November, he was diagnosed with a tumour on the spine and a secondary tumour on his chest. For approximately a year, this couple, with the help of others, cared for and watched over him.

The tribute that Ken and Heulwen Robling wrote for this book was headed, *The Man with the Large Heart*. They gave this description of Cyril Rosser: "He was a loving, caring pastor with a big heart and a concern for all... There was no chemotherapy for him, so these were very trying months as he became limited in what he could do, but he would always see the funny side of things and turned his difficulties into jokes. He was courageous through it all, especially when suffering great pain and weakness of body. During this time, he saved diligently for the missionary offering for the Penygroes Convention (1965), but sadly this was not to be..." (Robling, 2016)

Cyril Rosser died on 12th August 1965 and over 700 people attended his funeral. On his death a local newspaper published an article with this heading: *The Apostle to West Africa*. The introduction was as follows: "They sat with their few possessions, their bedding, their cooking pots, water filters, mosquito nets and medicines on the side of the African road waiting for the once daily 'Mammy wagon' to carry them on the next stage of their missionary journey. Already, the morning sun was a hard taskmaster. The man was ill with malaria. The woman, always at his side, was his wife. One minute he suffered almost intolerable heat, the next, he shivered with the chill of his illness. The woman heard the noise first, for the man was slightly deaf. She said with relief, 'The Mammy wagon is coming at last.' He was glad. The perspiration ran from him as if from a tap. He stepped into the road and signalled the lorry... but the Mammy wagon was full and it roared on in a cloud of dust... Wearily, they burdened themselves with their possessions and trudged along the dusty road to the next village... The man and woman were a long way from their home at 10, Windsor Road, Neath. They were Cyril and Ida Rosser, who had dedicated their lives to God and the people of Nigeria." (The Neath Guardian, 1965)

Pastor Adegboyega gave this tribute: "Pastor C.H.G. Rosser was... greatly used of the Lord for the upliftment and development of the Apostolic Church vision in the country. He also went on missionary tour throughout the whole country, teaching, establishing, and comforting the souls of the saints in the Apostolic Church. He was a minister of courage, truth, righteousness and justice... Those of us who had opportunity to work with him would never forget his activities and usefulness for the establishment of our feet in the Apostolic vision. He and his wife had experienced difficulties which they were able to overcome by patience and long-suffering." (Adeboyega, 1978)

Heulwen Robling wrote, "My lasting memory will be the visit of the two African pastors, who attended the convention that year (August 1965) and asked if they could visit. Uncle Cyril was 'lying in state' in our lounge. They came in so quietly, knelt beside his coffin and sobbed and cried, and then suddenly they lifted their faces upwards and started to pray in their native tongue. This got louder and louder until they stood to their feet, laid their hands on the coffin and repeatedly said in English, "Thank you God, thank you God. Thank you for the sacrifice and service of Pastor and Mrs. Rosser for our land." (Robling, 2016)

"O Lord, send faithful men and strong,
Who fight for right against wrong,
To these sin-shadowed, heathen parts,
With comfort for men's aching hearts.

We ask nor health nor wealth. We plead
For men to meet the crying need,
O, may some heart obey Thy call
And boldly come forsaking all;

Surrendering everything for God,
To follow where His feet have trod;
To bear the cross; with grace divine,
His lonely plea not to decline.

T'will be. Our faith anticipates
Thine answer and nought underrates
Thy power. We know Thou hearest our cry,
Dost know the need and wilt supply."

Cyril Rosser (Apostolic Herald, 1935)

CHAPTER TWELVE
OUR RESPONSE

"Now to Him who is able to do far more abundantly beyond all that we ask or think, according to the power that works within us, to Him be the glory in the church and in Christ Jesus to all generations forever and ever. Amen"
Ephesians 3:20-21

In the preface I mentioned a well-known minister to whom God said, "I've seen your ministry, now do you want to see Mine?" I hope that, as you have read the stories of these early Apostolic fathers, you have seen something of God's ministry - how He does church.

As I have been researching and writing this book, what has impressed me particularly is how fast the Holy Spirit can work. The accounts of the UK pioneers, such as Williams, Turnbull and Purnell, bear witness to how swiftly and dynamically the Holy Spirit can move and build churches. The Holy Spirit also worked powerfully and quickly through the early pioneers who went to

Australia and Africa. In Nigeria that momentum continued for years after the initial missionaries had been sent. This encourages us to believe that the Holy Spirit can also move quickly in our day and generation.

In writing this book, I have been fully aware that some are uneasy about looking at the past. However, the truth is that our history is God's story. We cannot simply write a "new" story and forget that we are to continue the story that started on 8th January 1916. Actually, we are to continue the story that God started in the Book of Acts. Surely the early days of the Apostolic Church were a continuation of the story of the Acts of the Apostles?

Philip Greenslade, theologian and teacher, comments, "Nostalgia need not breed inertia but can be a powerful incentive to seek God's favour again." (Greenslade, 2003) As we remember the past we find inspiration and faith to believe God for the future.

Ivor Cullen, writing in the foreword to James Worsfold's book, *The Origins of the Apostolic Church in Great Britain*, presents this view: "Any spiritual movement raised up by God to bring a spirit of revival to His Church and reveal precious lost truths loses its impetus and blessing after two or three generations. The movement not only needs a fresh outpouring of God's Spirit but a reminding of its beginnings and of how God has miraculously revealed Himself at times." (Worsfold J. , 1974)

My purpose in writing this book has been to help us understand afresh why the Apostolic Church came into being; to consider what contribution it has made, through the ministry of the Holy Spirit, to the overall Body of Christ; and to see how Jesus built His Church through the sacrificial and anointed leaders that God gave us.

I think of the example of Israel. Their history became fixed in the hearts of God's people through the feasts and holidays. They were told by God to repeat the stories to their children and their children's children. Their history revealed both the character of the Lord God and His ways. Why should we ignore such guidance for ourselves? For the Apostolic Church, the conventions; the monthly missionary prayer meetings; the ministries of apostle and prophet; the "tarrying" meetings and the ministry of the Bible College were its "feasts and holidays". It was in and through these events and ministries that our DNA was imparted to younger generations. It was here that new generations of young people were filled with the Holy Spirit, received missionary calls and had the opportunity to know and experience the truths that captured their "fathers" and thrust them out on world mission with faith in their hearts.

What should our response be? There might be a place for weeping and repenting before the Lord; for humbling ourselves and confessing and acknowledging that without the Lord, we are nothing, and without a Biblical and Holy Spirit vision that is centred on Jesus, we have nothing that is of any eternal value. I am not part of the "doom brigade", who would seem to suggest that all is bad and getting worse. I believe that, with a renewed focus and a determination of heart, we can discover a way forward that is linked to our original, spiritual DNA.

J.I. Packer makes this observation: "Christian minds have been conformed to the modern spirit: the spirit... that spawns great thoughts of man and leaves room for only small thoughts of God." (Packer, 1973) Let us determine to seek a greater vision of the Lord God of heaven and earth.

I believe that the Apostolic Church was birthed under the work of restoration that the Lord was advancing in His will and purpose for the 20th century. We are a restoration movement. At a National Leadership Meeting in September 2013, the Lord spoke through the late Pastor David Williams and challenged the leaders to re-dig the wells. The theme of the prophecy was total recovery.

The "wells" that the Lord directed the leaders to consider were the baptism of the Holy Spirit; deliverance ministry; "the pioneering spirit of days gone by"; and a Bible-based commitment to the Great Commission of Jesus Christ.

Jesus began His Great Commission with these words: "All authority has been given to me in heaven and on earth..." Apostolic history clearly demonstrates the truth of Jesus' words.

The Great Commission encompasses the whole world, but the streets where we live and the people that we meet from day to day are our first challenge. The tools for this Great Commission are the gifts of the Holy Spirit. The Lord has given us dynamite. We have been promised the Holy Spirit and power.

David Williams' prophecy continued: "God is looking for a total recovery of the New Testament experience of the Acts of the Apostles; a baptism in the Holy Spirit that will challenge people and quicken people and give people purpose to throw them into the front of evangelical work and purpose for God."

I want to finish with this final thought. Many of our existing churches were birthed by some remarkable people – ordinary people who became extraordinary in the hands of God. In writing this book, I have not sought to promote their ways but I have sought to portray their God. I trust that, as you have read the book, a thirst has been created in you to know more and more of the "God of our Fathers".

GOD HAS NOT CHANGED. HE IS STILL IN THE BUSINESS OF BUILDING GREAT PEOPLE FOR HIS GREAT CHURCH.

APPENDIX 1
A CLOUD OF WITNESSES

"Therefore, since we have so great a cloud of witnesses surrounding us, let us also lay aside every encumbrance..."
Hebrews 12:1-2

The book has focused on the lives and ministries of nine early Apostolic men of God, but, if truth be told, there were many others, both men and women, who would have been worthy of a chapter. The Apostolic Church has been blessed with some truly remarkable people.

In this appendix we will consider, in much less detail, some of those other individuals who are part of our one hundred years' story. Some may be relatively unknown, but they are numbered among of the "cloud of witnesses" that God would use to challenge us today to *lay aside every encumbrance and the sin which so easily entangles us, and... run with endurance the race that is set before us...*

HERBERT V. CHANTER

Herbert Chanter was born in Bradford in 1890. He proved to be one of several key men, such as Daniel and Jones Williams, Andrew Turnbull and Frank Hodges, whom God used to draw together the various strands of Pentecostal groupings that united to form the Apostolic Church. Gordon Weeks puts it this way: "These men, from different backgrounds and with different personalities... were in the right place and time in the purposes of God." (Weeks, 2003)

This account of Herbert Chanter's early Christian experience appeared in the *Apostolic Herald,* August 1936. "Pastor H.V. Chanter... is a native of Bradford, Yorkshire. His spiritual history dates from 1916, when, in response to the prayers of friends associated with the Pentecostal movement there, he made a decision for Christ, afterwards seeking the baptism with the Holy Spirit. As a result of incisive study of the Bible he arrived at the conclusion that prophecy was a manifestation of the Spirit which ought to be in evidence in the Church today, and this opinion isolated himself and those who shared it from the body of people with whom they had till then been worshipping. In November 1916, an independent service was started in a house, in which, during the following year Pastor Chanter was called to be an elder. Thereafter, a public room was procured and in 1918 he was called and anointed as a prophet in the rapidly-increasing company. Finally, in 1919, the call to the apostleship came, and Pastor Chanter became the youngest apostle in the church. Early in 1922, the Bradford Pentecostals joined the Apostolic Church. Then, following a period of productive effort during which the Bradford Church grew enormously, the Pastor dedicated himself to the work entirely, having left his employment in July 1922." (Apostolic Herald, 1936)

The Pentecostal church that Chanter and others broke away

from in November 1916 was led by Smith Wigglesworth, a well-known Pentecostal evangelist. Actually, they were told to leave because of their belief in directive prophecy. The church was known as the Bowland St. Mission and Wigglesworth said, "I will have nothing to do with the prophetical word here. I cannot trust or believe it, and therefore it is not going to be here." As soon as he said this, it is reported that a young woman prophesied, "Being that you have finished with Me and My voice, I finish with you, and there is a day coming when you will see the door of this assembly shut, but I will have another place, and I have faith in the heart of some of the young in this congregation." In 1917, the owners of the Bowland Street premises repossessed the hall and the meetings were stopped. (Weeks, 2003)

In November 1916, the breakaway group from Bowland St. Mission started to meet at the home of Herbert's parents in Cunliffe Terrace, Bradford. His parents were among the first in Bradford to be filled with the Holy Spirit in 1908. On 7th January 1917, this house group became "The Apostolic Church of God" and started to meet in a Hall in Fearnley St., Otley Road, Bradford. At this time, they were under the cover of an apostle from Bedford, Pastor R. Jardine, and he visited this group, with a prophet, Pastor Boulton, "to set it in order". Herbert, his father and A.W. Rhodes, his brother-in-law, were recognised as elders. Herbert's mother was called as a deaconess. When the Bowland St. Mission meetings were closed in 1917, many of the congregation started to go to Fearnley, including the Cousens and Perfect families who were significant in the development of the Apostolic Church. By November 1917, this Apostolic Church of God had moved to a bigger hall in Albert Street, Otley Road, Bradford.

Weeks tells a fascinating story from this time. At a fellowship meeting for elders and their wives, a prophecy was given that if those present would go home and seek the Lord, He would give them the words and the tune for a hymn. Two hymns were produced that have blessed the Apostolic Church for many years: "Jesus My Eyes Are unto Thee" and "Jesus Was Slain For Me". (Weeks, 2003)

By the end of 1921, the Apostolic Church of God in Bradford had grown to include assemblies in the North of England, Bedford, London and Kent. Pastor R. Jardine had a supervisory role over this church grouping. Herbert Chanter, now a pastor, had also been recognised as a prophet and an apostle. Jardine had been involved with the Apostolic Church in Wales but withdrew sometime in 1917. However, Chanter was challenged with this question, "Why are we not a united Apostolic Church?" Aware of movements with similar names and not wanting to be in competition, Herbert Chanter sought the Lord for guidance. (Weeks, 2003)

Chanter and his brother-in-law visited the Glasgow Apostolic New Year Convention in 1922 and he started to correspond with Pastor D.P. Williams. In March 1922, the Williams brothers visited Bradford but no merger was agreed at this time, although there had been prophecy that further revelation would come in regard to Bradford.

Gordon Weeks recounts the remarkable story of the 1922 Bradford Easter Convention which resulted in the Apostolic Church of God in Bradford, and its associated churches, becoming fully incorporated into the Apostolic Church: "In Bradford the Easter Convention was advertised to be held in the Apostolic Church of God, Albert Street from Good Friday to Easter Tuesday 14-18 April. Pastor H.V. Chanter decribes how, unexpectedly on the Thursday, Pastors D.P. and W.J. Williams and then Pastors A. and T.N. Turnbull arrived at his house seeking accommodation. Later Pastor F. Hodges and Bros. U. Pearson and W.A.C. Rowe arrived. All these brethren explained that by prophecy they had been directed to come to the convention." (Weeks, 2003)

Pastor Herbert Chanter wrote, "This coming together without

premeditation was so remarkable that we could only say it was the Lord; there must be some purpose in which we were all concerned." As detailed in a previous chapter, out of meetings in Bradford a Missionary Council was established with Bradford as the base. The eleven tenets were accepted as the doctrinal statement. Penygroes would be the main headquarters but each section (Bradford, Hereford, Glasgow and Penygroes) would be responsible for their own area of the country and their own finances.

Chanter was called into full-time ministry during these meetings in Bradford. However, what was notable about this convention was that it set in motion the fulfilment of a prophecy given in 1917. A woman in the Apostolic Church of God in Bradford had prophesied that if the church would be faithful then God would lead them to a time when from Bradford He would send missionaries to many parts of the world. The prophecy said that Bradford would be the hub of a great wheel, whose spokes would go in all directions across the world and "the purpose of God would be fulfilled by belting the globe." (Weeks, 2003)

A Missionary Council was established with representatives from Scotland, London, the Midlands and Wales. This Council would meet at least three times a year. Responsibility for the work in Ireland, and also for the new endeavours in Argentina, was transferred to the Council. Bradford became the Missionary headquarters; Pastor Chanter became the editor of The Apostolic Missionary Herald; Mr. H. Cousen, who had been Smith Wigglesworth's right-hand man, became the treasurer and A.W. Rhodes became the secretary. Pastor D.P. Williams was appointed President of the Council. A monthly missionary prayer meeting and offering were put in place across the assemblies.

In the October 1923 *Apostolic Church Missionary Herald* Chanter reports another church opening in Bradford, in the district of Great Horton.

Working alongside Herbert Chanter was his brother-in-law, Arthur Rhodes, who was a recognised prophet, George Perfect, a recognised teacher, and Herbert Cousen. Pastor Hugh Dawson gives this summary of how the work spread under Chanter's ministry: "From the years 1919 to 1927 he was located in Bradford and from there pioneered the Apostolic Vision in the North of England, covering such places as Stockton, Middlesborough, Callerton, North Walbottle, Horden, Easington Lane, Beamish and South Hetton. During this time also he pioneered in the South of England, covering such places as London, Stonehall, Dover and Folkestone." (Riches of Grace, 1966)

In 1927, Pastor and Mrs. Chanter moved to Sunderland, but, in February 1931, they were sent to North America. They encountered visa difficulties with the US authorities and settled instead in Nova Scotia, becoming the first resident UK Apostolic missionaries to Canada. There was already an Apostolic presence in Nova Scotia. This had been established by Pastor Joseph Larkins, the superintendent of the work in America, in 1927. He had been the first UK apostle to go overseas to pioneer and was based in Philadelphia. It was through a Nova Scotian attending the Apostolic Church in Philadelphia, that the link was established.

Herbert Chanter continued to pioneer other congregations in Nova Scotia. Hugh Dawson gives an insight into the challenges they faced: "During this time both he and his dear wife, Alice, faithful and devoted, suffered very much hardship because of the intense cold and the long distances to be travelled with very indifferent means of transport." (Riches of Grace, 1966) Once the visa problems were resolved, they relocated to the United States in November 1932, residing in Altoona, Pennsylvania.

In April 1934, Pastors D.P. and Jones Williams visited North America and it was decided that Pastor Joseph Larkins should move from East Lansdowne to Toronto. This was a step of faith as there were no contacts in Toronto at that time. It was further decided that Pastor Chanter would replace him in East Landsdowne, Pennsylvania, which had been the Apostolic base in the US since 1922.

The Chanters moved in November 1935 but not before Pastor Chanter's own father, Pastor A.B. Chanter, had ministered in the States for six months. He "ministered throughout five assemblies and healings and restorations to the church were experienced. The Altoona Convention in November was richly blessed with three hundred people present at the Sunday morning service and two hundred children in the Sunday School. Five men were called through prophecy to be elders and five ladies to be deaconesses." (Weeks, 2003)

T.N. Turnbull gives this overview of Herbert Chanter's ministry in the US: "During his sojourn in East Lansdowne the work as a whole in the United States grew and was in a very good condition, Pastor Chanter adapting himself exceedingly well to the people of that country." (T.N.Turnbull, 1959)

In 1941, the Chanters were called to return to the UK and found themselves in the midst of a war zone: "He was located in London during the worst days of the awful bombing, the Blitz, when his faithful care of the flock called forth the highest praise from the saints and neighbours and the other assemblies in this country." (Riches of Grace, 1966)

After London, Herbert Chanter served as pastor in Edinburgh and Keighley, retiring in 1953 due to ill-health: "His physical condition, heart trouble, no doubt caused or aggravated by the hardships suffered in Nova Scotia, was, and continued to be, of such a nature that he was never able for thirteen years of his life to minister regularly or travel away from home." Pastor Chanter died on 1st August 1966, at the age of seventy-six, and was remembered in this way: "He was a man with a great, warm heart; generous, kind, and thoughtful for others." (Riches of Grace, 1966)

VIOLA GARDINER

Viola Hagemann was born in Denmark and in 1925 began her missionary service in Lin Cheng in northern China. She was a single woman and went to support another Danish Apostolic missionary called Miss Dagny Pedersen. Dagny Pedersen had been in Lin Cheng since 1911.

In the late 1920s Miss Hagemann, while on furlough in the United States, married a Mr. Berg. They had a son called Junior, but Mr. Berg died in 1931. In January 1932 Viola arrived back in Lin Cheng with her son to continue working with Dagny Pedersen, who travelled with them on her return from furlough. Pastor Herbert Cousen, the Chairman of the Apostolic Church Missionary Board, was in Shanghai to meet them.

Sadly, just a few months later, this announcement appeared in the July 1932, *Apostolic Herald*: "As a Body we wish to extend to our sister, Mrs. Viola Berg, our Danish Missionary in China, our expression of sorrow and deepest sympathy at the sudden home-call of her darling little boy (aged 4) after two days illness with fever. Since arriving back in China, Mrs. Berg has been going out almost every day preaching and visiting among the Chinese. It was necessary on these occasions to leave the little boy at home and during the first days he cried and desired to accompany her. Mrs. Berg took him one day to a Chinese idol temple and showed him one of the big idols, saying, 'Look at this. It is to such a stone god that the Chinese pray, and he cannot help them. That is why mamma must go out and tell them about Jesus.' 'Just go, mamma,' he replied, 'I shall not cry, but will be a good boy at home.' From that day he was perfectly satisfied when Mrs. Berg left him at home." (Apostolic Herald, 1932)

In May 1935, a missionary from the Australian Apostolic Church came to work with Mrs. Berg and Miss Pedersen in Lin Cheng. His name was Hector Gardiner and he had been converted in 1930 under the ministry of William Cathcart in Perth. He was called prophetically to China by Pastor Jones Williams during Convention meetings in Melbourne at the end of 1934. He was a single man of thirty. Gardiner was able to help the Danish missionaries complete the church building and mission compound that had been started with the purchase of land the previous year. He and Viola married later in 1935.

In 1936, tragedy again visited this missionary group. Mrs. Viola Gardiner died on 1st July, three days after the birth of a baby boy. The child was born by caesarean section at a Presbyterian Mission Hospital, some fifty miles from Lin Cheng. After the birth of the child, she underwent further surgery, but she never recovered. The baby, who was named Terence, survived. Mrs. Gardiner was buried beside her first son, Junior Berg.

At the graveside opportunity was given for people to give testimony of how Mrs. Gardiner had helped them. One elderly Chinese gentleman told how he had been put into prison on a wrongful charge. He said that it was Mrs. Gardiner who worked tirelessly to get him out.

Sometime later, at the British Consulate in Peking, Pastor Gardiner married an Elim missionary, Miss E.M. Baker and Terence had a new mother.

ALFRED L. GREENAWAY

Pastor Alfred Greenaway, from Skewen, and his wife Eufron, from Pontardawe, left the UK for New Zealand on 8th March 1934. They had only just married. Eufron was the sister of Pastor William James, the pioneer of the Pontardawe assembly in South Wales.

Prior to leaving for New Zealand, Pastor and Mrs. Greenaway were based at Stockton in the North of England. In the January 1932 *Apostolic Herald* there is a report of an evangelistic mission that Pastors Greenaway and Richard Turnbull held at Houghton-le-Spring: "Fifteen adults and many young people have been saved, many more we know are under conviction, and many have been ministered to for healing." (Apostolic Herald, 1932) There were other reports of Pastor Greenaway's evangelistic drive in the North East, before his missionary call.

In 1934, the New Zealand church had appealed to the UK for help with the growing Apostolic work there. In response, two men were chosen to go: Alfred Greenaway, who was an apostle, and Pastor John Thompson, who arrived with his family in April 1935.

The background to this Macedonian call from New Zealand was the pioneering work of Pastors Cathcart, McCabe, Hewitt, Evangelist Isaac Hewitt and New Zealand contacts, Edward Weston, Len Jones and Alf Jackson. On Sunday 7th January 1934, an Apostolic Assembly was established in Wellington and "put in order." At that service, and under the cover of an apostle and a prophet one hundred and twelve people accepted membership of the Apostolic Church and, through prophetic direction, over twenty individuals were placed into local church roles. Edward Weston was the pastor/teacher and Alf Jackson the pastor.

In the months leading up to the arrival of the Greenaways in April 1934, further pioneering was undertaken in six other places in New Zealand. Pastor Greenaways role was to be superintendent of the work in New Zealand, with his base in Wellington. As the work in New Zealand was expanding, a UK pastor, Dickson, was transferred from Australia to Auckland in July 1934.

By August, Pastor Greenaway had been instrumental in establishing another Apostolic Church. At the end of 1934, Pastors D.P.

and Jones Williams visited New Zealand, bringing ministry at the New Year Convention, just one year after the inauguration of the work in New Zealand.

Perhaps the greatest breakthrough that Pastor Greenaway made in his first year there was with the Maori population. An appeal was received from some missionaries working among the Maoris to come and help them to find a deeper experience in God. Alf Greenaway went to meet them and other Apostolic ministers followed to give ministry. In October 1937, the first Apostolic Maori Mission Church was opened in the Bay of Plenty District, on the North Island.

Pastor John Thompson arrived to join the team. This brought the total of UK pastors arriving in one year to three. Pastors Dickson and Thompson, with several indigenous leaders, were involved in the continued expansion and establishing of churches in New Zealand and Pastor Ivor Grabham, a prophet, arrived in February 1936.

Alf Greenaway continued his own pioneering work, conducting revival services. As a result a church was established in Hastings. When Joshua McCabe visited from Australia, thirty-two were accepted into membership and over ten people were placed into local roles. Here again, in Hastings, we see the ministry of apostle and prophet operating together to establish a local church. Worsfold writes, "because of the strong opposition from some evangelical congregations, the pioneering of the Apostolic Church in this place was referred to as 'The Battle of Hastings'." (Worsfold J., 1974)

In July 1937, Pastor and Mrs. Greenaway, as a result of a prophetic word through Pastor McCabe, left Wellington, New Zealand for Japan. There were other members of the group who also went to Japan. Gordon Weeks explains: "They travelled to Japan to assist the work of the Japan Apostolic Mission and to begin the Apostolic work there." Due to various reasons, Pastor and Mrs. Greenaway left Japan and went to Australia in 1938. Weeks writes, "After lecturing in the Ikoma Bible College on the Church and Apostolic principles Pastor A.L. Greenaway returned to Australia where he suffered a severe nervous breakdown, due to the distressing nature of the Japan climate." (Weeks, 2003)

He later took up a pastorate in Adelaide. We know from the book, *Remember I Sent You*, that in 1946 he became Principal of the Apostolic Church Bible School in Melbourne, Australia. (Stanton, 2012)

From Australia, the Greenaways came back to the UK in 1948 to take charge of the re-opened Bible School in Penygroes. It had been closed for eight years. Omri Bowen, a later Principal of the Bible College, writes, "Pastor Greenaway D.D., D.Theol., brought along with him two students from New Zealand, one of them being Ivor L. Cullen, who later became a pastor, and eventually President of the Apostolic Church in New Zealand. Though Pastor Greenaway remained Principal for only two years, his scholarship and expertise laid a sound theological basis for the post-war period of the School." (Riches of Grace, 1960)

Jonathan Black, in his blog, Some Early Pentecostal Communion Choruses, gives us this insight into why Pastor Greenaway went back to New Zealand in 1950: "He found it difficult to work under a system where graduates of the Bible College could be bypassed when it came to ministerial appointments, and so ended up returning to New Zealand." (Black, 2015)

The Greenaways arrived back in New Zealand in November 1950 and, after a period of itinerant ministry and local church leadership, they moved to Hamilton in 1954. On 18th February 1957, a Bible Training Centre was opened in Hamilton. This was

New Zealand's first attempt to provide training for those who felt the call of God. Pastor Greenaway was the Principal.

Jonathan Black continued his blog with this commendation of Pastor Greenaway: "Dr. Greenway was also a pioneer in encouraging pastors to undergo formal, higher theological study, although Council came out against such study at the time: 'This Council deplores its ministers seeking degrees and feels that general Bible study mixed with prayer and devotion and crowned with the power of the Spirit of God is absolutely indispensable for the ministry.'! That was 1951, and it would be another 18 years until Council changed its position – in response to prophecy – and decided that 'theological degrees can be of advantage with the anointing of the Holy Spirit.' Although even then, there were still several restrictions surrounding pastors taking degrees. Those of us who know the advantage of a theological education today should be grateful for pioneers like Alfred Greenaway." (Black, 2015)

E. FRANK HODGES

Frank Hodges was born in 1872 and wrote this about his conversion in 1905: "During the Welsh Revival the Lord called and found a man in the City of Hereford and brought him under conviction of sin, into a knowledge and experience of salvation in Jesus Christ. Being truly born from above the Holy Spirit planted a deep desire for the things of God and a particular longing for the church as seen in the written Word to be again in operation." (Weeks, 2003)

He owned a gentlemen's outfitters business in Hereford and described himself as a "man full of the world, living without Christ." He was saved during a Torrey Alexander mission in London. "Sometime after his conversion, Hodges was prayed for and healed of an enlarged heart condition; something he was happy to testify to until his old age." (Worsfold J. E., 1991)

He was baptised in the Holy Spirit in Wales and spoke in new languages in a house quite near to the home of Evan Roberts. He wrote of this experience at a later date: "I got a wonderful baptism in the Spirit. I had a Welsh tongue, and I spoke in Welsh... I was told what the tongue meant, in English; and everything has been fulfilled. I witness here of that; not only does the Lord speak in known tongues, but He speaks also in unknown tongues." This was truly remarkable because, before this experience, he confessed to hating the Welsh but that, after his baptism, he 'now loved them.'" (Worsfold J. E., 1991)

Frank Hodges came back to Hereford and bore witness to his experience of the baptism in the Holy Spirit. This resulted in him gathering a group of believers around him. In 1910, a plot of land was donated by a woman in the group and Hodges himself provided the funds to build a hall. Unsure what name to give it, he decided to visit a woman he knew in Wales who had a gift of prophecy.

He recalls what happened: "The Lord told me through a sister (in Cardiganshire) through prophecy... that He wanted me to build Him a house; for He knew all about me; and He would send people that would 'go all the way'; also He said to me that it was to be called the 'Apostolic Church'; I did not know what that meant; I could not help it; I put up the name 'Apostolic Church', and it was up for seven years before Pastor Dan Williams came along. The Apostolic Church was the talk in Hereford." (Riches of Grace, 1962)

Frank Hodges married Ellen ("Nelsie") Odell Vinter, from Cambridgeshire in 1916. Ellen, who could trace her ancestry back to John Wesley, had been filled with the Spirit in 1908 when Mrs. Boddy[20] prayed for her in a house in Croydon. William Rowe comments, "She brought to the union a passion for the Word of God and a maturity of experience in the royal service, having as a

---

20   Wife of Rev. Alexander Boddy, leader of the Sunderland Revival, 1908

full-time deaconess served with some of the greatest ministers in the land; but ever true to the leading of the Holy Spirit, she stepped out into Pentecostal fulness and Apostolic Faith." (Weeks, 2003)

Frank Hodges, who had previously met D.P. Williams and heard him preach in the days of the Apostolic Faith Church, went to the Penygroes Convention in 1918. He had been told that the Apostolic Church was in error, but because of the title "Apostolic" he came to see what it meant, since he had been given the same name prophetically for the hall in Hereford. He recognised the voice of God at the convention and went back to Hereford feeling "there was something yet to come" for them, which he "could not quite understand."

He returned to the Penygroes Convention in 1919 and invited D.P. Williams, with other leaders, to visit Hereford. When they arrived they saw the name above the door, the *Apostolic Church*. Frank Hodges told them, "That name has been waiting for you for seven years." The ministry brought by this visiting delegation, by way of both teaching and prophecy, was readily accepted and the church was "set in order" with the calling, through prophecy, of an overseer, elders, an evangelist, deacons and deaconesses. From that time the Hereford Apostolic Church became part of the Apostolic Church in Wales. (Weeks, 2003)

In February 1920, Pastor and Mrs. Hodges were guest speakers at the opening of the Swansea Apostolic Church. Mrs. Hodges preached twice during the eleven days of meetings.

In April 1922, a significant event took place in the life of Frank Hodges. Herbert Chanter was the leader of an independent Pentecostal church in Bradford, with five related churches coming under his cover. Without any prior arrangements with one another, three groups of Apostolic leaders arrived at this church in Bradford for the Easter Convention: the Williams brothers from Wales;

Pastors A. and T.N. Turnbull from Scotland; and Pastor Hodges and two leaders from the Hereford Church. This God-appointed coming together resulted in Chanter and his group of churches joining the Apostolic Church and the UK missionary headquarters being established in Bradford. During the convention, Pastor Frank Hodges was called as an apostle and the two leaders from Hereford, William Rowe and Uriah Pearson, were called and ordained as prophets.

Pastor Hodges then became responsible for the Hereford section of the work, with two prophets alongside him. By the end of 1922, it comprised ten assemblies and became known as the "England (Midlands) Section". Each assembly had either a pastor or an overseer. After 1922, this section grew to include: Hereford, Leominster, Ross, Madley, Wem, Shifnal, Brierely Hill, Smethwick, Handsworth, Wolverhampton, Ludlow, Gloucester, Shrewsbury, Ponyesberry and Hay. A further apostle, William Guest from Smethwick, was also ordained in this section in 1923.

A caravan was donated and used for evangelism in the villages throughout Herefordshire. In the summer of 1924, two women, Miss Ross and Miss Hunter, spent the summer living in the caravan and taking the Gospel to villages in Monmouthshire. They did this at their own expense. In the summer of 1925, two other women, Miss Lloyd and Miss Dickinson also used the caravan to evangelise the villages around Leominister and the Hopyards.

It was from Hereford that Apostolic truth was also taken to Cornwall. Two women from the Hereford District were on holiday at St. Ives when they heard someone preaching in the open-air. They went to talk to the man, a Mr. A. Phillips, and told him about the baptism in the Holy Spirit. The two women invited him to the 1926 Hereford Whitsun Convention and helped with the costs. It was later reported: "There he received his baptism with the Holy Ghost and fire, bringing the fire back to Porthleven. Then God began to pour out His Spirit upon some of the earnest Christians of other churches in the town. A fine company of baptised saints were soon assembling together in a cobbler's shop for worship." (Williams. D. ,1933)

Pastors Hodges and Rowe made their first trip to Cornwall, a distance of three hundred miles, in October 1926. They stopped in Newport and Bristol to meet with people who wanted to know more about Apostolic truth. When they arrived in Helston on 14th October, Mr. Phillips was there to meet them. This was the start of pioneering in Cornwall.

In the 1933 *Apostolic Souvenir*, there is this update on the position in Cornwall since that first contact in 1926: "Since then a fine church has been built at Porthleven, and four other assemblies have been opened in the district. Some 130 to 140 have passed through the waters of baptism, and numbers have received the glorious baptism of the Holy Ghost. Many have had miraculous touches from God in the healing of their bodies." (Williams. D. , 1933)

Pastor Hodges also travelled overseas to minister. In 1922 he accompanied the Williams brothers and Andrew Turnbull to the United States. This was the first overseas trip after the Missionary Council was formed. It was on this trip that the team experienced a serious car accident while driving to San Francisco, but miraculously there were no significant injuries. From America they moved on to minister in Canada.

In the remaining years of Frank Hodges' ministry in Hereford, the churches under his care continued to grow and develop. His wife died in 1941 and five years later he moved to Australia with Pastor William Rowe and his family, who were being relocated there. Rowe had been a close colleague for over thirty years and their relationship was described as father and son in the faith.

Hodges believed that the Lord had a work for him to do in Australia, but, as the time drew near for him to leave, he became desperately ill with bouts of severe haemorrhaging from a stomach ulcer. He was not expected to recover, but by faith he booked his passage to Melbourne. His doctor told him it was impossible for him to go and his condition was so bad that, for two weeks, he lived on nothing but milk and water. He later wrote, "Then the Lord began to raise me up. I began to gain strength in spite of what the X-ray had revealed about my state. I was eagerly watching to get a boat to sail, although they said it was impossible... I got on that boat on April 1st 1945 and landed in Australia, May 1st 1945, having had a splendid voyage by sea... I ate my food well, slept well and arrived in Melbourne looking quite a different man. Now I have been here eighteen months. I have put on a stone and a half in weight. My friends say I never looked so well in my life... It is nothing but a miracle: but He is the miracle-worker. I give the Lord Jesus all the praise and glory! (Riches of Grace, 1948)

After four years in Australia, Pastor Hodges died on 20th April 1949 at the age of seventy-seven. This was the tribute of the Hereford Church: "We shall miss him for his gracious disposition; his generous spirit; his largeness of heart, and for his liberty and likeness to Christ. We in Hereford especially mourn his loss, for he was the founder of this work, as well as the father of so many in the faith." (Riches of Grace, 1949)

WILLIAM H. LEWIS

William Henry Lewis was born on 22nd April 1883 in Birchgrove, a village near Swansea in South Wales. In 1918, he married Gwen Davies and they went on to have three daughters: Mary, Ruth and Lois. When Pastor Idris Vaughan's first wife, Nancy, died of cancer in 1931, William and Gwen also took in Idris' and Nancy's son, Bertie.

William Lewis was one of those who lived through the Welsh Revival but was not converted. Testifying many years later, he explained, "I was more of a spectator of the Revival than a participator." Although he was a religious man who never cursed, gambled or drank, he says, "In spite of all this there was an aching void in my heart." (Lewis W. H., 1942)

After a period of deep conviction of sin, he eventually accepted Christ as his personal Saviour. He worked as a miner in South Wales and describes how his attitude to work changed after his conversion: "The change made me a better workman, more conscientious towards my employer as well as towards my fellow workmen. I experienced the power of God even down in the bowels of the earth, enabling me to live a Christian life as well as to testify of such." (Lewis W. H., 1942)

After some time with the Welsh Independents and then the Calvinistic Methodists, in 1911 William Lewis became a member of the Apostolic Faith Church. Initially he attended the assembly in Pontardawe, but, in 1914, he was appointed overseer of a newly established AFC in Birchgrove. He was still the overseer in January 1916, when Birchgrove assembly and others broke away to form the Apostolic Church in Wales with D.P. Williams.

From January 1916, William Lewis' involvement and ministry in the Apostolic Church developed and grew. In 1922, he was part of the Welsh representation on the Missionary Council which was formed at the Bradford Easter Convention.

Later that year, while Frank Hodges was in the United States ministering with the Williams brothers and Andrew Turnbull, William Lewis took care of the Hereford and associated churches. During his ministry there were people saved and, according to the *Apostolic Missionary Herald*, "The Church was much built up on the lines of holiness and separation from the world during Pastor

Lewis' ministry. About 30 followed the Lord through the waters of baptism at the Hereford Church during the three months he was in charge." (Apostolic Church Missionary Herald, 1923)

William Lewis was called and ordained to the apostleship in 1925 (see Chapter 9). For a few years, there had been concern about the development of the Apostolic work in London so, in 1926, he was sent to the three existing London churches, which were located in Peckham, Dulwich and Hammersmith. In his first few months there, an assembly opened in Brixham and, before the end of 1926, Pastor Cecil Ireson was appointed the overseer of this new church plant (see Chapter 5). (Ireson, 1970)

The work in London continued to flourish under the ministry of Pastor W.H. Lewis. By 1933 there were also churches in Barking, Kennington, Romford and Burnt Oak. Linked to the London District of the Apostolic Church were assemblies in Stonehall, Dover, Folkestone, Bexhill and Worthing. Working alongside Lewis as a prophet was Pastor J.D. Eynon, originally from Hereford. This is another example of the linking of apostle and prophet for the growth of the Church, a practice which runs through the early history of the Apostolic Church.

Pastor Lewis' granddaughter, Mrs. Miriam Fuller, related this story: "W.H. was a great man of prayer, spending hours on his knees. One day he went to pray in his room and told my grandmother not to disturb him 'even if the king of England comes to the door'. Later that morning, D.P. Williams knocked on the door. My grandmother invited him in for a drink and explained that W.H. didn't want to be disturbed. After D.P. had left, Grandpa came downstairs. When he heard that D.P. had called, he reprimanded Nana saying, 'But D.P. is much more important than the king!'"

In 1932, a serious moral issue arose involving Sigurd Bjorner, the leader of the Apostolic Church in Denmark. The subsequent fallout from the discipline imposed resulted in Bjorner, six elders and two hundred and fifty members leaving the Copenhagen church. Pastor Lewis was sent to Denmark for two months to navigate the Danish Church through the difficulties. His ministry proved successful not only in Copenhagen but in the country as a whole. The report of the Easter Convention in Copenhagen was that "many were baptised with the Holy Ghost, backsliders restored and not a few dedicated their lives anew to God." (Weeks, 2003)

On his return home, Pastor Lewis spent a week in Paris. He had been given the responsibility of joint leadership of the Apostolic work in France, with instructions to visit France every two months from his base in London. As his ministry trips to France continued, the work there also developed. In 1933, there was news of a new building in one town and good numbers attending the meetings in Paris. In November that year, after a convention in Paris, it was reported: "Up to four hundred people attended the services addressed by Pastors D.P. Williams, W.H. Lewis, V. Wellings, W. Gummer and Bro. H. Mitchell. Thirty eight people were saved, a demon possessed person was delivered and many were healed." (Weeks, 2003)

In 1933, William's younger brother, Arthur, was also called as a pastor and, by the end of that year, was appointed as the first Principal of the Apostolic Church Bible School in Penygroes.

1934 was an important and strategic year in the development of the Apostolic Church. Discussions started with a view to changing from seven self-administrating sections to one administrative unit. The General Headquarters was to remain in Penygroes, the Missionary Centre was to continue in Bradford and a new centre would be established in Glasgow for finance. Such changes demanded a constitution with guiding principles. Pastor Lewis was part of the team set up to determine those guiding principles and he was appointed to the role of General Secretary, based in Penygroes. (Weeks, 2003)

Various other UK pastors continued to visit the churches in Denmark, but in 1936, Pastor W.H. Lewis was sent back to resolve another crisis. Weeks explains: "The subject Of British Israelism was still causing problems in Denmark and the teaching of the Oxford Group (Buchmanism) was also affecting the work there. This group (not to be confused with the Oxford Movement), founded in USA, laid much emphasis on the public confessions of failings, especially on sexual matters, in the pursuit of the moral absolutes of purity, unselfishness, honesty and love. In 1938 it became 'Moral Rearmament' and continued to preach self-reform rather than sanctification by the work of the Holy Spirit." (Weeks, 2003) The teachings of both British Israelism and Buchmanism were rejected by the UK Apostolic Church Council.

However these were not the only issues causing concern. Bjorner had been shown grace and compassion by the UK Apostolic Church and, after a time, he returned and was restored to his leadership position. Before long, as Weeks explains, "He tried to make changes in the organisation of the assemblies to non-Apostolic methods" and then decided to leave once again. This time he took two hundred and fifty people with him and a few of the Copenhagen churches were affected. The remaining twenty-four Apostolic assemblies and thirty house groups in Denmark weathered the storm. (Weeks, 2003)

William Lewis was sent into this very difficult situation in April 1936. After a thorough investigation of what had happened in Denmark and how Pastor Bjorner had administered the church, the conclusion was that he had operated as a "one man movement" and had done nothing to implement advice from the UK regarding administration. Another fact came to light: "The full-time staff had not received their full wages for eight years!" (Weeks, 2003)

Lewis, with the help of Danish colleagues like Christensen, Friberg, Beck and Facius, set about re-establishing the Danish

Apostolic Church. Worsfold writes, "It must be said that it was largely as a result of the grace and ministry of Lewis, a widely-respected Bible teacher, that a good foundation was relaid for the Apostolic Church in Denmark to recover from this schism." (Worsfold J. E., 1991) In 1937, Lewis was asked to continue his ministry in Denmark for another four years.

At the August Penygroes Convention that year, Pastor Oluf Christensen spoke of the 'trying times' through which the Danish Church had passed and of a Danish newspaper that had published a report claiming, 'The Apostolic Church in Denmark is going down'. Christensen paid this tribute to the work of William Lewis: 'Our church was at one time like a big ship on the reefs, but we sent a wire to Penygroes and asked for a pilot. He came and was a good pilot. We love him and learnt much. He is still with us, lifting us higher in the realms of God." (Worsfold J. E., 1991)

In October 1938, William Lewis went to Estonia for three months of mission. He was supported in this by the Danish and, later, the UK Apostolic Churches. When he left Estonia he returned to the UK, but, because of Britain's declaration of War on Germany in September 1939, he did not go back to Denmark till January 1940. Just three months after his arrival, German forces occupied Denmark and Lewis was detained and interned in Germany in June 1940. (Weeks, 2003)

An unmarked newspaper cutting kept by W.H. Lewis' family describes his arrest: "Pastor Lewis was 'picked up' on May 6[th,] just after opening the service at church. Two plain clothes detectives took him to the police headquarters. He spent the night in a cell and, despite assurances that he would be released, he was taken again to another prison in the 'Black Maria.'"

Lewis, who was fifty-seven years old at this time, was transferred to Nuremberg within days of his arrest. He later wrote, "We were considered very dangerous men, we ministers. The Germans thought we were paid by the British Government to do secret service work... In the first months we had no Red Cross parcels and we often had nothing to eat in the morning but German bread." He goes on to describe how the bread was often soaking wet and the potatoes were no better than a British farmer would have given to the pigs. He spent the next four years and three months between two civilian internment camps in Germany.

In a letter to one of his daughters, dated 7th April 1941, Pastor Lewis wrote, "It is with a measure of joy I am again writing you this week because I am conscious that day by day, though separated physically, our spirits meet at the throne of grace and there we have hallowed fellowship with God and with one another."

This update was included in the December 1941 *Herald of Grace:* "DO YOU KNOW that Pastor W.H. Lewis, our Superintendent Missionary Representative to Denmark, has been transferred to another concentration camp in Germany? That friends may correspond with him, and that he himself will be eager to receive news from all at home? Here is his new address: Internee Post (to be written in capitals in the left-hand corner of the envelope). British Civilian Internee, W.H. Lewis, 17473-W, Ilag VIII, Germany." (*Herald of Grace*, 1941) Many people did write and the Missionary Board Secretary, Pastor Hugh Mitchell, in particular, kept in contact with Pastor Lewis. The letters were reproduced in the *Herald of Grace*.

At times in the camps, Pastor Lewis suffered from ill health, but he was not inactive. In the March 1945 Herald of Grace, a copy of a sermon, "The Face of Jesus" was reproduced. Pastor Lewis was due to preach it on 8th March 1942, at the 11a.m. service held inside the concentration camp. However, a Pastor Bell had to read it instead because William was laid up in hospital.

He would also often try to help to lift the spirits of his fellow internees. They were constantly fed Nazi propaganda and there could be long periods with very little news from home. He describes how morale would plummet: "Men would sometimes throw themselves on their beds – nothing to do, they couldn't concentrate, and above all, no news. Then one of them would receive a letter from home, censored of course but there were sentences which conveyed a great deal to the prisoners that the Germans could see no harm in... 185 grouse were shot down this week... and it was not the grouse season... our cousins were over last night and stayed a number of hours, bringing many presents." (Apostolic Herald, 1945)

The family at home were not forgotten. Mrs. Lewis sent this message to the Church: "Mrs. Lewis desires to thank the numerous friends who have joined us in prayer on their behalf and to acknowledge the receipt of the many letters of sympathy and encouragement sent during these anxious days." (Apostolic Herald, 1940)

Pastor Lewis finally returned to the UK in 1945. Weeks writes, "In 1940, in the darkest days of the war, a prophecy was given in the Kennington Church in London that a day would come when the Lord would bring back His servant from the Far East (Pastor C.C. Ireson) and also His servant from Germany (Pastor W.H. Lewis) and that they would meet at the door of that assembly. This prediction was literally fulfilled in 1945." (Weeks, 2003)

William Lewis was called, through prophecy, to go back to Denmark. This testimony reveals his undaunted spirit: "I am not getting younger in body, but I am feeling young in spirit... The burden of Denmark has been on my spirit. I cannot shake it off. It was no surprise to me when the word came. I feel I am a Welshman, an Englishman and sometimes a Dane. I don't know if I am an international man... I am a monument to the grace of

God and His preservation because of the prayers of His saints. I am asking you to pray for me continually for I want to finish my course not in retirement. I want to die in harness." (Apostolic Convention Report, 1946)

By the time William Lewis returned to Denmark in 1946 he was sixty-three years of age, and there were eighty assemblies. Plans were also in place for a building complex in Kolding. This would comprise a language school and a hall for convention purposes, with ground left over for anything else that was required. A farmer had given thirty acres of land. (Apostolic Convention Report, 1945)

The Danish Church had come a long way since those days of crisis and defections in the 1930s. It had already re-established contact with the Apostolic Church in Hungary and started to work into Norway, Switzerland and Greenland.

It was William Lewis who officiated at the funeral of Pastor D.P. Williams in February 1947. In 1948, Pastor Lewis reached the age of 65 and he and his wife, Gwen, retired to Streatham, in London. He died on 1st October 1959.

Pastor Cecil Ireson paid this tribute to him: "We in London largely owe the foundational work of the Assemblies here to God's servant, and some of our best men received their early training under him... This man of God has now gone to his reward, and how great his reward will be, for he served the Lord untiringly and unswervingly, never deviating from the line God set him." (Riches of Grace, 1959)

DAGNY PEDERSEN

Dagny Pedersen was born in 1888 in the Danish city of Roskilde, approximately twenty miles west of Copenhagen. She had a deep encounter with the Lord Jesus Christ at her conversion in the early 1900s. One night she cried out in distress, "Jesus, you know I desire to follow you. Help me cleanse my heart." She describes how she felt when she woke the next morning: "My burdened heart was now relieved, and I had a great, great joy and a deep peace and rest within. I could not understand it. After dressing, I was on my way to leave the bedroom and, just as I put my hand on the door handle to turn it, what seemed like a firm hand was placed on my left shoulder and these words sounded out mild and clear, 'Thy sins are forgiven thee.' I was amazed and in my happiness I said to myself, 'How long will that last?' Again I heard the voice in these words, 'It will be for eternity, for it is I', and I had assurance that it was the voice of Jesus. My burden of sin was taken away; I was free and very happy." (Apostolic Herald, 1932)

In February 1905, Dagny was baptised in water and three years later, as a result of a visit by Pastor Barrett[21] from Norway, she was filled with the Holy Spirit and spoke in new languages. However, the Baptist church she attended did not understand this experience and she joined a Pentecostal church in 1909. (Apostolic Herald, 1932)

She writes, "With this wonderful visitation of the Holy Spirit in my experience, God laid a burden on my heart for the heathen, especially those of China. I could pray and pray... and as I prayed the love for them grew more and more and I felt that no sacrifice was too great that they also might have part in eternal life. Two years after this it was clear to me that Jesus desired me to sacrifice myself for China and gladly I said, 'Yes, Lord.'" (Ireson, 1970)

With the support of her local church in Roskilde and that of her mother, who had previously had a prophetic word about a member of her family going to the "heathen", Dagny left Denmark on 4th April 1911, bound for China. She was twenty-three years

---

21 Barrett was leader of a 1907 Revival in Norway

old and alone when she set off, but she was joined on the journey by two women from Norway. She settled in the north of China in a city called Lin Cheng (Lincheng). This is situated in Hopei (Hebei) Province, approximately 1,500 miles south-west of Peking (Beijing). (Apostolic Herald, 1973)

In 1924, a group of Danish Pentecostal churches, led by Pastor Sigurd Bjorner, joined the Apostolic Church in the UK This Pentecostal group included Dagny Pedersen's home church and altogether they had ten missionaries in China. Nine of the missionaries left the group, not wishing to be part of this affiliation. The one missionary that remained was Dagny Pedersen.

In fact the affiliation of these churches with the Apostolic Church UK was not without opposition. Pentecostal leaders and groupings throughout Scandinavia spoke out and wrote against this union, but Pastor Bjorner stood his ground. Thank God he did, because the Apostolic work that developed in Denmark, in those early years, brought spiritual and practical blessing to other Apostolic churches in Europe. It also brought a truly inspirational missionary called Dagny Pedersen.

Between 1924 and 1948, Dagny faced some enormous challenges: civil war, a Japanese invasion, serious illness, the deaths of Mrs. Gardiner and her son, gangs of bandits, natural disasters and Catholic opposition. Her strong faith and her never-failing efforts to take the Gospel to the city of Lin Cheng and its surrounding areas were exemplary. Several evangelists worked with her, both men and women, and Pastors Cecil Ireson and Hector Gardiner were sent to establish and further develop the Apostolic work in the region. All the missionaries and Chinese workers frequently had to cross the military lines between the Chinese and the Japanese and they often had to travel through areas where bandits were operating. Floods would come and sweep away the walls of the compound but, undaunted, they would set about rebuilding them. Mission stations were established in and around the base and long distances were travelled, either on foot or by bicycle, to visit these outstations. Chinese evangelists were also trained to take the Gospel to their own people.

Gordon Weeks gives this brief insight into the work in 1934: "Throughout 1934 the evangelistic work had continued in N. China in spite of the danger from bandits and the offer of Roman Catholic leaders to their workers of ten dollars 'for every earnest Christian they can win over'. Miss D. Pedersen was very ill and had to have an operation in Peking but by the end of the year she had recovered full health. The hall in Lin Cheng Hsien was too small for the numbers of people meeting there, especially when they gathered from the surrounding villages, but in December 1934 they were able to purchase a very suitable piece of land with the help of an American Pentecostal Missionary, Pastor Heidal. He had a good knowledge of Chinese law and so he was able to help overcome the opposition of the local mandarin and get the site registered in the name of the Apostolic Church for a mission-station." (Weeks, 2003)

Dagny wrote this about the purchase of the land: "In the many years I spent in China, many were the difficulties I experienced, for disturbances oft flared up; still God gave me grace to meet the different situations. Indeed such were a challenge to us to fight through to victory. It was our desire to build a worthy structure to hold the many who wanted to listen to the Gospel. With this strong desire in my heart, I tried to put a little money aside each month. God was good to us, and eventually we secured a piece of ground." (Ireson, 1970)

The foundations were laid in the spring of 1934 and the church building was completed in October 1936. Dagny writes, "We had bought three large marble blocks, and on these were inscribed the words over the door, 'All ought to praise God'. Then, on either side respectively, the words 'To fear the Lord God is wisdom,' and 'To depart from evil is understanding'. Then over the platform inside, I had the words, 'Enter into His courts with thanksgiving.'" It was Pastor Gardiner who brought the project to completion, after his arrival in May 1935. The compound became home to the missionaries and the Chinese evangelists and their families. (Ireson, 1970)

The Sino-Japanese war broke out in 1937 and lasted for eight years, during which time the Japanese were stationed in the village where the compound was situated. Cecil Ireson writes, "Miss Pedersen's rooms were built up to the wall, so that from her room, through a small window high up, light could be seen shining out beyond the wall of the village, out to the open countryside, and that in the direction of Free China... Each night the Japanese soldiers would ride out to the surrounding villages, bringing in men and women as hostages to be shot! Miss Pedersen would hear the returning horses and that in the small hours of the morning, for often, being unable to sleep, she would be reading the Psalms by the light above described." (Ireson, 1970)

The Japanese mistrusted the missionary group and were very suspicious of their activities. Ireson further recounts how, one night, the Japanese came into the locked compound and took away the Chinese evangelists, Dagny Pedersen and her adopted daughter, Adina, who was twelve years old at the time. Dagny describes what happened when they were taken for questioning: "We were both accused of having connection with the Chinese army. I was called a liar and with fists banging on the table, it became too apparent that they were not prepared to believe our story." (Ireson, 1970)

The Japanese accused her of making signals to the enemy by the light in that small window. However, Dagny, Adina and the Chinese evangelists were all finally released. During the Sino-Japanese conflict, many Chinese Christians were imprisoned, tortured, and even executed by the Japanese. What protected the Mission initially was the fact that is was registered with the Danish rather than the British authorities.

The whole situation became very threatening and Dagny wrote, "Often through days and nights, all we could do was to sigh and supplicate God to help us through." (Ireson, 1970)

The missionaries and Chinese evangelists continued to put their lives on the line for the Gospel, reaching out from their base to the many outstations.

Dagny describes some of the suffering of those times: "The last years of the eight years' war were very hard. No one was allowed to receive wages from foreigners... We had to give a report of all our meetings, and were threatened with hard punishment if we went outside the Japanese controlled areas... In those days many were taken prisoners, and many were tortured, while many were brought to a painful death." After October 1941, Dagny Pedersen was the last remaining missionary on the compound in Lin Cheng. Hector Gardiner had returned to Australia and his colleague, Pastor Aubrey Newland had been interned by the Japanese. There were, however, some other Danish missionaries who were working in the area. (Ireson, 1970)

After three days of fighting the Red Chinese troops finally overthrew the Japanese in Lin Cheng. Dagny wrote, "During the first two nights of fighting, Adina, my Chinese daughter who was now 19 years old, and I remember we both sat under our big table, whilst outside the war was raging dreadfully! We could only cry to God for His protection, and we were so thankful to see the dawn breaking, for the night was so long, and the roar from the big cannon unceasing. The last night we hid in a room under the church, for it was safer from bullets of the enemy than my house." (Ireson, 1970)

While the initial months under communist control were peaceful and Dagny Pedersen was able to visit the outlying stations again and even witness to the communist troops in the town, the situation began to turn. When visiting the villages, she found that there was nobody to listen to the Gospel because the villagers were forced to attend communist meetings. Then the compound was raided, windows were broken and doors smashed. There was no correspondence filtering through from the UK, Denmark or Australia and Dagny did not know what to do. Restrictions for meetings were imposed and if a meeting was discovered, it was broken up.

The communists started to use the church building in Lin Cheng to torture and execute people. Accusations were made against Dagny Pedersen and her life was in grave danger. While she was praying, the Lord gave her a word from Isa. 43:2: *When thou passest through the waters, I will be with you.* The intimidation and accusations continued and the compound was stripped bare of its contents. Threatening crowds would gather outside. People were banned from visiting her or even speaking to her. The Lord gave Dagny this further promise: *I will deliver thee in that day.* (Jeremiah 39:17-18) (Ireson, 1970)

She describes how the Lord undertook dramatically: "One morning I was sitting on the edge of my bed knitting, when I heard a voice say, 'Go quickly. Now is the time'. I threw my knitting down, tidied myself a little and went to the mandarin and police superintendent. He said, 'If I give you a passport, will you return?' I answered, 'No, I am now old.' He told me to return in two days, which I did, and I was told to go." (Ireson, 1970)

On the 1st December 1948, Dagny Pedersen started her journey back to Denmark. With little money and meagre food rations, but, with the help of Chinese Christians and American missionaries and a clear word of knowledge at one checkpoint, she was able to reach Peking and the Danish Embassy. There she obtained a passport and eventually arrived in Denmark in 1949. The promises of deliverance that the Lord had given her all came to pass and she settled once more in her home town of Roskilde.

Dagny Pedersen's faithful and courageous service in China brought much fruit in the countless lives which were won for Christ and the many workers that were trained in preaching the Gospel. Only eternity will reveal the true extent of the fruit of the work that she initiated in Lin Cheng.

Cecil Ireson, a fellow worker in China, described her as: "One who counted not her life dear unto herself... She was a true 'mother in Israel' for the hundreds of Chinese who were saved and delivered." (Ireson, 1970)

Weeks pays this worthy tribute to Dagny Pedersen: "She is the most outstanding example of dedicated missionary service in the whole history of our Fellowship." (Weeks, 2003)

JONES WILLIAMS

Jones Williams, the brother of Daniel Powell Williams, worked alongside his brother as a prophet from the day the Apostolic Church in Wales was birthed on 8th January 1916 until his death on 15th April 1945. His brother Dan died less than a year later. Pastor Warren Jones, in the preface to the book, *Cradle of Mystery*, wrote, "That a worldwide movement should begin in a small Welsh mining village, with two coal miner brothers, is amazing." (Williams, D., 2006)

D. P. Williams tells the story of how his brother, Jones, was ordained before he was saved. It was during the Welsh Revival and Jones found himself sitting between Evan Roberts and another minister, Dr. D.M. Phillips, on the platform. Pastor Dan writes,

"While the large congregation was ablaze with praise and prayer, Evan Roberts turned to Jones and asked him, 'Do you love Jesus?' He answered, 'Of course I love Jesus!' Then he asked, 'Would you like to be a minister?' Jones answered, 'Yes! I would love to be a minister, sir!' Mr. Roberts called the attention of Dr. Phillips and said, 'This young boy would like to be a minister for God', and laid both hands on his head and asked God to make him a preacher of the Gospel. Often, afterwards, Jones said that God ordained him then to the ministry, before he was saved, and before the Apostolic Church was established." (Williams, D., 2006)

Jones Williams, who was nine years younger than his brother, was saved sometime after the Welsh Revival. The majority of the family were saved in 1905. Jones writes, "God visited our home and saved father and mother with the majority of the family. I was one that was not saved, with another sister. For six and a half years, from the time the others were saved, I lived at Garnfoel (the family home) unregenerate." (Williams, D., 2006)

One of D.P. Williams' early experiences of prophetic guidance involved his own brother. At a cottage meeting in Penygroes, this prophetic word was given to D.P., "Go thou, My servant (naming the house to which he was to go) there are two persons in that home, sitting, and the smaller in stature is an ordained and chosen channel to travel with thee through the nations." This was a crucial moment in the life of D.P. Williams in regard to following prophetic revelation. He and his wife went to the house as directed and found the prophetic word to be true. Jones later wrote, "My brother said to his wife that he was going to obey this word. If he found it true, then no man would hinder him from believing and following the voice of God; but if he found it was not true, he would say nothing about it and no one should hear anything about the spoken word. I was one of them and I was smaller in stature. Now no one could have known that I was in this particular house but God Himself." (Williams, D., 2006)

In January 1912, Jones Williams married Ann Evans, from Llandeilo. "It may seem unusual to us now but it was not untypical of the times that, while the reception was taking place in one room for Mr. and Mrs. Jones Williams, 'many saints were in another', the report says, 'feasting on heavenly manna and one man received the baptism and spoke in tongues.'" (Worsfold J. E., 1991)

In February 1913, at an Apostolic Faith Church meeting in Swansea, a prophet from the Bournemouth assembly prophesied that Jones Williams was a prophet and Pastor William Hutchinson ordained him. He had come to the meeting still in his working clothes and straight from his shift underground. "Soon afterwards he was recognised as the prophet for Wales in a service in the Pontardawe Assembly." (Weeks, 2003)

Pastor Jones Williams was a very able preacher and teacher of God's Word. His pastoral work was exemplary, particularly during the Second World War, when he lived in Cardiff and London. While in Cardiff, his own home was completely demolished but that did not hinder him in his care of the local church. "In the period of national emergency the pastor proved himself a true shepherd. After every evening raid, by German planes, he was to be found visiting the saints, ministering to their need both spiritually and naturally. The older folk cannot speak too highly of him and those that were 'bombed out' can only speak of his devotion to them as members of the flock." (Williams, D., 2006)

Pastor Richard Turnbull told this story about Jones Williams and his own father, Pastor Andrew Turnbull, ministering at an Edinburgh Convention: "After the last War, in our Edinburgh Convention when Pastor Jones Williams and my late father were ministering, a soldier came out walking on crutches; they prayed over him, and in the name of Jesus he was commanded to walk; and later I saw him walking carrying his crutches, really healed, and he came right onto the platform. Jesus is the same today." (Apostolic Convention Report , 1943)

During his ministry in the Apostolic Church, Jones visited twenty-seven countries. On many of these overseas visits he was accompanied by his brother, but sometimes he travelled with others. For instance in 1925 he went to Denmark with Pastor H.V. Chanter, and in 1926 to Italy with Pastors F. Hodges and A. Turnbull.

In 1926, Jones Williams visited the American churches. He had been previously to the States in 1922 with Pastors D.P. Williams, A. Turnbull and F. Hodges. Jones Williams prophesied that the main assembly in Philadelphia would be severely attacked and spoken against, which is exactly what happened. When he came back in 1926, he found the assembly in a very poor situation. Pastor Jones got to work and, through private and public meetings, turned the situation around. "His ministry was richly blessed and well received, people were restored to fellowship, some were baptised in the Holy Spirit and the collections increased four-fold! All the erroneous rumours and attacks were refuted and the assembly re-established in Apostolic truth." This paved the way for an apostle from the UK, Pastor Larkins, to come to the US in May 1927. The leaders in the Philadelphia assembly wanted Pastor Jones Williams to stay with them. (Weeks, 2003)

Jones Williams was used greatly in revelatory prophecy, of which these are just a few examples:

A cottage meeting had commenced in Skewen in early 1916. Towards the end of the year, the assembly had an evangelistic campaign in the village and borrowed a Methodist chapel called, "Salem." D.P. Williams writes, "The Word of the Lord came at the Mission on November 7th 1916, through Prophet W.J. Williams, 'Even as I promised unto Joshua, that every place where he would put the sole of his feet, I would give him, if thou wilt be faithful, My servant, thou shalt have this place of worship to gather Mine own together." (D.P. Williams, 1933)

The leader of this group in Skewen was Pastor J.J. Williams. In 1919, the Methodists offered "Salem" to the Apostolic Church for a specific sum of money. Pastor J.J. Williams wrote, "The same night the Elders at Penygroes were directed by the word of the Lord to wire, offering the very sum of money for the chapel that they had asked me for. So the previous word in 1916, that it should be our place of worship, came true. The evidence and the fulfilment were undeniable. The wire is still in my possession. Our God is a living God!" (D.P. Williams, 1933) "Salem" was opened as an Apostolic Church on 29th November, 1919.

Another example concerns a lady, known as "Aunty Margaret". This woman had undergone surgery to remove a large lump from under her arm, but the operation was not completely successful. In a meeting she was attending Pastor Jones Williams prophesied, "There is one here who is disturbing Me, saith the Lord. What dost thou want?" Aunty Margaret shouted out "Healing, Lord!" Jones Williams continued, "Take it, it is thine!" When some of the women helped her to remove the bandages, it was found that the wound and the affected area were renewed like the flesh of a child. (Davies & Yeoman, 2008)

On the 1st January 1920, at the Glasgow New Year Convention, Pastor Jones Williams prophesied, "For I even call that one in the midst from the little nation (Pastor William Phillips from Wales) to send him forth unto that place (Ireland) that I may work indeed... I have amongst those, and amongst that nation, My choice." Ireland was in turmoil at that time, but the Lord said through the prophet, "Thou shalt not fear for I will give thee strength; I will give thee light and I will give thee power that, by the name by which you are sent forth, many shall bend, many shall bow indeed, saith the Lord." (Williams, D., 2006)

It is important to remember that at this time there was no Apostolic Church in Ireland. All the leaders of the Apostolic

Church had was an invitation from a Pastor Fisher to visit a small Pentecostal church in Belfast. On 10th January, a team including Pastors D.P. Williams, A. Turnbull, W. Phillips and others arrived in Belfast for a two week mission. At the end of the two weeks there was an Apostolic assembly in Belfast with 87 members. Pastor Phillips went back to Northern Ireland in the October and, with others, went on to plant several assemblies in the city of Belfast and in the wider province. Another product of Jones Williams' ministry was the prophetic identification of local men, such as Cardwell, Ferran and Lauder, who would take the work forward in Northern Ireland.

In February 1924, an Apostolic delegation, including D.P. and Jones Williams, went to Denmark. During this visit over 700 people stood in a meeting in Copenhagen to declare their acceptance of membership in the Apostolic Church. But this visit was also memorable in another way:

"During this period in Denmark Pastor W. Jones Williams prophesied (at a time when people still looked back to the 'war to end all wars in 1918'), 'Europe will again be bathed in blood, and your country will not escape.' Those of us who have visited Gestapo headquarters in Kolding and lived through the 1939-45 war know only too well how amazingly accurate was that courageous word of prophecy." (Weeks, 2003)

Jones Williams paid a high price for this prophetic ministry to which God had called him. His first wife, Mary Ann, only had her husband home for one Christmas during all the years of his ministry. When Pastor Jones was leaving with his brother for Australia, in September 1934, his wife was unwell and not expected to recover. She said this to him: "Jones, you must go, the Lord has called you. I have never said, 'No!' to His will during all these years and I will not say it now. If he takes me while you are away, then all will be well." (Williams,D., 2006) Mary Ann died in November 1936.

The suffering also included public ridiculing and mockery. Jones Williams wrote, "I have suffered much from outside opposition and misunderstanding of God's ways and purpose. As I have walked the streets some have shouted after me, 'That's the god of the Apostolic Church.' Then they have spoken in imitation of the 'tongues' and sneeringly asked, 'What is the interpretation?'" The mockery not only came from the unsaved but also from the saved. "Then, again, even while God was speaking through my lips as His appointed channel, children of God have come to me and shouted in my face, 'You are a liar!'" (Williams, D. , 2006)

Pastor Jones Williams died on 15th April 1945. "Death occurred from cardiac trouble while the deceased was a patient at St. Andrew's Hospital, London and it was no surprise to his numerous friends to hear the medical opinion that his 'journey's oft', and care for the flock in Kennington, London District, had hastened the end." (Williams, D. , 2006) He left a wife and four children. His brother, Dan was in America and was unable to come home.

Many tributes were given at his funeral in Penygroes. Pastor T.N. Turnbull, a fellow prophet, gave this tribute: "One thing that was outstanding in my brother Jones' life (I was very much with him in the early days) was his courage and convictions. He was a man of great courage."

This is the first verse of a poem, called "Love's Elegy", which D.P. Williams wrote in honour of his brother:

"'Twas not my lot in thy last hour to see thee,
Nor bid farewell when in the valley's night;
But we shall meet when morning dawns in Glory,
And sing God's praises on fair Zion's height."

There were many more individuals whom I could have included in this appendix, but space does not permit. Men like

Pastor Joseph F. Phillips who pioneered the Apostolic vision in Southern Ireland; Pastor Ian MacPherson who blessed the Body of Christ with his preaching and writing; Pastor George Evans who served in Argentina, Italy and Canada; or Pastor Joseph Larkins, who went with his family to the USA in May 1927, the first UK apostle to go to another land.

I could have written about the able administrators with whom God has blessed the church; men like Pastors Harry Croudson, Thomas Davies ("The Scribe"), and Percy Johns. There are also other women I could have included such as Ivy Lewis and Vera Allan, who both went to Nigeria and Miss Clark, who was a missionary in India.

In regard to other nationalites, I think of Dr. Carl Naeser from Denmark, who was the first to pioneer in France, opening an assembly in Paris in September 1924; the Derrys from New Zealand; and Pastor Roy Williams and family from the USA.

Another area which I could have explored was how the missionary zeal in the UK was reproduced in other countries around the world. The Australian Apostolic Church was the first to send a missionary to India, Pastor Fred Hurst. Japan, Papua New Guinea and the New Hebrides were pioneered by the Apostolic Church "down under". The Canadian Apostolic Church branched out into the West Indies. Nigeria and Ghana pioneered into surrounding countries in West Africa. The Danish Apostolic Church was a means of blessing to many countries in Europe, such as Italy, France and Estonia. We must remember that behind all these Gospel endeavours were people, with families, who had a heart for service and a faith in the Lord of heaven and earth. God still uses people to take His will and His purpose forward today.

I could also have written about David Ferran, the brother of Pastor A. Ferran, who owned a shipping business in Belfast and supplied Gospel vans to evangelists, not only in the UK, but also to our missionaries overseas.

Then there is Herbert Cousen, a businessman from Yorkshire, who for many years served on the Missionary Board, first as Treasurer and then as Chairman. Herbert Cousen, and his wife showed great hospitality to our missionaries as they travelled from and returned to Bradford. Also, at his own expense, he visited our missionaries in China and Nigeria. He escorted two engaged brides, Miss Myfanwy Williams (niece of Pastors Dan and Jones) and Miss Netta Johnson out to their respective fiancés, George Evans and James Turnbull, in Argentina in 1926. Herbert Cousen was recognised as a prophet and later, in 1929, as an apostle.

I have spent many hours reading Missionary Committee Minutes from the 1940s, when Pastor Cousen was the chairman. It was a massive responsibility he carried in regard to the continual raising of finance, the determining of strategy for individual countries, recognising the vast differences in culture and climate, arranging the resources for the purchase of cars, land and houses, and, finally, handling, with grace and care, the many personal difficulties that arose within the missionary staff overseas. Some of our missionaries died on the mission field leaving widows with children.

Finally there was Mr. C. Munday, a representative of a British Trading Company in West Africa, who allowed his personal accounts to channel wages and grants from the UK to our missionaries in West Africa and also supplied loans as needed. Mr. Munday had a remarkable deliverance on one trip back to Nigeria during the war. There were two ships returning to Nigeria and they were part of a naval convoy. Arriving at Liverpool, he was directed to the wrong ship and set sail. Sad to say, the convoy was attacked and the vessel that Mr. Munday had been due to travel on was torpedoed and went down with the loss of all those on board.

We also need to remember the unnamed company of people who graced our movement across the nations of the world after 1916. Through their sacrificial giving, their unrelenting service, their untold acts of kindness and their devotion to Apostolic truth, they saw a movement raised that was part of God's restoration purpose in the 20th Century. Through such people a building portfolio worth millions was established across the world; Bible schools to train future leaders were brought into being; a school programme was established in West Africa that helped many children learn and aim for bigger things and missionary outposts were established across the globe. All the while the Gospel was being spread far and wide, the kingdom of Satan was being defeated and Jesus was being revealed as King of Kings, and Lord of Lords.

There are two further appendices included in the book, where you will find others mentioned who have blessed the Apostolic Church over the years. In addition, blogs have been written highlighting other pastors and missionaries, including Pastor Hugh Mitchell and Miss Esther Knight and more will be added before the end of this centenary year. They can be accessed online by visiting ac-100.org.

APPENDIX 2
MEMORIES

The following memories of previous Apostolic pastors and missionaries have been written by family members or colleagues. In some cases they have been edited and condensed.

STEPHEN BOWEN: Nerina Williams (granddaughter)

Stephen Bowen was born again during the 1904 Welsh Revival at the age of 24. He became one of the founding members of the Apostolic Church in Penygroes. He was a business man and had a motor garage in Llandybie, near Penygroes. He was amongst the first people in the village to own a motor vehicle, which became known as the "Apostolic Chariot". He was able to drive Pastors Dan and Jones Williams around to various places to minister.

On one such occasion they were holding a service in Llanon, Cardiganshire, on December 18th 1915, where there was great opposition. It ended in quite a serious incident, including shots being fired and stones being thrown at them. One of the injured was Stephen Bowen.

The incident was taken to court by a local man from Llanon. After the court hearing the case was dismissed.

As a business man, Stephen owned three quarries and was able to supply building materials to build churches in Llandybie (where he became the first pastor), Cwmdu, Bethlehem (near Llandeilo not Israel!!), Crosshands, Tumble, Dafen and Llwynhendy. When he moved to Edgware, outside London, in 1926, he built up another business and eventually built the church in Burnt Oak, Edgware in 1929 and became its first pastor.

He always said that he didn't want to be in full time ministry because as a business man he could then give financial support to the Lord's work. He was a humble man and did not want any recognition. It was all the Lord's doing.

Author's note:
Pastor Stephen Bowen died in November 1962 in Lodi, California. He and his wife had moved there in 1961 to help his son-in-law and daughter, Mr. and Mrs. Noel Meredith, pioneer an Apostolic church on the west coast of America.

Pastor Owen Roberts, in his tribute to Pastor Stephen Bowen, wrote, "He was a brother of whose faithfulness to the Apostolic Vision we cannot speak too highly. He exemplified this faithfulness in every aspect and we can truly say of him what the Apostle Paul said of Tychicus: 'A beloved brother, and a faithful minister and fellow servant in the Lord.' He possessed a bright and cheery disposition and it can be said of him that he was a personification of the chorus he frequently sang: 'I'll carry my sunshine with me everywhere I go.'"

HARRY COPP: Christine Williams (daughter)

The following is a summary of the notebook we found after my mother's death, which was a part of an early draft of my father's life.

My father had made the decision for salvation as a very young boy of 8 years old, at a series of children's special services at a Baptist Church in Dublin. Returning to his hometown of Bridlington in Yorkshire he continued to attend a Baptist Church, where his father was a deacon and his mother taught Sunday school. After being baptised in water at the age of 16, he became a more fervent witness, taught in the Sunday school, visited the workhouse, spoke in the open air services, and delivered tracts.

It was at this age that my father felt the call to become a missionary in Africa. He was encouraged to lead meetings, speak and continue to study, so he enrolled at Wellesby College. He had also trained as a heating engineer and plumber and these skills were to stand him in good stead in many and various projects on the mission field.

He then started to attend an independent mission at Bridlington. Here, he responded to a call for missionaries and went to work for Southern Spain Mission, near Gibraltar in 1933. He lived by faith; firstly working with a co-worker, then on his own.

Following his return from Spain, he attended a fellowship in Halifax, where he met my mother. This fellowship became the basis of the Apostolic Church in Halifax. My father was invited to become a missionary in Durban, South Africa for the Apostolic Church in 1938. My mother joined him shortly afterwards and they were married in Durban. I and my sister, Sylvia, were born in South Africa.

We returned to Britain at the end of the war on a troop ship but my father was sent to Nigeria to minister at the Apostolic Church Training College. On his return to Britain he went as pastor to Porthleven, Cornwall, then Blackburn.

My parents then served two terms of two and a half years as Apostolic missionaries in the Gold Coast, now Ghana. On their return to Britain, my father became the pastor at Castleford but we saw less and less of him as he was often away at conventions, special services or executive meetings. Whilst he was home he was on call 24/7 as he dearly loved his folk in these assemblies.

My father was designated to move to Bradford to become Missionary Secretary in 1966, but before that was asked to return to Ghana alone for 6 months. He felt fully fulfilled in his work on the mission field and planned, on his return to the UK, to ask the Missionary Committee if he could return to Ghana again for a full term of office. This was not to be as he died on the return journey. It would have been a greater benefit to have known him for longer and gain from his wise counsel.

In some ways it was a privilege to have my father as a pastor as he was based at home, so was often around in the early days. This made the parting when my parents went to Ghana all the more difficult, as we had to be left in boarding school and missed the love, care and security of home life. In those days pastors had the responsibility for several assemblies and visiting took up a great deal of time as it was by public transport. My father also spent much time in prayer and study of the Word. Each evening we would end up with family altar.

My father ended his journal with this statement: "How true are these words, 'Lo, I am with you always even unto the end of the age'"

TOM FORD: Elizabeth Vincent (daughter)

Pastor Tom Ford with his wife, Edith, left Brynmawr in South Wales for Nigeria in 1946. He was 38 and she was 33. They had been married for 10 years, and when they left the UK they had no children. When they returned in 1952, they brought home one daughter, Elizabeth. She was born in Calabar. The doctor who helped was drunk and was plied with lots of coffee to sober him up as much as possible. Elizabeth is married to Pastor Peter Vincent, originally from Swansea, and now resides in Glasgow.

It took the pastor and his wife six weeks to arrive in Lagos, Nigeria in one of the Elder Dempster Line ships from Southampton. They were stationed in Calabar and worked alongside Ps. Donald McGill, Ps. Sandy Taylor, Ps. Derry, Ps. W. Grabham and Ps. Charlie Hopkins. They learned and spoke the Efik language while there.

They loved the work and particularly working with the African people. Elizabeth remembers that the family at one time were given snake to eat for an evening meal, unbeknown to them. It was only when her mother asked what the nice meat was that they had just eaten, they were told. The other thing she remembers was, that her father was participating in a funeral with other pastors, when mid ceremony there was a knocking sound from inside the coffin lid! Needless to say, the funeral came to an abrupt halt!

Pastor Ford worked hard preparing many Bible studies, and spent a lot of his time teaching, which was effective and he found it very rewarding. They returned to the UK in spring 1952.

ISAAC HEWITT: Pastor W. John Hewitt (nephew)

Pastor Isaac Hewitt was the brother of Pastor John Hewitt, and together they pioneered in Australia, New Zealand and South Africa.

The Hewitt family, mother, father, two daughters and Isaac, followed John to Australia in the 1920s. The family became involved in a Pentecostal work in Brisbane, while John was in Sydney leading a Pentecostal church. He would eventually return to the UK, but the family stayed in Australia.

The church in Brisbane was called the "Canvas Cathedral". This was a Pentecostal work begun by William Booth-Clibborn from the USA. Isaac became involved in the church.

When Booth-Clibhorn decided to return to the USA, he made contact with John Hewitt who was at that time involved in revival and divine healing meetings in the UK John accepted the invitation to take over the role as leader of the Canvas Cathedral, a huge marquee in Barry Street, Fortitude Valley. Booth-Clibborn did not realise that Isaac was related to John. When he was told of Booth-Clibborn's decision to return to the United States of America, Isaac asked the obvious question, "Who is going to come and take your place?" The response was, "Actually, he is a namesake of yours. It is John Hewitt, the great Welsh revivalist." With delight Isaac said, "That's my brother!"

John became the Senior Minister and Isaac served alongside in different areas of church leadership and so commenced the team ministry of the Hewitt Brothers. Because of repeated storm damage to the marquee and the challenges of maintenance, it was decided to build a permanent building, that was named "Covenant Christian Church". This later became known as "Glad Tidings Tabernacle" and now "Brisbane City Church". It was at that time the largest Pentecostal assembly in Australia.

One particular Sunday morning in 1933 Isaac Hewitt, now a youth leader and choir leader, arrived at church for the service. Meeting with his brother John in the office, he pulled out an envelope from his pocket. Speaking with his elder brother, who he looked upon as a father and mentor, he said, "This is my resignation to be handed to the secretary." "You have wonderful leadership opportunities here in the fellowship so you can't hand in your resignation", he said. Isaac responded with, "But John, I must. God has spoken to me." Nothing would change Isaac's mind. He knew that God had spoken to him. At this point of time, John, with a wry grin, reached into his inside pocket and withdrew an envelope saying, "God has also spoken to me about the same thing and this is my resignation." In an amazing way, without collusion, God had spoken to them both clearly about his redirection for their future. So was launched a powerful pioneering duo — the "Hewitt Brothers",

At this time, John was invited to travel to Adelaide to join William Cathcart, whom he had met in the UK He was now pioneering the Apostolic Movement in Australia. John took Isaac with him as the song-leader, and together they worked as the Hewitt Brothers in great campaigns across Australia and also pioneering New Zealand with amazing results. These included the Adelaide Town Hall for 16 weeks, then on to the Melbourne Auditorium and Unity Theatre, Perth, to mention a few. Hundreds were accepting the Lord every week and many signs, wonders and miracles took place.

Isaac married Joy Evans from Perth, WA, the daughter of one of the early apostles in Australia. He became a great pastor and apostle, loved by everyone who knew him. He ministered in churches across the nation and became State Superintendent in WA. His astute business ability was applied to his function in the Body of Christ, resulting in church growth and planting, including the Dianella assembly, now known as "Summer Lakes".

For three and a half years, Isaac Hewitt was superintendent of the Apostolic Missionary work among the Australian aborigines at Jigalong, on the edge of the Gibson Desert. During this time water holes were dug and animal flocks and herds developed. This established the mission as a going concern from a business standpoint and further enhanced the spiritual effectiveness.

After returning from Jigalong, Isaac worked with the AOG in WA. During these years he became a mentor to many young men who still serve the Pentecostal church across Australia today.

Upon the return of Isaac Hewitt to the Apostolic Church, he pastored at Dianella and travelled across the nation. He also preached in many churches in New Zealand. There are few left who recall the early years, but, speaking with those who remain, there is always an expression of awe at the mention of Isaac Hewitt, or "Pastor Isaac" as he was known.

Our early pioneers deserve to be honoured for the faith steps they took and the challenges faced. Isaac James Hewitt was a powerful man, mightily used of God in the early pioneering days of the Apostolic Church Australia. With his wife Joy, and children - June (musician) and David (song-leader and preacher) - they exemplified a family united in serving the Lord.

JOHN HEWITT (SENIOR): Pastor W.John Hewitt (son)

In Nantyffyllon, November 1915, John Hewitt made a commitment to follow and serve the Lord. He was mentored by Stephen Jeffries, and started preaching in his hometown. There probably wasn't a street in the district where he didn't preach the Gospel. He then travelled to Australia in 1923 leaving the Colliery in Maesteg, in the Llynfi Valley, to work at the coalface in Ipswich Queensland.

He soon left the mining and accepted the role as leader of the Silkstone Baptist Church, also holding campaigns for the Baptist denomination. He soon became known as the "Great Welsh Revivalist". He was an apostle in gifting and an evangelist at heart. In his first campaign at Dinmore there were 100 decisions and he baptised 80 in water. At one church, while he preached, two people were baptised in the Holy Spirit, bringing much persecution.

In December 1926, Lily Newton from the Swansea assembly left for Australia to marry her fiancé, John Hewitt, in Silkstone, Queensland. He had been invited to take over the Pentecostal assembly in Sydney, so they were soon married and took up that position.

During subsequent years he travelled to Auckland, New Zealand 1927; and then was invited to lead the largest NZ Assembly of God in Wellington. He then travelled to South Africa where his campaigns saw many miraculous healings. He returned to Wales in 1929 for a holiday, was invited to a Council meeting in Bradford and attended the Penygroes Convention.

After a further successful ministry in South Africa for 16 months, John Hewitt returned to the UK where he joined Evan Jones, singer, and Frank Warburton, pianist, to form the First International Evangelistic Band, campaigning throughout the British Isles.

He again travelled to Australia in 1932 to pastor Australia's largest Pentecostal Church, the Canvas Cathedral in Brisbane, Queensland. Then in 1933 John Hewitt with his brother Isaac, were miraculously led, independent of each other, to resign their position in Brisbane and join William Cathcart and Joshua McCabe in Melbourne - John Hewitt as evangelist and Isaac his brother, 11 years younger, as leader of song - for successful revival and divine healing meetings, where signs, wonders and miracles were the norm. In Adelaide City, the Town Hall was packed for 16 weeks as the revival continued there and in other cities.

For a short period in the 1950s, John H. Hewitt filled the role of Acting President while W.A.C. Rowe was on an extended ministry tour of the UK churches.

D. CHARLES HOPKINS: Ernest Williams (colleague)

In January 1957 I first met Charlie (Pastor D. C. Hopkins), who was in charge of the Efik/Ibibio Area of Eastern Nigeria. It was the Latter Rain period at that time (although Charlie certainly enjoyed the blessing of Latter Rain, he had none of the baggage that sometimes accompanied it). It was my duty to work under him and support him. He clearly displayed his qualities as an anointed apostle, excellent leader, faithful teacher and able developer of an Apostolic Church.

He constantly majored on the development of indigenous ministries. He led his fellow apostles and prophets in many major public campaigns - usually when it was full-moon, since there was no electric light in many localities at the time, and the public was able to come together in thousands. He provided amplifying equipment which contributed greatly to the success of such meetings. Many souls were saved, and there were miracles of healing (often in the crowd as preaching progressed), blind seeing etc. Sometimes assemblies were opened as a result. Another emphasis for which he was responsible was what he called Men's Conferences.

He chose some eight or nine centres - to which all men in the geographical area were invited to attend. The first evening ministry was given either by himself or by an indigenous apostle, followed by food provided locally. Next morning there would be two teaching sessions on Apostolic principles, both practical and theological, before all were free to go home. The team leading the conference would then depart to the next centre to repeat the programme. This produced many elders and some pastors.

He established a residential Bible College for full-time deeper teaching. Principals included Pastors Alex Ferran and Joe Kirkwood, with Nigerian apostles taking over later.

Annually he also held four-day staff teaching conferences; and at every opportunity he not only emphasised the baptism of the Spirit, but led sessions for the receiving of the Spirit - sometimes with as many as 50 receiving at a time. All this points to the development of an Apostolic Church which, in the two and a half years I first served with Charlie, opened 250 new assemblies.

D.C. was my "boss" for all my service until Cameroon split off from dependence on Nigeria and I thank God for him.

JOSHUA G. MCCABE: W. John Hewitt (Colleague of J. McCabe and son of John Hewitt)

As a young man Joshua McCabe worked in the printing industry in Scotland and had a wonderful conversion. Even though his mother was a member of the Apostolic Church, he attended a Christian Brethren Assembly. He was instructed that "tongues and healing were not for these days". However, God had a plan for Joshua and sent a pastor to visit Mrs. McCabe. Conversation led to conviction and he was soon filled with the Spirit, with signs following.

Joshua McCabe, soon after, was called to be an evangelist and ministered in various assemblies in Scotland. Later came the revelation that he was a prophet in the Body of Christ.

In 1931, a request came from William Cathcart, a Scottish Apostle who had been sent to pioneer in Australia, for a prophet to work with him in the pioneering venture. Joshua McCabe wholeheartedly accepted the call and, in January 1932, he arrived with his wife and daughter in Perth WA.

His obvious gifting as a prophet was outstanding throughout the years. He would travel into a district and prophesy, naming people into various functions without having met with them or heard their name.

Joshua McCabe was appointed President of the Australian

Apostolic Church upon the sudden death of W.A.C. Rowe in 1960. He was a man with a great love for the Apostolic vision and he loved to preach about the Holy Spirit. I had the privilege of him being in my assembly for over 20 years in his retirement, before he passed away peacefully at 99 years of age. Well into his 90s, though clinically blind, he would still preach on his favourite subject. Yes! You've got it - the Holy Spirit.

SAMUEL M. MCKIBBEN (Senior): Anna Parker (daughter)

In his youth, Dad accepted Christ as his Saviour in the Railway Mission in Glasgow. Not long after in the 1914-1918 War he was recruited as a soldier. The first night in the barracks, he knelt by his bedside to pray. Soon boots were thrown at him, but he ignored them, and his fellow conscripts came to accept him as a Christian. He rose through the ranks to become a sergeant and the Lord preserved his life. He was gassed, sent back to the UK to recover, and never returned to the trenches, but served elsewhere till the War ended.

After he returned to his home in Glasgow, he went on holiday to his cousins in Ireland who had been saved, and recently baptised in the Holy Spirit. They were very enthusiastic about their experience so, as soon as Dad returned to Glasgow, he found "The Burning Bush" in Renfrew St., and became sold out for God himself. In the late 1920s my Dad was appointed overseer of Coatbridge Assembly, and editor of the Scottish Magazine called the *Apostolic Messenger*. It was full of testimonies and campaign reports.

In May 1929, he married his Danish bride. Theirs was the first wedding in the recently acquired large church in North Frederick St., Glasgow. Pastor D.P. Williams gave Mum away and Pastor Andrew Turnbull married them. She shared all Dad's enthusiasm for the Lord's work.

In 1931, I was born, and a few months later Dad accepted the call to full time Ministry. Dad's remit for Bradford was to pastor the assembly in Manchester Rd. serve on the Missionary Committee, be the editor of the *Apostolic Herald*, and do some gospel campaigns. At the height of its publication, 32,000 copies had to be packed and posted monthly by my Dad and some volunteer young folk including Hugh and Kenneth Mitchell.

In 1935, my brother Samuel was born. I was 4 years old. Mum had been ill during the pregnancy. It was only much later we learned that the problem was the onset of MS. It was to be our "thorn in the flesh" for 23 years till the Lord called her home. Constant prayer, even fasting at times, by ourselves and faithful prayer warriors kept us hopeful, but when God chose not to heal her, He gave us the grace to press on.

It was particularly difficult for Dad while my brother Samuel and I were little children, but he remained diligent in his calling to serve the Lord. Later, when she became bedridden for the last 11years, Dad and I became her sole carers.

In 1937, Dad was called to move to Stirling. I learned to pray every day that the bungalow would sell quickly, and God would provide a ground floor flat for us in Stirling. It was to be my first real experience of answered prayer and for my parents, the proof they really were moving in God's will. He was pastor of 5 assemblies in the Stirling District.

About 18 months later, Dad was asked to cover as Pastor of the Copenhagen Apostolic Church for 3 months while Pastor W.H. Lewis (their missionary from London) went to Estonia to set up a fledgling church plant there. Dad was willing to go to Denmark, but concerned about leaving his ailing wife to cope with a 3yr. old and a 7yr. old, but also the fact that another war was threatening. God saw and met our need. A lady in the Stirling Assembly paid for Mum, me and Samuel to go and stay in Denmark. Although Mum could no longer walk well, she could still cook, care for us and interpret for Dad.

Our next move was to Aberdeen. Dad had the care of 3 assemblies, and was away quite a lot, being on the Executive. Towards the end of our stay Mum was hospitalised twice, each time for 2 or 3 weeks. So at 13, I quickly learned to cook, clean, and do piles of home -work. I had to leave school at 14, when Dad was called to Dover in Kent. In my short school life, I had been taught in 6 different schools!

We found the Saints in Dover greatly relieved that shelling by the Germans in France had stopped. Their town was sadly very boarded up, and many people had given up, and moved away. Spiritually there was great blessing for the faithful church, and for me, the chance to get to church as we had acquired a wheel chair for Mum. We took her to all the meetings including my water baptism, and the night I was baptised in the Holy Spirit! There was great joy! We were able to hold open-airs on the beach every Saturday night in summer.

Sadly, as the UK rejoiced in VE day celebrations on 8th of May 1945, my Mum collapsed and became bedfast. Apart from a district nurse calling daily for a short time, we had no help. The following year we moved back to Scotland. It was an extremely difficult move for Dad to organise, and for me to travel in ambulances, and sleeper train with Mum, but we made it with the Lord's help.

Dad had the care of 7 assemblies in the Clyde Valley District. No House Groups in those days, so each assembly had 2 meetings on Sundays, and at least one week night service. He had no car, so relied on public transport. He was also Chairman of the Church's Finance Committee at that time. Mostly I cared for Mum during the days, and he did the nights but when he was at home, I cooked and he would feed her. We still did some hospitality, so I got news of the meetings, but missed them, except for youth rallies, and Sunday School, where Dad was not needed. My friends got married, and I despaired sometimes that our trial would never end.

Annually, Dad generously spared me one week of his holidays, plus some free time each week. To me, it was a miracle when I met Frank who was living in Wales. Despite having to wait years, our love for each other deepened. One of our friends said ours was not a courtship but a correspondence course! Over 900 letters passed between us. It was not until some years after Dad became pastor of the Edinburgh District, that we finally married in 1956.

Six months after we married, Mum passed away, aged 63. Dad waited 4 years then married married Pastor Isaac Martin's widow, Netta. She was a fine lady, whom we all loved. They were extremely happy, and she was very heart broken when he passed away 11 years later, aged 76. Samuel had his gravestone inscribed, "Fought the good fight, Finished the course, Kept the faith".

Author's note:
Pastor T.N.Turnbull, son of Pastor Andrew Turnbull, gave this tribute to Pastor Samuel M. McKibben on his death; "He was a man of God, a godly man, who lived the life he preached. He did this, whatever the cost to himself. He was also dedicated to the call which God had given him. He also lived a life of devotion. He had a spirit that surmounted all difficulties, and pressed on to victory throughout the many years of his Christian life." (Riches of Grace November 1972)

BEN NOOT: Anne Davies (daughter)

My father, Benjamin James Noot, lived in Skewen, a village in South Wales. As a young man he attended the Methodist Church where he was the pianist. He also played the piano to accompany the silent movies at the local cinema!

His mother, having heard stories of how God was blessing the group of people meeting at Salem, began to attend. On hearing this, my father told her, "If you're going there you'll end up in the lunatic asylum before long". But, as time passed, and he heard more stories of what was happening at Salem he decided to see for himself.

Not wanting to be seen by anyone, he arrived after the evening service had begun and slipped into a seat at the back. His plan worked to such an extent that prayer having begun before he entered, both the deacons who were supposed to be watching the door were kneeling with their eyes closed and hands in the air, confirming his suspicions that this was indeed the first step along the road to the asylum!

However, he found a place at the back and sat down. Just then a prophet sitting on the platform began to speak: "I see you my servant. You are uncertain and sitting on the fence. I am telling you this day to come down on the right side."

Although never having heard prophecy before, he knew without any doubt that God was speaking directly to him and so joined the Apostolic Church which met at Salem, Skewen, identifying himself with the scorned Pentecostals. At that time he was a heavy smoker but told us soon after he "just stopped".

Eventually he was called into the pastorate and ministered in several churches in South Wales. One of these was our church in Swansea. At that time the Swansea eldership was in turmoil. Mrs. Evelyn Williams, Pastor Dan's daughter-in-law, told me that one Sunday morning the police were called because two of the elders had come to blows over the communion table! After my father was sent there things settled down. "We asked God to send us a lion to sort out the church" she said, "but He sent us a lamb!"

It was in his early forties that he, my mother and my sister, Beth, then aged 2, left by sea for Canada to pioneer churches with other pastors, some of whom had also been sent from Britain. I was born 6 years later in Toronto. In those early years the family moved many times and thriving churches were established. In 1948, the Latter Rain Movement arrived.

At the age of 7, I was too young to remember, but what happened next became part of our family history because, after serving for 14 years in Canada my father asked to be brought home to Britain. He felt that, as President of the Canadian Council for 13 years, he was bound to maintain loyalty to the British church which had sent him to Canada. He was alone in opposing the desire of the other Canadian pastors to overthrow Apostolic principles of guidance and governance in the Canadian churches. In a letter sent on 3rd. November 1950 he writes, "I fail to see why these people demand that we throw over our name and government before they have anything to do with us."

This request was granted and we were sent to Lurgan, in Northern Ireland. At that time, it was the custom to publicly welcome returning staff from abroad at the Penygroes Convention (the highlight of the Apostolic year). My parents were not welcomed and my mother felt it deeply, saying we had been brought home in disgrace.

But this is the story of God's faithfulness: He began to bless the Lurgan assembly and district. There was a real visitation of the Spirit that touched many across the island of Ireland.

We were there for just 3 years and my father was then moved to the Rhondda Valley in South Wales. He served there until retirement and afterwards in support of the District Pastor, David Morris, with whom he formed a very close and personal relationship. A year after he retired my mother died at the age of

52. He told me once that after that he was only truly happy when he was in a meeting. He died at the age of 75 at peace with God and with man.

Author's note:
Pastor J. Omri Jones, who knew Pastor Noot for over 40 years, gave this tribute "Pastor Noot was a sterling character, very wise and prudent in all his dealings with officers and saints, and great peace prevailed amongst the saints. He always had the unity of the body before his mind's eye, and strove at all times to keep the work in line with the tone and tenor of scriptures." (Riches of Grace, August 1967)

FRED POOLE: John Poole (son)

How do I remember him?

I remember him in his study – diligently, carefully, preparing teaching material, answering correspondence, me listening for the sound of his portable typewriter as he worked long hours.

I remember him in the pulpit, authoritative, confident, sure of the message he was delivering, always calling us to a place in our faith that was higher and deeper.

I remember his sermons were filled with illustrations from his early days in Wales.

I remember his altar calls during days when the Sunday night service was an Evangelistic Service.

I remember him walking down from the platform to where the communion table was and the reverence and honour he gave to "doing this in remembrance of Him."

I remember his courage in being willing to follow his convictions, even when it brought him great trial and difficulty, and sometimes separation from people he had great respect for.

I remember the delight and joy on his face when he first opened our pulpit to ministers from "old line denominations" who had experienced the baptism of the Holy Spirit and as they testified to what "walking in the Spirit, being led by the Spirit" now meant to them.

I remember his love for the Epistle to the Ephesians and the fact that he became known in many places as "the Apostle to the Ephesians" since he took his text from that letter so often.

I remember him as a pioneer – using radio as a medium of communication when few others did.

I remember the opportunities he gave me as a young man, opportunities to develop my gifts and abilities, making room for me, by stepping back from a place and role that he would always have filled.

I remember him in "open air meetings" in Montreal, in Peterborough and in the heart of Philadelphia, he loved witnessing in and outside of the church building and encouraged us all to do the same.

I remember the look of respect that other ministers and leaders had for him all of this country and in other countries as well.

I remember the frustration he had when he could not convince people to embrace a God who could do "exceedingly, abundantly, above and beyond all that they could ask or think."

How did God use him?

God used him to bring many individuals to a place of faith and trust in Jesus and to seek to follow him.

God used him to open the hearts and minds of so many people to a vision of the body of Christ that was greater and bigger than anything they had imagined.

God used him to help people accept gifts and ministries from places that we had previously rejected.

God used him to bring countless numbers of people into the experience of knowing the Holy Spirit as a real person and power in their lives.

God used him to mentor younger ministers and helped them to grow in their gifts and callings.

God used him by counselling denominational ministers who

had been baptized in the Holy Spirit not to leave for Pentecostal denominations, but to stay in the place they were and witness to what God had done and was doing in their lives and ministry.

God used him to help young people experience the joy of their faith, and that serving God did not mean you had to have a long face and a sour countenance.

God used him to help people believe they could do more individually and as a faith community than they thought was possible. As an example, I am thinking of the move that the congregation in his first pastorate in Pennsylvania made going from a small suburban location to purchasing a much larger building in the center of Philadelphia and of paying off the mortgage in one year. Something that amazed even the mortgage lenders.

God used him in West Africa when, through his relationships, he brought a team of men with the gift of healing to lead large meetings which brought so many people to faith.

Impressions on me:

I gained from my father a lifelong respect and reverence for Scripture and the need to study it consistently, diligently, with an open mind and heart.

I gained from him a lifelong respect for the work of the Holy Spirit and in the fact that you can never, ever set limits or boundaries – "the wind blows wherever it wants to" and no one can stop it.

I gained from him an appreciation of worship in Spirit and in truth, an understanding that if our gratitude and praise did not come from the heart, that it was also much "religious activity" and profited nothing.

I learned that success in the ministry comes from a full and total commitment to God, as you understood God, and that nothing else could come first.

WILLIAM A.C. ROWE: W. John Hewitt (colleague of W.A.C. Rowe)

Among those earliest of Apostolic pioneers in the UK was a young man named W.A.C. "Billie" Rowe. Among those early apostles, many of them mature in years, stood out this fresh young man. He was used widely in ministry and had a strong teaching ministry presented with a compassionate understanding of his audience.

During the early 1940s, during World War 2, he travelled to Australia and New Zealand with Hugh Dawson (who I believe was the Vice President in the UK at that time). This was at great risk considering the many battles on the high seas as well as in the air. They were away for two years offering administrative and spiritual assistance.

In 1946, when there was need to replace William Cathcart as President of the Apostolic Church in Australia, W.A.C. Rowe responded to the call and travelled to Australia with his wife and two daughters, and Pastor Frank Hodges.

When the possibility arose for a missions outreach in the Highlands of New Guinea, it was W.A.C. Rowe who prepared the way, travelling to Port Moresby to meet with the Administration of the Territory of Papua and New Guinea. He then travelled to the Highlands, meeting with the District Commissioner, patrol officers and tribal chiefs, settling on Laiagam as the place.

One Lord One Faith, his well known book covering many of the "Distinctive Apostolic Truths", was completed just before his sudden, untimely death in 1960, just over 13 years after arriving in Australia.

CHARLES SERCOMBE: Christine Moore (daughter)

I remember my father as a man who loved life. He loved his ministry in the Apostolic Church, took his pastoral responsibilities very seriously, and rated home-visiting as of equal importance to actual preaching. He drew enormous encouragement from being part of the overall leadership team, and embraced in obedience a prophetic call to the mission field before ever he heard that call for himself.

He loved having visitors, especially those with Ghanaian connections, and the heartiness of his ensuing laughter with them gave me a glimpse of his character that I might otherwise never have seen. Fellow American missionaries were an added encouragement to him, and he thrived on the sense of making a difference during his many years in Ghana.

He was glad to continue his service to the Lord well into retirement, and never spoke to me of any regrets. He thanked the Lord sincerely for good health, and only began to fail after he turned 80, though he kept secret much of that encroaching illness.

I'll remember him always as totally committed both to the Lord and to what became his life's calling to the Apostolic Church. But it falls to others who knew him better to reflect in greater detail as to what that actually entailed. These are - as requested - merely a daughter's reflections... the more personal ones being, of course, far too many to record.

IDRIS J. VAUGHAN: David Vaughan (son)

Idris J. Vaughan was born on 13th March 1901 in Abertriwr in Mid-Glamorgan. A few weeks later his father was one of eighty-one miners killed in an explosion at the nearby Universal Colliery at Senghdd.

As time moved on, the family moved to Cwmtwch in the Swansea Valley and then to Ystalyfera, where his mother was converted and became a staunch member of the local Pentecostal Church. Some years later Pastor Stephen Jeffries was the guest speaker over the Easter period. On Easter Monday, after the services and appeal, Idris was saved. In 1916 at Maesteg, under the ministry of Stephen Jeffires and Mrs. Cripp, he was baptised with the Holy Spirit. Back home in Ystalyfera, through time, Idris was recognised as an evangelist and prophet.

Pastor I.J. Vaughan was ordained at the home of D.P. Williams at Pontypridd and in 1921 he was called to the ministry full-time as an evangelist and prophet, to be located in Northern Ireland, where he served for some years, living by faith. In this he found God to be faithful in meeting all his needs.

In 1931, Pastors G. Perfect and I.J. Vaughan, were called to be the first missionaries of the Apostolic Church to Nigeria - Pastor Perfect as an apostle and Pastor Vaughan as an evangelist and prophet. They arrived in Lagos on 2nd June 1932 to be royally welcomed by Pastor D.O. Odubanjo and some of the other leaders.

At the end of November 1932, Idris was called to Calabar for a 12 week gospel campaign. However, because of a mighty work of God in revival, the twelve weeks became 12 years. The revival in those early days went on for years and thousands were converted and hundreds of churches opened.

The following report of Pastor Vaughan on the early days of revival will prove most interesting: "Truly, there was revival in the air: there was revival on the ground and there was revival as, going down into the water of Calabar, I baptised eight hundred from those who had found Christ in those six weeks of divine visitation, for such it must be claimed to have been, in view of the apparent suddenness of it and of the humble black and white agents involved in it!.. It is still with great wonder that I recall a first holy communion service in the new building, where instead of the original small company of about thirty or so, I ministered to a congregation of somewhere nearer a thousand eager, happy Christians."

One could ask – what was the secret? The answer clearly given would be prayer. The prayer meetings in Nigeria were of great importance, and still are! I can also testify that my father, Idris Vaughan, was a man of prayer and the Word. He belonged to a generation of men and women who were truly captivated by the love of God - true warriors of faith.

APPENDIX 3
THE ULTIMATE COST

by Pastor Philip Powell: retired Vice-President of the Apostolic Church UK and Chairman of the Overseas Mission Board.

Nothing has moved me more than reading of missionaries who paid the ultimate cost in serving the Lord on the mission field. Some died young while others lived to a good age.

In this article it is my intention to pay tribute to missionaries of the Apostolic Church who died serving the Lord in missionary service. Writing about them is no easy task and therefore is undertaken with the greatest respect for those who laid down their lives and are buried in the soil of Africa, at sea or repatriated and buried in the UK.

In some cases, I have drawn on extracts from various Apostolic documents, and I am grateful for the information supplied by Pastor Len and Cathy Howells, Pastor Hugh Mitchell's article *Early Recollections* and Pastor Gordon Weeks' book, *Chapter 32*.

The following Apostolic missionaries laid down their lives in Africa paying, the ultimate cost:

PASTOR WILLIAM TAYLOR

The first Apostolic Church missionary to die on the mission field was Pastor William Taylor, who died in Nigeria on 1st July 1938 from dysentery aged 52 and is buried in Kaduna. Pastor G. Perfect gave a tribute to him at the Penygroes Convention in 1938 on the occasion of the unveiling of a plaque in memory of his sacrifice. Pastor Perfect was with him when he died.

The call to Nigeria came to him whilst he was the pastor of the church in Porthleven and, although suffering from a heart condition, it did not stop him seeking to fulfil the will of God for his life. This call was deep rooted in him and so nothing was going to prevent him fulfilling his life's call.

He went to Nigeria leaving his wife in Porthleven. They had four children, two boys and two girls, and the loss of their father was certainly a great blow to them as a family. After her husband's death, Mrs. Taylor stayed in Porthleven with three of their children.

A service of dedication in memory of him was held during the 1939 Penygroes Convention. Pastor G. Perfect gave a very fitting tribute to him on behalf of the church - sympathy and condolences were expressed to Mrs. Taylor and her family. During the service of remembrance Pastor D.P. Williams made an appeal for someone to replace Pastor Taylor and several came forward including Pastor Taylor's son.

PASTOR WILLIAM GRABHAM

Pastor William Grabham was born in Ystradgynlais, a village located at the top of the Swansea Valley in South Wales.

He attended the Apostolic Church there where he committed his life to the Lord Jesus Christ whilst in his teens. He made rapid progress spiritually and as an evangelist often preached in the open air in the surrounding villages.

He was a full time minister for almost 25 years, serving the Lord and the Apostolic Church in the UK and Nigeria. His pastorates included Porthleven, Shrewsbury, and N. Ireland.

He undertook three tours of missionary service and his third tour was to be his last. His first tour was in 1938 when he responded to an appeal for a missionary to replace Pastor William Taylor who died and was buried in Kaduma in Nigeria.

Pastor Grabham was the pastor in Shrewsbury when he responded to fill the vacancy in Nigeria. He was one of 14 pastors and others to go forward at the Penygroes Convention following the President's appeal for Pastor Taylor's replacement. It was at the Thursday evening service of the 1938 Convention that the President, Pastor D.P. Williams, announced that Pastor and Mrs. Grabham had been chosen to go to Nigeria - at the same time Pastor Grabham was ordained to be an Apostle in the body of Christ.

Pastor Grabham testified at the Convention: "Now I can see how the Lord has led. Even if I die on the field, one thing I know, I feel I am in the will of God". He was ready to lay down his life. He loved the Africans, labouring among them, and leading many to know the Lord Jesus as their Saviour.

He and Mrs. Grabham were sent to Nigeria on their first missionary tour prior to the outbreak of the Second World War. During their third tour, Mrs. Grabham returned home to Wales alone leaving her beloved husband's body in the soil of Nigeria in Enugu.

PASTOR WILFRED RHODES

Pastor Wilfred Rhodes took over as the Superintendent of Calabar, Nigeria in 1942, and in August 1943 laid down his life in the Master's service - his death being a great loss to the Church.

Pastor David Rennie reported, in the special Calabar Issue of the Apostolic Herald, March 1961 that he "visited the grave of Pastor Rhodes of Bradford (near to the grave of Mary Slessor) which tops the green slope of Calabar's cemetery hill overlooking the beautiful wooded shores of the creek below".

Before becoming a missionary, Pastor Rhodes was a lay member of the Missionary Committee, appointed in 1934 along with F. Bairstow (father of Dr. Edward Bairstow). All the members of the Committee were situated around Bradford.

Despite his and the Missionary Committee's dislike of mixing secular with spiritual work in Africa, he said, "we must take up education"; and so secular education was now coordinated with Gospel work in Nigeria.

In *Early Recollections* Ps. Hugh Mitchell wrote "A major loss to the missionary work was the death of Ps. Wilfred Rhodes. I well recollect accompanying him to Glasgow to take ship to West Africa. It was wartime and all the shipping left under great secrecy. Mrs. Rhodes (a medical doctor) and I bade farewell to him at the gates of the main dockyard in Gourock. We never saw him again. He safely reached Africa but within one year he had succumbed to yellow-fever and was called home to his eternal rest. News of his serious illness was telegraphed from Calabar to Lagos and the late Ps. Idris Vaughan (a missionary serving in Nigeria) hastened to be at his side - but was too late. This was a great blow to the Lord's work at the time, a blow to faith as well as the serving staff. Like others before him and since he had made the great sacrifice and yielded up his life for the cause of God and the souls of men".

Following the death of Ps. Rhodes his widow attended the Bradford Apostolic Church in Yorkshire.

PASTOR ALBERT SEABORNE

Pastor Albert Seaborne was brought up in Beaufort, South Wales, a town in the Monmouth Valley. His father was converted through the preaching of Pastor Jacob Purnell, who founded the Apostolic Churches in Monmouthshire.

After serving the Lord faithfully in the Beaufort, Brynmawr and Ebbw Vale District, where it was evident that the hand of the Lord was upon him, he and Mrs. Seaborne were called into full time service.

In 1948, they were called to serve the Lord as missionaries in Ghana, West Africa. During their first year in Ghana 500 were born again and on one occasion he baptised 110 candidates in water. The blessing of the Lord witnessed that they were in His will in Africa.

In May 1955, at the direction of the Missionary Committee and the General Council, they were relocated to Ilesha, Nigeria in West Africa. The following year to direct the work in Calabar and, following the death of Pastor W. Grabham, they moved to Iboland. Towards the end of 1957 they returned to the Ilesha Area, labouring for some time at Kabba.

In 1961, they returned to Ghana, which was to be their last missionary tour before being located in the UK to take up pastoral ministry. The way the Lord preserved them in missionary service is worth a mention here for, on one occasion whilst on trek, their car veered off the road and plummeted down a ravine landing upside-down and the roof of the car taking the impact of the crash, but both their lives were preserved.

In December 1961, Pastor and Mrs. Seaborne went to a Christmas Convention in a Northern Area where he preached - he had said it was the best convention he had ever attended. On the evening of 25th December they returned to their home which was in Somanya. He was then taken ill and passed into the presence of the Lord.

Pastor Seaborne had a meek spirit and a kindly character. His life was dedicated to the call and service of God as a missionary in West Africa. He was always willing and ready to be directed by the divine government of our Church, whether revealed in apostleship or by the word of the Lord.

Varied aspects of his missionary work, calling and location revealed outstanding virtues of spiritual insight. He found delight in the outworking of God's perfect will and plan in his life. Of him it could be said, "Willing to go or willing to stay, what mattered was what was pleasing to the Lord."

A memorial plaque was dedicated to him and placed alongside the plaques of Pastors W. Taylor, W. Grabham, and W. Rhodes, missionaries who also laid down their lives in Africa. The plaques can be seen in the cemetery of the Apostolic Temple, in Penygroes, South Wales.

PASTOR HARRY COPP

Saved at the age of 8 in Dublin, Southern Ireland, and at the age of 16 he went through the waters of baptism in a Baptist Church in Bridlington. In 1933 he answered a call for help from the Southern Spanish Mission and in 1935 came back to the UK and took charge of a Pentecostal work in Halifax in Yorkshire and it was here he had the experience of the baptism in the Holy Spirit and this was followed by his commitment to the Apostolic Church. In 1936 he was given the charge of the Assemblies in Halifax and Huddersfield and was there until 1938 when he responded to a call to go to South Africa as a missionary. Pastor and Mrs. Copp laboured there until 1945. From South Africa they moved to West Africa and became involved in establishing the Bible College in Ilesha, Nigeria. Owing to his ill health it necessitated a return to England, and was followed by a period of recuperation in Porthleven in the South West of England. As his health improved the family were located in Blackburn until 1952 and then moved to Shrewsbury until 1954. He was appointed the General Superintendent of the Sunday School Movement, which he fulfilled extremely well.

A further call was extended to him to serve as a missionary in Ghana with Mrs. Copp and they proceeded to Ghana until being recalled to the homeland in 1959. The family were located in the Castleford District in Yorkshire where he ministered until his final journey to Ghana. During his period at home he served on the Missionary Committee and the General Executive.

He and Mrs. Copp went to Ghana for the last time to supervise the work there during the furlough of Pastor and Mrs. Frank Johnson. The Pastor travelled on his own, but soon Mrs. Copp joined him, labouring together until their period of service was over.

On their way home to the UK Pastor Copp died on board the ship bringing him and Mrs. Copp home from Ghana. A service was conducted and he was buried at sea just off the coast of Spain.

PASTOR GERRY BRODERICK

Gerry was our first missionary to be located in Mozambique

with Vanessa his wife. He originally came from America, and moved to Latvia, pastoring the Church in Ogre. It was whist he and Vanessa served the Lord in Latvia that Pastor Ken Rees made contact with them and a very strong bond of friendship and fellowship developed. Gerry was a natural missionary and Pastor Ken Rees, who at the time was chairman of the Overseas Board, recognised the ministry for mission that burned within Gerry. It was proposed to them as a missionary couple that there was a need of missionaries in Mozambique. They responded and went to take up residence there in 1995. The work progressed under the ministry of Gerry, but unfortunately he contracted cerebral malaria (which is the severest form of malaria). His condition deteriorated and he died 6th November 1996 and is buried in Chimoio, Mozambique. Pastor Granville and Heather Johnson, Arwel and Anne Davies, comforted Vanessa at the time. It was a personal privilege, during a visit to Africa as Missionary Chairman, for me to visit the grave in Chimoio where Gerry is buried.

A memorial thanksgiving service was held in the Apostolic Church All Nations Church in Kennington, and was attended by his wife and children, Pastors Ken and Eva Rees and Philip and Sheila Powell represented the Overseas Missions Board.

MRS. BETTY LEWIS

Betty was the first wife of Pastor Joel Lewis and served with her husband in Nigeria for many years, being there when Pastor Willie Grabham died. His death necessitated them moving on to another part of Nigeria to take over the work. After some time working in Nigeria, they moved to Bulawayo, Zimbabwe, in 1963. She was an excellent missionary wife, serving the Lord and doing a good work alongside her husband for 26 years, and was involved in welfare and community work beside her involvement in the church, where she was the pianist. It was during the difficult time before Independence that she and Pastor Joel were there living and travelling, and it was extremely dangerous. Although the country was at war with terrorists, she was not afraid to return after a furlough in the UK

Betty Lewis (Dunn) was born in Lanarkshire Scotland and died suddenly on Sunday 19th October 1980 at the age of 57. Her funeral took place on Thursday 23rd October 1980. The service was conducted by Pastor Eric Horley. Betty is buried in the Athlone Avenue Cemetery in Bulawayo, Zimbabwe.

MRS. HEATHER JOHNSON

Heather was the first wife of Pastor Granville Johnson. She was born in Glyneath, a village near to Neath in South Wales. After her marriage to Granville they pastored in Manchester, Swansea, Edgware (London), Newport and finally in Durban in South Africa, where she travelled extensively to Zimbabwe, Mozambique, Malawi and other places throughout Africa. Heather was a great missionary who cared for the underprivileged, supplying them with necessary aid. There was not one place where she was not adored by the African children. Children from the villages they visited flocked to see her and to listen to the Bible stories she told them. I had the privilege of travelling 7000 miles throughout Africa with Heather and Pastor Johnson and saw the love and respect the people had for them.

Following one of the extensive trips to the various mission fields, Heather began to feel unwell. Pastor Johnson, on arriving back home at Kloof, Durban, took Heather to hospital where her condition worsened, and she subsequently passed into the presence of the Lord just after midnight on 16th June 1998, the date in the UK was 15th June as South Africa is one hour ahead of the UK Heather's body was repatriated to the UK and a memorial and thanksgiving service was held in the Mount Pleasant Baptist Church, Swansea - which was filled with those who wanted to pay their last respects to a faithful missionary. Pastor Warren Jones, the President of the Apostolic Church officiated. Pastor Philip Powell Chairman of the Overseas Board gave the sermon on "The Kings Daughter is all glorious within" from Psalm 45 v 13. Other representatives from the Overseas Missions Board were also present. Heather is buried in Glyneath Cemetery, South Wales.

PASTOR JOHN PRIDIE

Pastor John Pridie, although retired, visited Nigeria and died there. He is buried in Lagos.

NIGEL PEARSON

Pastor and Mrs. David Pearson's son, Nigel, died whilst they were serving their Lord in Nigeria and is buried in Uyo.

It is with the deepest of sympathy and thankfulness to God - to the Pearson family who tragically were bereaved of their son in Nigeria, and all the families of those missionaries who paid the ultimate cost of serving the Lord in the various countries of the world.

BIBLIOGRAPHY

(n.d.). Retrieved May 2016, from BBC History Website.
(n.d.). Retrieved May 18th, 2016, from Arts and Humanities Research Council Website.
(1922). Riches of Grace .
(1923). Apostolic Church Missionary Herald .
(1924). Apostolic Missionary Herald .
(1928). Apostolic Church Missionary Herald .
(1929). Riches of Grace .
(1931). Apostolic Herald .
(1932). Riches of Grace .
(1932). Apostolic Herald .
(1933). Apostolic Herald .
(1934). Apostolic Herald .
(1935). Apostolic Herald .
(1935). Riches of Grace .
(1936, September, Convention Issue). Riches of Grace .
(1936). Riches of Grace .
(1936). Apostolic Herald .
(1937). Riches of Grace .
(1937). Apostolic Herald .
(1939). Apostolic Herald .

(1939). Apostolic Herald.
(1940). Herald of Grace.
(1940). Apostolic Herald.
(1940). Riches of Grace.
(1941). Herald of Grace.
(1941). Herald of Grace.
(1943). Herald of Grace.
(1945). Apostolic Herald.
(1945). Herald of Grace.
(1946, September 10th). Apostolic Missionary Committee Minutes.
(1947, February). Apostolic Church Council Minutes.
(1948). Riches of Grace.
(1949). Riches of Grace.
(1951). Apostolic Herald.
(1955, October). Apostolic Church Missionary Committee Minutes.
(1957). Apostolic Herald.
(1959). Riches of Grace.
(1960). Riches of Grace.
(1961). Apostolic Herald.
(1962). Riches of Grace.
(1962). Riches of Grace.
(1962). Apostolic Herald.
(1963). Apostolic Herald.
(1965, August 20th). The Neath Guardian.
(1965, August). The Neath Guardian.
(1966). Riches of Grace.
(1966). Jubilee Riches of Grace.
(1970). Riches of Grace.
(1971). Riches of Grace.
(1973). Apostolic Herald.
(1979, May). Riches of Grace.
(1979). Riches of Grace.
(1989, December). Riches of Grace.
Adeboyega, S. (1978). Short History of the Apostolic Church in Nigeria.
Allen, D. (2004). There is a River. Milton Keynes: Authentic Media.
(1936). Apostolic Church Convention Report.
(1940). Apostolic Church Convention Report.
(1946). Apostolic Church Missionary Report.
(1943). Apostolic Convention Report.
(1945). Apostolic Convention Report.
(1946). Apostolic Convention Report.

(1946). Apostolic Convention Report.
(1947). Apostolic Missionary Report.
Asare-Duah, R. &. (2014). The Gallant Soldiers of the Church of Pentecost. Ghana: Wise Print.
Black, J. (2016, January). Happy 100th Birthday to the Apostolic Church. Apostolic Church Theology Blog .
Black, J. (2015, July). Some Early Pentecostal Communion Choruses. Apostolic Theology Blog .
Black, J. (2016, January 13). Why What Happened in 1916 Happened. Apostolic Church Theology Blog . UK.
Brooke, J. (1911). Showers of Blessing .
Brown, J. The Missionary.
Burgess, S., & Mass, E. V. (2002). The New International Dictionary of Pentecostal and Charismatic Movements. Grand Rapids, Michigan: Zondervan.
Carradice, P. (2010, October 21st). Frongoch Prison Camp. Retrieved May 18th, 2016
Cathcart, W. (1976). From Gloom to Glory. Dallas: Christian Communications Trust.
Chant, B. (2011). The Spirit of Pentecost. Lexington, KY: Emeth Press.
Charman, T. (2014, August 9th). Daily Mail .
(1925). Convention Report.
D.P.Williams. (1933, August). Souvenir Exhibiting the Movements of God in The Apostolic Church .
D.P.Williams. (1931). The Prophetical Ministry In the Church. Llanelly: Mercury.
Davies, J. (1993). A History of Wales. Penguin Books.
Davies, J. (n.d.). The Legacy of WWI. Retrieved May 18th, 2016, from BBC Wales History Website.
Davies, T., & Yeoman, P. (2008). Born in the Fire. Swansea: Kingdom First Publishing.
E.M.Bounds. (2004). The Complete Works of E.M. Bounds on Prayer. Grand Rapids, Michigan: Baker Books.
Ellis, M. (1930, January). Riches of Grace .
Evans, E. (2000). The Welsh Revival of 1904. Bridgend: Bryntirion Press.
Fielder, G. (2000). Grace, Grit and & Gumption. Fearn, Ross-shire: Christian Focus.
Flynn, J. (2014, August 4th). World War One Centenary.
Gardiner, A. (1988, May/June). A History of the Apostolic Church. Melbourne, Australia.
Gee, D., (2010) The Pentecostal Movement, Masterson Press

Gibbard, N. (2005). Fire on the Altar. Bridgend: Bryntirion Press.

Gibbard, N. (2006). Fire on the Altar. Welwyn Garden City: Evangelical Press and services Ltd.

Greenaway, A. (1926, July). Riches of Grace.

Greenslade, P. (2003). Songs for all Seasons. Farnham: Crusade For World Revival.

Harper, M. (1974). As at the Beginning. London: Hodder & Stoughton.

History of the United Kingdom During World War I. (n.d.). Retrieved May 17th, 2016, from Wikipedia.

Home Front. (2014, October). Retrieved May 18th, 2016, from Cymru'n Folio - Wales Remembers.

Hutchinson, W. (1911, February). Showers of Blessing.

Ireson, C. C. (1970). My Life and Thought. Bradford: Puritan Press.

Jennings, C. A. (n.d.). 20th Century Testimonies.

Johnson, G. (1982, May). Apostolic Church Riches of Grace.

Jones, J. (1965, September). Riches of Grace.

Jones, J. (1933). Souvenir Exhibiting the Movements of God in the Apostolic Church.

Jones, O. (1953, March). Riches of Grace.

Jones, W. (1939). Apostolic Missionary Report.

Jones, W. (n.d.). The Timeless Secret.

Joyner, R. (1993). The World Aflame. New Kensington: Whitaker House.

Joyner, R. (1993). World Aflame. Charlotte: Whitaker House.

Kay, W. (2000). Pentecostals in Britain. Milton Keynes: Paternoster Press.

Leonard, C. (1989). A Giant in Ghana. Chichester: New Wine Press.

Lewis, T. (1933, March). Riches of Grace.

Lewis, T. (1973, March). Riches of Grace.

Lewis, W. H. (1942, July). Personal Testimony Statement.

Lloyd-Jones, D. M. (1987). Revival. Crossway Books.

Mac Pherson, J. (1933). Souvenir Exhibiting the Movements of God in the Apostolic Church.

MacPherson, I. (1936). Ploughman's Progress. Bradford.

Malcolmson, K. (2008). Pentecostal Pioneers Remembered. Xulon Press.

McCabe, J. (1990, September).

McCabe, J. (1990, September). (B. Chant, Interviewer)

McCabe, J. (n.d.). Pioneer of Faith.

McKeown, A. (1985). A Man Named Adam.

Morgan, D. D. (2011). The Span of the Cross. Cardiff: University of Wales Press.

Morgan, K. O. (1981). Rebirth of a Nation, Wales 1880-1980. Oxford University Press.

Morris, E. (1973). Testimony.

National Library of Wales. (2015). Retrieved May 18th, 2016, from Wales at War.

Noot, B. (1936, November). Apostolic Herald .

Owen, W. (1930, January). Riches of Grace .

Packer, J. (1973). Knowing God. London: Hodder and Stoughton.

Pawson, D. (1998). Word and Spirit Together. Hodder & Stoughton.

Phillips, W. (1936, April). Apostolic Herald .

Prince, D. (1998). Who is the Holy Spirit? Summit Publishing Ltd.

Purnell, J. (1933). Souvenir Exhibiting the Movements of God in the Apostolic Church.

Robinson, J. (2005). Pentecostal Origins: Early Pentecostalism in Ireland in the Context of the British Isles. Milton Keynes: Paternoster Press.

Robling, K. H. (2016). The Man with the Large Heart.

Rosser, C. (1934, November). Blasphemer becomes a Believer. How God Laid His Hand Upon Me for the Nigerian Mission Field. Apostolic Herald .

Rosser, C. (1933). Souvenir Exhibiting the Movements of God in the Apostolic Church.

Rowe, W. (1962, January). Riches of Grace .

Seaborne, T. Testimony.

Shinn, M. (n.d.). Pulpits, mutinies and 'khaki fever': World War One in Wales. Retrieved May 18th, 2016, from Arts and Humanities Research Council.

Spurgeon, C. (2004). Morning and Evening. Christian Focus Publications.

Stanton, M. &. (2012). Remember I Sent You: Rachel L. Derry, A Memoir.

T.N.Turnbull. (1959). What God Hath Wrought. Bradford: Puritan Press Ltd.

Tenney, T. (1999). God's Favorite House. Shippensburg, PA: Destiny Image Publishers, Inc.

The Apostolic Church - Its Principles and Practices. (1937). Bradford.

Thomas, A. (2015). Family Memories of W.R. Thomas.

Thomas, B. (2016). The Influence of Directive Prophecy on the Apostolic Church UK. Bangor.

Thomas, V. (2015). Family Memories of W.R. Thomas.

Turnbull, T. (1965). Apostle Andrew. Bradford: Puritan Press Ltd.

Wallis, A. (n.d.). Restoration of the Church article 12769. Retrieved

October 15, 2014, from articles.ochristian.com.

Weeks, G. (2003). Chapter Thirty-Two. Barnsley.

Weller, K. (2005). A Critical Analysis of the Apostolic Church's (United Kingdom) Understanding and Use of P and Prophetsrophecy. Bridgend: Evangelical Theological College of Wales.

Williams, D. (2006). Cradle of Mystery. Swansea: Kingdom First Publishing.

Williams, D. (1933). Souvenir Exhibiting the Movements of God in the Apostolic Church.

Williams, D. (1931). The Prophetical Ministry in the Church. Mercury.

Williams, P. Testimony of Phillip Williams.

Williamson, D. (2016, February 19th). How war mums wrote the name Verdun into generations of families in Wales. Retrieved May 18th, 2016

Workhouse Tales. (2015, December 21st). Retrieved May 18th, 2016

Worsfold, J. (1974). A History of the Charismatic Movements in New Zealand. Bradford: Puritan Press.

Worsfold, J. E. (1991). The Origins of the Apostolic Church in Great Britain. Wellington, New Zealand: The Julian Literature Trust.

Contact Marcus Thomas:
marcus@thebridgecommunitychurch.org.uk